Faith

That Makes You

Think

Dr. Gerard M. Verschuuren

En Route Books and Media, LLC
Saint Louis, MO

Make the time

En Route Books and Media, LLC
5705 Rhodes Avenue
St. Louis, MO 63109

Contact us at contactus@enroutebooksandmedia.com

Cover credit: Sebastian Mahfood

© 2022 Gerard Verschuuren

ISBN-13: 978-1-956715-72-9
Library of Congress Control Number: 2022942104

All rights reserved. No part of this book may be reproduced, stored in a retrieval system, or transmitted in any form, or by any means, electronic, mechanical, photocopying, or otherwise, without the prior written permission of the author.

C.S. Lewis (in *The Problem of Pain*)

"*From the moment a creature becomes aware of God as God and of itself as self, the terrible alternative of choosing God or self for the center is opened to it.*"

Praise for this book

"This lively and accessible work should awaken or reawaken many Catholics to the glories of their Church as a beacon of faith and reason. It's a real contribution to the New Evangelization."

Mary Ann Glendon
Emeritus Professor of Law, Harvard University,
Former US Ambassador to the Holy See

"After a lifetime in the academy, I am convinced that the highest priority in the New Evangelization is intellectual evangelization, and specifically, apologetics—answering the major questions which so deeply concern our young people: Does God exist? Are we mere matter? Is there a conflict between the bible and science? Does evolution have to be rejected? What is happiness? Are we really free? How can suffering be reconciled with a loving God?
This book does all of this in an incredibly accessible, engaging, and intelligent way—which paves the way into the mind and heart of the living God.

Fr. Robert Spitzer, S.J.
President of the *Magis Center of Reason and Faith*,
Former President Gonzaga University

"We live in a time and place in which vague religiosity unattached to belief in anything in particular has apparently become an attractive option for a large and growing number of people, including some who call themselves Catholics. Gerard Verschuuren's book is a bracing antidote, well-reasoned and clearly written, to this peculiar affliction and a timely reminder to us all that the pillars of authentic faith are grounded in truth."

Russel Shaw

Professor at the Pontifical University of the Holy Cross, Rome Former Secretary of the National Conference of Catholic Bishops/US Catholic Conference

Table of Contents

PRAISE FOR THIS BOOK i

TABLE OF CONTENTS iii

PREFACE vii

1. THE AVALANCHE OF ATHEISM 1
   Atheists who are unaware of God 1
   Atheists who are undecided about God 3
   Atheists who are argument stoppers 7
   Atheists who have closed their minds 9
   Atheists who have been brainwashed 12
   Atheists who are militant 15
   Atheists who are enslaved 17
   Conclusion 22

2. YOU ARE ONLY… 25
   Only a speck of dust? 26
   Only a bag of genes? 30
   Only a string of DNA? 33
   Only a blob of cells? 37
   Only a pack of neurons? 39
   Only an automated machine? 43
   Only a glorified animal? 46

  Only a member of a colony? 51
  What is the bottom-line? 54

3. THE GOD WHO IS, THE GOD WHO ISN'T 57
  God is not a part of the universe 57
  God is not a physical being..61
  God is not an absent landlord 65
  God is not a deity among other deities 67
  God is not a hypothesis...72
  God is not "a god of the gaps" 74
  God is not a dictator 79
  God is not all there is..82

4. DO WE REALLY HAVE A FREE-WILL? 85
  Genetics: perhaps we do have a free-will...............................85
  Neuroscience: perhaps we do have a free-will 93
  Philosophy: yes, we do have a free-will................................104

5. SCIENCE AND FAITH REUNITED 111
  Galileo stoked the fire..112
  Born in the cradle of religion..119
  Science, a Judeo-Christian project...124
  God is the author of both 129
  How to read the Book of Scripture? 133
  Science and faith back together again...................................138

Table of Contents

6. MADE IN GOD'S IMAGE 147
- The soul has two parts 147
- The mind is the intellectual part of the soul 149
- A triune God--is that possible? 170
- An incarnate God--is that possible? 171
- From possibility to reality 177
- The will is the voluntary part of the soul 182

7. HOW EVIL IS SUFFERING? 215
- Moral evil 216
- Natural evil 220
- The man Job 227
- The God-man Jesus 235
- A matter of life and death 240

8. GOD'S PRESCRIPTION FOR HAPPINESS 249
- Why "ten words"? 250
- What does each "word" command? 256
- Coming to the end… 294

INDEX 297

ABOUT THE AUTHOR 305

Preface

The title of this book probably baffles many of us: how can faith ever make you think? For most people, thinking contradicts having faith. People who think do not have faith. And people who have faith do not think. That is the most common perception nowadays. But that perception is seriously flawed.

In fact, there is a strong connection between thinking and having faith. St. Augustine expressed this quite clearly saying, "Believers are also thinkers: in believing, they think and in thinking, they believe.... If faith does not think, it is nothing." In the Catholic tradition, this connection has been known as "faith and reason." Pope John Paul II even wrote an encyclical on this issue, making them two sides of the same coin.

On the one hand, we can't be asked to accept in faith what we can't understand, can we? God gave us brains and minds. He expects us to use them to understand even the mysteries of faith, to the extent such understanding is possible. So, faith must have something to do with reason. That's why Blaise Pascal, a scientist and theologian, called the Church "a body of thinking members."

On the other hand, we can't be asked to put all faith aside either, can we? Reason itself depends on some kind of faith—faith in our senses, faith in our intellect, faith in our memories, and faith in what others have discovered. Besides, there is more to life than reason—and that's where religious faith comes in. Seen this way, faith provides answers to questions that would otherwise be unanswerable. So, reason must have something to do with faith.

But somehow, the deep connection of faith and reason has been lost in the life of many believers. The faithful may have to be "evangelized" again in the faith that makes us think. In his 2012 letter of January 24, Pope Benedict XVI expressed his deep concern for the new evangelization efforts of the Catholic Church. He wrote, "faith is in danger of being put out, as a flame that finds no more fuel. We find ourselves before a profound crisis of faith, before a loss of the religious sense, that is the greatest challenge for today's Church." Therefore, we need to hear, read, and practice the Gospel again and again—the whole Gospel, and nothing but—not some halfway compromise.

Let me warn you for one serious complication. Sometimes, intellectual arguments do not convince people, no matter how strong those arguments are. The reason for this is quite simple. St. Thomas Aquinas summarized it in one sentence: "Whereas unbelief is in the intellect, the cause of unbelief is in the will." The will can cause us to dismiss what the intellect tells us.

It is my intense hope that this book may provide some fuel for the dwindling flame of our faith—for the faith that makes you think, if you are willing to. It was specifically written for Catholics—fallen-away Catholics, lukewarm Catholics, struggling Catholics, would-be Catholics—for all those in search of the truth, as it gives life-saving answers to life-size questions. In this book, I want to promote religious and Catholic literacy, which is dwindling more than ever in our society, in our culture, and even in our Church. This book belongs basically to the genre of apologetics, evangelization, and catechization, thoroughly rooted in the Catholic tradition, with a mild philosophical touch based on the tradition of St. Thomas Aquinas.

In the chapters to come, we will see what this entails for our Catholic faith. Each chapter can be used as a guideline for discussions and seminars; each chapter can be read independently (that is why there are some repetitions). This makes the book also a perfect tool for the new evangelization. Call it a form of catechization if you will—teaching us the principles of the Catholic faith that make you think.

I want to express a special thank-you to Sr. Marianne Postiglione, RSM for polishing the English of a non-native speaker. And last but not least, I want to thank my wife, Trudy, for her constant support, even when my mind was so focused on writing this book. She also enriched and strengthened my faith by her example and tender loving care. Without her support, this book would have never seen the light.

1.

The Avalanche of Atheism

Atheists Come in Various Colors

- Paganism: unaware atheists
- Agnosticism: undecided atheists
- Empiricism: closeminded atheists
- Scientism: brainwashed atheists
- Antitheism: militant atheists
- Satanism: enslaved atheists

Here is a reply to these various forms of atheism.

Atheists who are unaware of God.

Here we encounter a form of atheism that most people would not even call atheism. It is the kind that feels no need to protest or deny God's existence, because atheists of this type do not perceive anything spiritual or religious in their lives. The Catechism of the Catholic Church (CCC) speaks of "spiritual blindness" (2088). These people can no longer hear God because they live in a very noisy world, filled with radio and TV, loudspeakers, and earphones. They are a breed of their own, entirely engulfed by a secular world. It has left a "God-shaped hole" inside each one of them that only God can fill. As St. Augustine put it in his *Confessions*, "What place is there in me to which my God can come, what place that can receive the God who made heaven and earth? Does this mean, O Lord my God, that there is in me something fit to contain you?" Unfortunately, this very place seems to have quietly become empty and vacant in the minds of these atheists.

That's why these atheists no longer feel any need to protest or even deny God's existence, because they believe only in what they can see, feel, hear, and touch in a physical sense. As far as God is concerned: out of sight, out of mind. In a world of what can be seen, there is no space for the unseen. This kind of atheism has forgotten that our culture is in fact steeped in Christianity, although that culture has become highly secular in habits and practices. How could anyone forget? Our freedom, our democracy, our health care system, our scientific achievements, our educational system, our charitable institutions, and many other blessings wouldn't be what they are, or they might not even exist, if they didn't have Christian roots. So, you wonder how some people can live in complete ignorance of such an obvious fact.

Let's keep in mind that, for centuries, it was unthinkable in the Western world to even deny God's existence. Times have changed dramatically and alarmingly. Pew Research Center telephone surveys in the USA conducted in 2021 show 28% are so-called "nones" (including 4% who describe themselves as atheists, 5% who are agnostics, and 18% who are "nothing in particular). Although atheists are still a very tiny, yet very vocal minority in the Western World, our society is changing fast. More and more people are no longer aware of this growing vacuum, as they have no memory of the way life used to be, so they now live obliviously in complete religious ignorance. The bottom has been taken out of their lives; they have lost their "sixth sense" and their "fourth dimension." They are spiritually illiterate. They never give God or religion a single thought.

Here we have atheism in its simplest form: I just never think of God. Pope Benedict XVI called it "secularism," which leads to a lifestyle marred with complete unawareness of God. He also called it "paganism," turning us into complete heathens. It doesn't deny God, doesn't fight God, it just ignores and neglects

God. Its only commandment is, "You shall never invoke the name of God, *unless* you do so in vain." A thoroughly secularized world is a world without windows or skylights—a prison cell. All of this will ultimately lead us to the edge of an abyss—which is *nihilism*, claiming that there is no law, no authority, no rationality, no morality, and no purpose to life. The only thing left is the "rock-solid" reality of food, money, sex, and material possessions—all of which will collapse for us when we die.

Do we really want to go that way? I would say it is not too late to turn around, for we are headed for a dead-end. This is probably the scariest kind of atheism, although mostly gone unnoticed—because it doesn't raise its voice in protest or denial; it just lives and grows like a mushroom in complete silence and ignorance until its season is over. It quietly lives in a world of materialism and relativism, where people are possessed by their possessions—and they seem to be happy there, because they no longer know any better. They are quietly leading a life of religious amnesia—aimless and clueless. Pope Benedict XVI once mentioned how the air we breathe in our societies is often polluted by a non-Christian, even a non-human mentality, concerned only with worldly things and lacking a spiritual dimension.

Atheists who are undecided about God

This version is called agnosticism—a word that Thomas H. Huxley invented; he described it as "not a creed but a method." Sounds harmless, doesn't it? Agnosticism asserts that we just do not know whether God does exist or not, and what is worse, we have no way of ever knowing one way or the other (but perhaps after we die). So, this version is not really atheism in the strict sense, for it also says that we have no knowledge that God does *not* exist. It just keeps us in limbo, and therefore refuses to give

God the honor and worship He deserves as our Maker.

How come there are so many agnostics, especially in scientific circles? Agnostics swear by logic, and they claim that logic cannot demonstrate the *falsity* of a belief in God—it is said to be an unbeatable, unverifiable hypothesis—but neither can it demonstrate the *truth* of a belief in God (it is said to be a daring, unsettled hypothesis). The latter part explains why the French astronomer Pierre-Simon Laplace is often quoted in this context. When given a copy of his latest book, Napoleon Bonaparte received it with the remark, "They tell me you have written this large book on the system of the universe and have never even mentioned its Creator." Laplace answered bluntly, "I had no need of that hypothesis."

What to make of Laplace's remark? First of all, I hate to ever call God a hypothesis that we stumbled upon or needed in our scientific endeavors; we will get back to this later. Second, I do agree that logic may not be the best tool to prove that God does exist or does not exist. G.K. Chesterton once said, "Atheism is the most daring of all dogmas, for it is the assertion of a universal negative." Chesterton is right; it is much easier to establish that there is a black swan somewhere on the earth than to prove that there is none at all. We may perhaps validly conclude that God is unknown (as agnosticism asserts), but it is very hard, if not logically impossible, to conclude that God is in fact absent (as solid atheism claims). It is just impossible to close a search for God with the conclusion that there is *no* God. No searches ever conclusively reveal the *absence* of their object. It is something like trying to prove that some accident has *no* cause at all; in fact, the real cause may still be eluding us—and so may God. On the other hand, I do think that we may be able to reveal the very *presence* of God, although probably never in a conclusive way. We will go into this debate later when we discuss other forms of atheism.

Chapter 1: The Avalanche of Atheism

Agnosticism may indeed appear as quite harmless, but very often agnostics do have a rather selectively negative attitude towards religious people in particular—they just declare them "stupid." Agnostics think that their own logic is so compelling that everyone who disagrees with their agnostic conclusions must be misinformed or just brainless. To be fair, I must point out that there are also agnostics who say they do not *know* of the existence of any deity, but still *believe* in God's existence. I wouldn't call those people atheists, though, at least not in the strict sense.

Is agnosticism really "not a creed but a method," as Huxley pretended? True, as a method, it boils down to a "philosophy of the Unknowable," but very often it excludes only *religious* truth from the domain of knowledge. In contrast, the Catholic Church declared during the First Vatican Council that "God, the beginning and end of all, can, by the natural light of human reason, be known with certainty from the works of creation." The Bible testifies to this: "The heavens are telling the glory of God" (Ps. 19:1) and that God "did not leave himself without witness" as St. Paul worded it (Acts 14:17), and that "since the creation of the world his invisible nature, namely, his eternal power and deity, has been clearly perceived in the things that have been made" (Rom 1:20).

Whatever way you want to define agnosticism, it should be criticized as a limitation of the mind's capacity to know reality. First of all, we do have plentiful evidence of God's existence that He has placed in His creation, as we will further demonstrate in the chapters to come. Catholic philosophers such as Peter Kreeft from Boston College point out, though, that agnosticism's demand for scientific evidence through laboratory testing is in effect asking God, the Supreme Being, to become our servant. Such philosophers argue that the question of God should be treated differently from other knowable objects in that this question regards not that which is *below* us, but that which is *above* us.

Second, Pope Benedict XVI, for one, accused agnosticism of limiting itself in claiming the power of reason to know *scientific* truth only, at the exclusion of religious or philosophical truths. Besides, it is contradictory in its own claim, since agnosticism in itself is not a scientific truth either. Therefore, the former pontiff considers agnosticism a choice of comfort, pride, dominion, and utility over truth, over self-criticism, humbly listening to the whole of existence, a readiness to be purified by the truth.

Third, each day in a person's life is an unavoidable step towards death—and therefore, *not* to decide for or against God, who is the all-encompassing foundation, purpose, and meaning of life, is essentially a decision in favor of atheism. The nearest atheists ever get to a spiritual experience is their own death.

The Catechism of the Catholic Church summarizes all of this as follows: "Agnosticism can sometimes include a certain search for God, but it can equally express indifferentism, a flight from the ultimate question of existence, and a sluggish moral conscience. Agnosticism is all too often equivalent to practical atheism" (CCC 2128). In other words, agnosticism tends to stifle the religious sense engraved in the depths of our nature.

During the 2011 Assisi gathering with some 300 representatives of various religions, Pope Benedict XVI gave an unexpected twist to agnosticism by acknowledging that agnostics are still engaged in a quest for God. He said that the inability of agnostics to find God is "partly the responsibility of believers with a limited or even falsified image of God. So all their struggling and questioning is in part an appeal to believers to purify their faith, so that God, the true God, becomes accessible." Let's try to do so in the rest of this book.

Chapter 1: The Avalanche of Atheism

Atheists who are argument stoppers

This form of atheism has been promoted by some philosophers who consider any talk about God a violation of the use of common language. They just silence people who still talk about God. Whereas agnosticism regards God-talk unverifiable but nonetheless meaningful, this form of atheism maintains that, if unverifiable, God-talk is *ipso facto* meaningless. These atheists claim that language is supposed to be either empirical (dealing with facts, like in science) or logical (adhering to rules, like in logic and mathematics), otherwise it is considered a nonsensical abuse of language.

In this view, religious talk about God would be neither empirical nor logical. One can say, for instance, that the *root* of a plant absorbs nutrients (an empirical statement), or that the *root* of four is two (a logical statement), but the statement that the root of a plant is two amounts to non-sense, as it violates the rules of language by mixing up two different kinds of using language. And the same presumably holds for God-talk—it is neither true nor false, but simply meaningless. As a consequence, we should, in the words of the Austrian philosopher Ludwig Wittgenstein, be silent about that which we cannot say—or in his own words, "Whereof one cannot speak, thereof one must be silent." The limits of language are supposed to be the limits of thought. All other use of language should be silenced. Period!

Is religious talk really meaningless? Claiming that it is, I think, may no longer be a serious form of atheism nowadays, but it used to be rather popular among members of philosophical schools that are called positivism, logical-positivism, and language-analysis—and they had quite some impact in scientific circles. The fundamental problem with approaches like these is that they determine ahead of time the outcome they like to see. They define what is legitimate by making sure they exclude what they do not *wish* to be legitimate. And besides, you wonder whether this claim in itself is either logical or empirical—or just meaningless... Some people just have this contemptuous habit of dismissing as meaningless those concepts whose meanings elude them. It is in essence an "argument stopper"—the end of the debate.

Currently, many have come to realize that religious discourse cannot be mere nonsensical babble. How could religious people ever disagree about what is considered non-sense? Isn't religion constantly dealing with disputes, dogmas, creeds, schisms, and heresies? How would disagreements on such issues ever be possible if religious talk were mere non-sense? There must be some mutual understanding here—otherwise religious people would have no idea as to what they disagree about.

This objection has some important and perhaps unexpected consequences, though. When religious people talk to each other, they should always say what they mean and mean what they say. If they do not, there could never be any sensible communication in religion. St. Paul puts it very bluntly, "I will pray with the spirit and I will pray with the mind also; I will sing with the spirit and I will sing with the mind also. Otherwise, if you bless with the spirit, how can any one in the position of an outsider say the 'Amen' to your thanksgiving when he does not know what you are saying?" (1 Cor. 14:15-16). According to St. Paul, even "speaking in the spirit" should never convey non-sense talk.

Well, the story doesn't end here, as it got an unexpected twist. The very Wittgenstein I mentioned earlier came to realize the narrow-mindedness of his original views and broadened them considerably later in life, when he rejected his earlier assumptions. In addition, he said once he hoped his Catholic friends would pray for him. Well, they did at his death bed; he died shortly afterwards and was given a Catholic burial at St. Giles's Church of

Cambridge in England. You never know what you are in for when you are an atheist.

Atheists who have closed their minds

These are the atheists who demand full-proof certainty for anything we claim to be true. They adhere to the philosophical theory of empiricism, which holds that all genuine knowledge is only possible when derived from empirical evidence. That means religion is on its way out and should be silenced. We found out earlier that it is hard, if not impossible, to prove that there is *no* God, but it is equally hard to prove the opposite—that there *is* a God. Does this mean atheists have found a safe strategy for victory? Let's find out why they think that only *empirical* evidence is acceptable as proof of God's existence.

Atheists in this category silence religion by declaring that empirical evidence and proof are impossible in religion, because God is not a measurable, quantifiable, or touchable entity. I would say they have a point here: indeed, God is not part of the empirical realm. Does this mean, though, that there is no empirical evidence for God's existence? Is religion merely based on a phantom world floating like a castle in mid-air, vanishing into thin air? I do not think so; there might very well be arguments for God's existence based on empirical data, while at the same time surpassing empirical evidence. I am thinking of the following philosophical questions. How could nature be intelligible if it were not created by an intelligent Creator? How could there be order in this world if there were no orderly Creator? How could there be scientific laws in nature if there were no rational Lawgiver? How could there be design in nature if there were no intelligent Designer? How could there be human minds if the universe were mindless?

We have a choice here when answering these questions. We either accept that there is *no* explanation at all for these observations in nature—which is basically irrational—or we look for a *rational* explanation of all of this. The only rational explanation would be that there is indeed an intelligent, rational, orderly, and lawgiving Creator God who made this universe the way it is. Is this manner of reasoning compelling? Perhaps not, but I believe it is a very forceful line of reasoning. We do need *some* beliefs so that we may understand. Imagine this is quite a turn of events: it is faith that makes us understand this world—that is, a faith based on empirical information.

More in general, we shouldn't forget that even in science, there is so much that we cannot prove in an empirical way but must just assume to be true. How do scientists know that this universe is comprehensible, that there is some underlying order connecting causes and effects, that there is a "law" stating that every event depends on some law of nature, and so on? If scientists couldn't *assume* all of this, they would have to give up on all their scientific endeavors. Even the principle of falsification—which requires for a theory to be considered scientific it must be able to be tested and conceivably proven *false*—depends on the fact (or belief) that like causes do produce like effects. This principle is based on the assumption of some kind of cosmic order operating in the "background." Besides, in a technical sense, there is never certainty in what we know, not even in science. Francis Crick, one of the two scientists who discovered DNA, couldn't have said it better: "A theory that fits all the facts is bound to be wrong, as some of the facts will be wrong." It would have been better if he hadn't said that facts can be wrong, but that those facts turned out not to be facts.

What can we learn from this? As far as science is concerned, there is much more believing in what we know than many want to believe. And vice-versa, in religion, there may be much more knowing in what we believe than many seem to know. Faith is certainly not blind to the facts but tries to make the best sense of everything there is. It does so on the basis of the limited evidence available.

Yet, the atheists we are referring to here remain suspicious of whatever religion comes up with. If there is anything "empirical" about religion, they would turn things around and declare religion a product of the mind, a form of wishful thinking, so they say. Hence, religion ends up being an illusion or delusion. When religion tells us that we were made in God's image, these atheists would point out that God was rather made in our own image. Sigmund, for instance, believes that the adoption of religion is a reversion to childish patterns of thought in response to feelings of helplessness and guilt. We feel a need for security and forgiveness, and so invent a source of security and forgiveness—God. Religion is thus seen as a childish delusion, whereas atheism is taken as a form of grown-up realism.

Did atheists such as Freud refute religion? First of all, if Freud claims that basic beliefs are the rationalization of our deepest wishes, wouldn't this also entail that his own atheistic beliefs could also be the rationalization of his own wishes? Don't we often think what we wish? Don't some people, like ostriches, choose to deny what they fear? Second, even if belief in God were wishful thinking, one could never prove that it is nothing else than wishful thinking. The God one would like to exist may in fact exist, even if the fact one wishes it encourages suspicion. Third, the Bible does not project a human being onto Heaven but shows us from Heaven what we as human beings can and should be like. Fourth, some religions admonish us to adjust our lives to the brute fact that things are *not* the way we would wish them to be in our dreams. A prophet's message may not be what we like it to be in our wishful thinking. How often did people beg the prophet Isaiah, "Prophesy not to us what is right; speak to us smooth things, prophesy illusions" (30:10). Instead, Jeremiah's response is, "How long shall there be lies in the heart of the prophets who prophesy lies, and who prophesy the deceit of their own heart?" (23:26). Prophets in the Bible are not fortune tellers but truth speakers.

Yet, the atheist we are talking about here have made up their minds and closed their minds for any alternatives. They are basically narrow-minded. They accept only what can be empirically proven in a strict sense and then reject anything that does not meet this excessive, unrealistic, and often unattainable standard. By doing so, they silence religion ahead of time. In short, empiricism, including the atheism that came from it, is an *a priori* standpoint that precludes any further discussion.

Atheists who have been brainwashed

And then we have those atheists who are very definite and sure there cannot be a God. Where on earth does this profound knowledge and certainty come from, I always wonder. The best explanation is probably that they have taken on the ideology of *scientism*—which is a "dogmatic belief" stating that science provides the only valid way of finding truth, thus eliminating everything that cannot be counted, measured, and analyzed in a scientific way with scientific methods. They claim that "the real world" is a world of quantified entities. Therefore, all our questions deserve, and even must have, a scientific answer phrased in terms of particles, quantities, and equations—and if not yet, we must work on finding those scientific answers. By saying this, they have put their trust entirely in science. In other words, they have taken on a new "religion" by replacing trust in God with trust in science, which means they have in fact been indoctrinated and brainwashed by science and its methodology. They kneel at the altar of science.

What are we to make of this? I find it quite ironic how believers in scientism can maintain that science is the only way of achieving valid knowledge. Somehow, they seem to be unaware of the fact that scientism itself does not follow its own rule. How could science ever prove on its own that science is the only way of finding truth? There is no scientific experiment that could do the trick! We cannot test scientism in the laboratory or with a double-blind experiment. The fact of the matter is that when scientism declares there is nothing outside the domain of science, it can only do so by making a statement from outside the domain of science, which cannot be tested with tools and methods from inside the domain of science. An instrument can only detect what it is designed to detect. In other words, science cannot pull itself up by its own bootstraps any more than an electric generator is able to run on its own power.

Scientism is therefore a baseless, unscientific claim that can only be made from outside the scientific realm, thus grossly overstepping the boundaries of science. It needs to step outside science to claim that there is no truth outside science. If we try to find God with scientific tools, we will never find God, as it is the wrong instrument to detect God. That is as silly as expecting a microscope to reveal the square root of sixteen. Yet, scientism rejects any religious faith and replaces it with its own "faith"—complete faith in science. This makes scientism a totalitarian ideology, for it allows no room for anything but itself.

Scientism acknowledges only one territory—the territory of science. Whatever is outside science's territory just does not exist in their view. If that were true, then it would follow that each time science makes advancements, these have got to be at the cost of religion. In their view, scientific expansion means religious withdrawal—so religion must be on its way out whenever science advances. But that is exactly where the misconception lies. Science doesn't gain territory at all, but it just learns more and more details about its own fixed territory—which is the domain of all that can be counted and measured. The rest is not part of its territory but was given away for other "authorities" to handle. If you want an analogy to picture the confrontation between science and religion, I suggest you think of a tennis field, where both parties have their own territory—instead of a football field, where advances of one party cost the other party.

Yet, many atheists have made science their "god." The idea is clear: atheism is based on scientific knowledge; religion is not, and therefore should be abandoned. When we look through our telescopes or microscopes, we will never see God, so we know there is no god—on scientific grounds, they say. This view is probably best summarized by the title of one of Richard Dawkins' books—*The God Delusion*. That's what God is according to this view—a delusion. Why? Because science tells us so! Of course, that is nonsense, for it is not science but scientism that tells us so. Their claim is that there is no other point of view than the "scientific" world-view. They believe there is no corner of the universe, no dimension of reality, no feature of human existence beyond the reach of science. When they tell us to "follow the science," we should ask: Why? And to where? Those are questions science cannot answer.

Therefore, we need to revisit the question as to what entitles these atheists to declare God a delusion. I do not see any valid reason whatsoever, because science cannot possibly reach God. God is outside its scope, just as everything else that is unseen and cannot be counted or measured is outside its scope. What an arrogance these atheists show when they claim universal validity for local successes in science—in defiance of the fact that the astonishing successes of science have *not* been gained by answering every kind of question, but precisely by refusing to do so. That is why there's no reason for megalomania in science. Always keep asking for "the rest of the story" that eludes science. Proclaiming that science has *all* the answers to *all* our questions is only possible if one would be all-knowing—which no human being can claim—or would have received divine revelation—which no atheist would agree to.

Yet, despite their weak arguments, these atheists have gathered huge crowds of "faithful" followers—partly because of their very influential books that have sold millions of copies all over the world. They abuse their scientific expertise to make you think they are experts in everything else too. They are like plumbers trying to also fix your electricity. I think they are asking a lot of "faith" from their followers—I would say, a baseless faith. Let's knock science off its pedestal and put it where it belongs—back in its cage. If we try to find God with scientific tools, we will never find God, as it is the wrong instrument to detect God. Our conclusion must be that atheism based on scientism claims more than it can prove.

Atheists who are militant

There is at least one more kind of atheism left; it is by its very nature a belligerent form that wants to spread far and wide by propagating itself through books, TV, and other media. It is becoming a real "cult"—a cult of people who vehemently *refuse* to believe in God and want you to *believe* that believing in God is dangerous and "evil." Hence, faith in God needs to be attacked or even eradicated. These people consider spreading their message of God-hatred to be their "holy war, "their "sacred mission." They do not just profess atheism but are actively involved in fighting *theism* with their own doctrine: anti-theism. They consider theism, or any belief in God, as a real and dangerous threat to society, and therefore should be rejected and attacked with all tools we have to our avail. This form of atheism is often referred to as "New Atheism." I will rename it as antitheism.

The term "New Atheism" was coined in 2006 by the journalist Gary Wolf to describe the positions promoted by some atheists of the twenty-first century. This modern-day atheism is advanced by a group of thinkers and writers who advocate the view that superstition, religion, and irrationalism are interconnected and should not simply be tolerated but must be counteracted, combatted, and exposed by rational argument wherever their influence arises in government, education, and politics, so that it can be eradicated.

In 2009, starting in Britain, advocates of the New Atheism got behind a campaign to put pro-atheist ads on buses. These were in fact antitheism ads. Gradually, the group grew with authors of early twenty-first century books promoting antitheism. Its authors include Sam Harris, Richard Dawkins, Daniel Dennett, and Christopher Hitchens—sometimes called "The Four Horsemen." The four New Atheists have sometimes been described in scornful terms as "evangelical atheists."

In the eyes of these New Atheists, belief in God has turned into a danger for society. Based on this shared belief, they basically started a church of non-religious believers. They don't have common services or a common book of prayer, of course, but they do have a common creed and doctrine. They reject all religions, they declare them all as equally anti-intellectual, and they challenge them as lacking evidence, more in particular scientific evidence. They think that a few deft blows to one of those religions, such as Islam, can disarm and destroy all of them as irrational. They mention weak arguments for the existence of God and then tear them down. However, the New Atheist definition of faith is a straw man. Needless to say that a false idea of God can easily be refuted. The Chief Rabbi of the United Hebrew Congregations of Great Britain, Jonathan Sacks, could not have said it better: "the cure for bad religion is good religion, not no religion, just as the cure for bad science is good science, not the abandonment of science."

The bad news for these anti-theists is that a world *without* God is more damaging to society than a world *with* God. When Aleksandr Solzhenitsyn, in his 1983 Templeton Prize lecture, tried to locate the root of the evils of the 20th century—two world wars, three totalitarian regimes with death camps, and a Cold War—he discerned a profound truth: "Men have forgotten God." What does this lead to? The writer Fyodor Dostoyevsky had already given us the answer when he said that, without God, all things are permissible. Once people remove God from their lives, the residue is self-celebration or egomania, and mayhem for society

What should we conclude from all of this? Because this form of atheism is basically fighting a straw man, it cannot be taken seriously. Anti-theism is in fact more dangerous to society than theism itself.

Atheists who are enslaved

There is something very peculiar about this particular form of atheism: It tries to constantly remind us of God while proclaiming God does not exist! How could you hate something that is not there? Why would you persistently prove to people the non-existence of a being not really there? Cardinal Stefan Wyszynski, the late Primate of Poland, who dealt most of his life with the aggressive atheism of Communism, has an astounding answer to these questions: In order to hate God, you must first have faith that there is a God, for only when you firmly believe in God will you be able to hate Him. That seems to be a paradox, but it was his explanation for the fact that the Communist media in his country used to persistently mention God in their atheist propaganda.

Why is this form of atheism so destructive? Why on earth would one want to fight religion, which doesn't hurt anyone in any way? We have nothing to fear from Christianity, for it doesn't endanger the common good but makes the deepest contribution to it; it actually gave a push to respect human rights and establish democracy, and it has been playing a main role in education and health care from its very beginning. If I were an atheist, I would say, let religion just die quietly! But I must add to this that religion keeps burying its undertakers.

On the other hand, if people were fighting a certain dictator, I could see why they would do so, because dictators take our freedom away. Yet, that is not the case with religion and theism, as we will discuss later in this book. So why would one want to fight Christianity and its beliefs? I, for myself, would feel no need to fight Islam, for instance; but I would fight Islam tooth and nail if it were trying to impose its Sharia law on me. But Christianity has no intention of taking over society life, for it gives to Caesar what is Caesar's.

Some might counter that just like Christianity has its missionaries, so atheism should be allowed to have its own "missionaries" as well, even its own "army chaplains." My response would be that Christianity has "Good News" to spread, with the goal of helping people in their daily lives and saving them from eternal damnation, whereas atheism has only "bad news" to bring—their message being that, at the end of life, "there is no place to go." I wonder why anyone would want such a message to spread or to help it spread. In addition, we discovered that atheism has no foot to stand on—so you wonder why anyone would wish to propagate something that is impossible to even defend or establish.

I see only one possible answer to all the questions I posed in the previous paragraph: there must be much more going on behind the scenes. The pivotal question is this: what is behind the deep-seated hatred that these atheists nurse against religion and against God? Let's face it, there is only one force that hates God's creation more than anything else—and that is Satan. Satan is not an atheist: he knows that God exists but wants no part of Him. It is Satan's ultimate goal to demolish all Christian elements in society and to damage the human image that was made in God's image. Could Satan be the real instigator of this aggressive form of atheism?

My answer would be a definite yes! Destructive atheism, in my view and in the view of the Church, is part of a much larger picture. It is part of a cosmic warfare, that is, between Good and Evil, between God and Satan. It is God's aim for each one of us to attain Heaven after death, whereas Satan's aim is to ensure that as many people as possible miss that eternal goal. Do not take these as two eternal principles locked in permanent conflict (like in Dualism and Manichaeism, CCC 285), for Satan and other demons are fallen Angels who were originally created good by God (CCC 391). Yet, Satan is a reality; evil is something to watch out for. As the First Letter of St. Peter (5:8) puts it, "Your adversary the devil prowls around like a roaring lion, seeking someone to devour." Prayer is the best weapon in this battle. Following the example of Pope Leo XIII, we should pray to St. Michael and ask him to defend us in battle against "Satan and all the evil spirits who wander through the world seeking the ruin of souls." Yes, it is a warfare, for what they are after is the ruin of souls. Our salvation is at stake in this battle.

It is only the religious "eye" that sees all of history as a cosmic and constant war between God and Satan, waged everywhere and daily—that is, "24/7." It "sees" how the power of evil, the force of Satan enabled men such as Hitler, Stalin, and Mao, to name just a few, to spellbind and enslave the minds and spirits of millions of people, creating hell ahead of time, right here on earth. This explains how such people have sold their souls by following "orders" that stem from sources far beyond their own resources. Only religious people are equipped to see this dimension in history that historians usually miss. They see the unseen behind all that is seen.

And now we see again how the power of Satan is enabling *atheists* to spellbind and enslave the minds and spirits of millions, creating havoc on earth with religious erosion and mudslides. That is why I call atheism a new, dangerous, and cancerous "cult," for its followers were happy to sell their souls to their new "master." No wonder the reality of evil goes far beyond material and physical powers; it goes even far beyond what human beings can do on their own. After all, could Hitler and his carbon copies have ever done what they did relying on human power alone? I know the answer is no!

Do I have any indication that this analysis is correct? I realize it is hard to prove its truth to people who do not have a "religious eye," but I am going to mention some confirmation from an unexpected source—exorcism. Exorcists always need to distinguish demonic possessions from mental or psychiatric disorders, and they use at least three symptoms to identify people as possessed. First, those people have the ability to see *hidden* sacred objects, which they always want to be removed. Second, they have an extraordinary physical *strength*. And third, they show an aversion to the *sacred* (e.g., they begin to curse, stop going to church, etc.)

I am not saying that all atheists are possessed, but they seem to be at least "under the influence" of evil forces—which is definitely true of those who follow this kind of atheism. They have become "enslaved" by evil forces. If there is a cosmic warfare going on between God and Satan—and in the Catholic view, there is—atheists are definitely on the wrong side in this battle. They show a clear aversion to anything *sacred* and try to remove it with all the *strength* they have. Unfortunately, they get tremendous help from the satanic realm of evil, which gives them the power to do even more than they could ever do on their own. This explains how such people can follow "orders" stemming from sources far beyond their own resources. The fuel behind all of their convictions is some satanic force engaged in a battle against God's creation—which is the role of Satan, the "father" of all lies, the great divider who knows how to remain hidden behind the scenes.

This reality reminds me of Adolf Hitler again. Dietrich Eckart claimed to have "initiated" Hitler into occultism—a rite by which "higher centers" are opened, enabling extrasensory powers. In reality, it entails the introduction of demonic entities into a person. Therefore, I ask the question again: Could Hitler have ever done all he did by just relying on human power alone? Satan is happy to lend people like him some "spiritual" help from "beyond." That is why these atheists seem to feel empowered from "on high" to declare to the whole world that there is no God, and that they are His prophets. They have sold their souls and are now "enslaved" by evil forces.

Conclusion

In this chapter, I tried to prove that atheism is as much a *belief* as the religious beliefs that it is trying to wipe out from the face of the earth. Nevertheless, atheism is a very powerful force in our secular society that has gathered a growing number of "converts" into its ranks. Atheism begins with eroding all Christian elements in society, layer by layer, and then sets off a mudslide that has the destructive capabilities of an avalanche, wiping out everything on its way. So, we all end up in the mud. Where God is absent, nothing can be good. This chapter was written as a counterattack, in an attempt to stop the mudslide by giving us back faith and hope in our Creator.

I think no one could do this better, though, than those "life-size" atheists who have gone through it all and, at last, came to see the Divine Light. There are many of them who finally discovered how they were deceived and had sold their souls. You will find their life stories everywhere—on the internet, in books, in articles. The list of former atheists and agnostics is quite impressive: Francis Collins (former leader of the Human Genome Project), Cardinal Avery Dulles SJ, Peter Hitchens (a brother of the atheist who recently died), C.S. Lewis, Gabriel Marcel, Malcolm Muggeridge, Joseph Pearce, Charles Péguy, Aleksandr Solzhenitsyn, St. Edith Stein, Allen Tate, Evelyn Waugh, Simone Weil, Dr. Bernard Nathanson (the abortionist who became a Catholic pro-life advocate)—and this list could go on for quite a while.

Let me mention one of them more in particular, the French philosopher and renowned atheist Jean-Paul Sartre. Toward the end of his life, by then blind, in poor health, but still in full possession of his faculties, the man whom most people know as an uncompromising atheist had a profound conversion. In the early spring of 1980, he shared much of his time with an ex-Maoist,

Chapter 1: The Avalanche of Atheism 23

Benny Lévy (writing under the pseudonym Pierre Victor), and the two had a dialogue in the ultra-leftist *Le Nouvel Observateur*. It is sufficient to quote a single sentence from what Sartre said during this dialogue: "I do not feel that I am the product of chance, a speck of dust in the universe, but someone who was expected, prepared, prefigured. In short, a being that only a Creator could put here; and this idea of a creating hand refers to God." Doesn't this sound like a profession of faith? It certainly caused much consternation to his life-long girlfriend Simone De Beauvoir, who spoke of the "senile act of a turncoat"? It seems to me that, at last, the blind and old man had been cured from his "mental myopia."

I hope and pray that you had a similar conversion yourself, if needed, when you made your way through this chapter, and that you feel better equipped now to face those atheists you might encounter. Atheism is a poison that requires an antidote. Just join Sartre who had finally seen a glimpse of the Light the Catholic Church has been speaking off so unrelentingly for two millennia. Isn't it better late than never? In Christianity, it is never too late in life. May this Light be our light as well, so we can live our lives by being drawn to God's Divine Light.

2.

You Are Only…

Not only are we being steadily attacked by atheism, but also by decrees like the following, which are probably closely connected with some form of atheism:

- You are only a speck of dust
- You are only a bag of genes
- You are only a string of DNA
- You are only a blob of cells
- You are only a pack of neurons
- You are only an automated machine
- You are only a glorified animal
- You are only a member of a colony

Each one of these decrees is basically a form of ideology, which reduces the complexity of the universe to the simplicity of some of its parts. Each one tells us that we are only—or put differently, "nothing but"—whatever they specify. Their shared message is in essence the following: You're only dirt, nothing else. What is missing consistently is any reference to the Creator of all there is, God. All these statements try to distort our human image and strip us of our human dignity which we received from our Creator. And therefore, all these ideologies ultimately equate to atheism.

Perhaps a Catholic philosophical approach can show us why these attempts fail and how we can defuse them. May this chapter help us retrieve our dignity, so we can realize again we are made in God's image and likeness, just as theism tells us. So let us defuse these decrees one by one.

Only a speck of dust?

You are *only* a speck of dust

Here is the message: You have no soul, no Maker, no significance. All that you are is a speck of dust. The astrophysicist Carl Sagan is known to have coined this idea. He called our planet "a lonely speck in the great enveloping cosmic dark." You heard it right. It's this speck of dust that we call home. Sagan tells us, "Look again at that dot. That's here. That's home. That's us. On it everyone you love, everyone you know, everyone you ever heard of, every human being who ever was, lived out their lives." No matter whether these expressions refer to our little planet, or to the ones living on it, ultimately they refer to you and me: We too are considered mere particles of dust. We become tinier by the minute and end up as star dust.

The idea is basically very old—it is the ancient pagan philosophy of *materialism*. It holds that the only thing that exists is matter; that all things are composed of matter and dust, and all phenomena, including the human mind, are the result of material interactions. In other words, matter is the only substance in this universe; physical matter has become the only or fundamental reality there is. In antiquity, the atomic theory of Greek philosophers had this notorious aura of claiming, not only that atoms are *everywhere*, but also that they are *all there is*. Ultimately, this means the visible world is all there is. That is how materialism started, and it has never really left us since. For some enigmatic reason, materialism has quite a spiritual appeal to it. However, the ironic thing is that, if you deny the existence of anything immaterial, you also deny the existence of your very own denial which is certainly immaterial as well.

I must admit materialism is not *only* bad. You could make the case that materialism inspired scientists to search for material explanations in their scientific research. And the marvelous results of their work are everywhere for us to enjoy. That is, for instance, how we discovered that infections are caused by "particles" and "germs." On the other hand, materialism is *also* bad: We still find it as a popular, but often hidden, ideology among scientists who inflate their sound methodology of searching for material explanations into the baseless doctrine that there *are* no other explanations than explanations in material terms. Carl Sagan is one of them.

It is in this latter sense that materialism shows its true colors. It inflates a sound scientific methodology into a flawed philosophical ideology. To quote Shakespeare, it is "A tale told by an idiot, full of sound and fury, signifying nothing." So, we end up as tiny beings in a minor solar system in a minor galaxy somewhere in the vastness of space and time. However, this view inflates a partial truth into the full truth. It is, in essence, a world view or doctrine that declares and explains *everything* in material terms. So, what is wrong with it then?

We are *more* than specks of dust

True, the Bible does tell us that we are made of dust: "the Lord God formed man of dust from the ground." But the story doesn't end there, for God "breathed into his nostrils the breath of life; and man became a living being" (Gen. 2:7). This tells us there is another side to the story. What materialism is portraying cannot be all there is. Why not?

Materialism is a form of what is called *reductionism*—or in the words of C.S. Lewis "nothing-buttery." It basically states that the whole is *nothing but* the sum of its parts (atoms or so). All forms of reductionism reduce the complexity of the *whole* to the simplicity of its physical *parts*, and then claim there is nothing else but those parts, those specks of dust. But we all know intuitively that love is more than a chemical reaction, that happiness is more than a release of chemicals, that guilt is more than an activity of neurotransmitters, and that grief is more than a cascade of stress hormones. Reductionism tells us only part of the story, but do not forget to fill in the blanks. We have gotten so used to this reductionist mindset that your typical American mother doesn't tell her children to eat their vegetables but to eat their vitamins.

Interestingly enough, even science itself has come to question materialism. Quantum physics, for instance, has revealed to us that matter has far less "substance" than we might believe. And then there is philosophy. If you turn a certain rule into an *all-inclusive* rule, you run the risk of refuting yourself. The very *idea* that "nothing exists except matter" is self-refuting because, if it were true, neither this idea nor any other mental idea would exist; as a result, it would deny its own existence. No wonder there are not many hardcore materialists left, other than some passionate Marxists of the so-called dialectical materialistic school.

But there is a much more serious philosophical problem with materialism: How can matter ever explain itself, its own existence? All philosophers are expected to walk a road to understanding, so they are supposed to explain why things are the way they are, asking themselves what the ultimate "root" is of all that exists. As a matter of fact, there is no ground for this to be found in the world itself, for the universe cannot provide its own ground. The world cannot give reality to itself—that would be bootstrap magic. Nothing can make itself exist; no child can make itself exist. Hence, from a rational point of view, there must be some power transcending this world, some infinite, absolute, and uncaused power—typically called God or Creator.

In this context, we should mention St. Thomas Aquinas, a

famous *Doctor of the Church*. Aquinas calls God the "Primary Cause," the first "uncaused cause" of existence, on Whom the universe depends perpetually and permanently for its very existence. This Primary Cause is *un*-caused, not self-caused, but the Source of all being; not some super-being among other beings but an *Absolute* Being; not a super-power among other powers, but the source of all powers; not a cause prior to and larger than other causes, but a *Primary* Cause on which all other causes depend.

I should probably clarify a bit more what St. Thomas is asserting here, for his statements may raise many eyebrows for some. You might ask: If the universe needs a cause or ground outside itself, why doesn't God need a cause or ground as well? The usual answer to this question is that the reason for God's existence is contained within itself—God is Absolute. But this may lead to the question why the universe itself cannot contain the reason for its own existence. And the answer to this question is that all things that have a beginning need a cause or ground outside themselves. This is also true of the universe. God, however, is eternal and absolute, and therefore doesn't have a beginning; As a matter of fact, He created time itself so that things can and do have a beginning. Consequently, the universe cannot be self-caused, because that would mean that the universe existed before it came into existence—which is a logical absurdity.

But there is another reason why the ultimate cause of being cannot be yet another thing in nature. It must be something *beyond* nature, something that has the power to produce the totality of nature without requiring a cause itself. Both the existence and intelligible order of the natural universe, therefore, show that everything in it exists because of an ultimate, Primary Cause—God. So, for now, I would conclude there must be more to this universe than specks of dust. The billions upon billions of stars and galaxies seem as nothing compared to the infinite depths of the Primary Cause, God.

Only a bag of genes?

You are *only* a bag of genes

Here we have another form of reductionism. It tells us that you have no creativity, no choices, no destination, for all you have is your genes—and you are nothing but your genes, and your fate is entirely determined by your genes. I must admit, though, that science is good at breaking things down into parts—and for geneticists those parts are genes. We have undeniably learned more and more about those genes. We even understand better how chromosomes, which carry the genes, are copied, and then pulled to opposite ends of the cell, before the cell splits in two, but further details are still quite fuzzy. What we do know, though, is that a gene can carry one of several variants called *alleles*. Since genes always come in duplex, one of the two goes to the next generation—but as to which one, that is supposedly a matter of chance. When George Bernard Shaw was approached by a seductive young actress who cooed in his ear, "Wouldn't it be wonderful if we got married and had a child with my beauty and your brains," Shaw replied: "My dear, that would be wonderful indeed, but what if our child had my beauty and your brains?" Yes, genetics can go either way, for it works with chances and probabilities.

It shouldn't surprise us then that many biologists love what they call the *gene pool model*—basically a glorified bag of genes. The atheist and biologist Richard Dawkins, for instance, is one of them. He loves to use this model to simulate a process of natural selection among the different variants of a gene (alleles) in a population. What he "sees" happening in the gene pool model is a change of allele frequencies, generation after generation. This view basically changes the organism into a "survival machine" for its genes. He even speaks of a "selfish gene" that is in a constant "survival battle" with other genes.

Some people call this kind of approach disrespectfully "bean-bag genetics": a bag of genes in a bag of chromosomes in a bag of cells. And from there on, humans have become a bag of genes as well—nothing more, nothing less. They are completely at the mercy of those genes, shackled by what genetics dictates. We are supposed to dance on the strings of our genes.

We are *more* than bags of genes

Is what genetics is telling us really all there is to it? Or is there another side to the story? I think we deserve to hear the rest of the story. Even science itself can show us that we are more than a bag of genes. As a matter of fact, you and I are surely more than the sum total of our genes. We have the power to rise above our genes. Does that mean our lives are controlled by genes? Not really. Genes are simply the hand that we are dealt; just as we may lose with a hand of "good" cards, we may be able to win with a "bad" hand. When problems loom, so do opportunities. As the legendary Congressman William Jennings Bryan used to say at the turn of the previous century, "Destiny is not a matter of chance; it is a matter of choice."

What is even more telling is that no two persons are completely identical, not even when their genes carry the same instructions, as is usually the case with identical twins. Identical twins do not even have identical finger-prints! Although they usually do have the same genetic program, they are distinct persons with distinct personalities and self-awareness. Sometimes, they strongly desire to be or become more like each other; sometimes, they want to distinguish themselves from each other. And when they get separated early in life and grow up in different families, they can become even less "identical," despite the genes they have in common.

Nevertheless, some biologists love to glorify the all-inclusive power of genes. When Richard Dawkins, for instance, promotes his gene-pool model, he concludes that the actual unit of selection is the gene. In reality, though, genes are not units of selection, not even in a purely biological sense. The late biologist Stephen J. Gould pithily rebuked, "Selection simply cannot see genes." Alleles, for example, that do not show up in the phenotype of an organism with two different alleles can never be subject to natural selection. The real unit of selection is the *organism*, but not the *gene* and its alleles—contrary to what the gene-pool model suggests.

What is wrong with Dawkins' approach? He doesn't seem to realize that we should never exchange the complexity of the whole for the simplicity of one of its parts. In addition, we also need to learn some important lessons from philosophy. Whenever geneticists speak of chance and randomness, we must be aware that the term chance can carry many different meanings, so each time a biologist says that something happened "by chance," we should ask: How do you mean? Biologists can define randomness in many ways, but they can never define it as meaningless or purposeless, as those words do not exist in science but derive from philosophy and religion. Yet, some geneticists love to adorn the scientific term *chance* with a capital C—changing it into some kind of goddess, the goddess of *Chance*, a sort of whimsical providence secretly worshipped and to be forcefully defended against rival deities. However, the concept of chance in genetics does not even comes close to fate, destiny, doom, or meaninglessness.

More on this later.

Religious people have always known this. What appears to science as a mere "random" event may in fact very well be a directed through a providential process seen from a religious point of view. As St. Padre Pio once said to a man who claimed such-and-such event had happened by chance: "And who, do you suppose, arranged the chances?" On the same note, John Henry Cardinal Newman wrote in an 1868 letter that accidental events in science are "accidental to us, not to God." In religion, there is just no place for good or bad "luck." As a matter of fact, St. Thomas Aquinas once said, "Whoever believes that everything is a matter of chance, does not believe that God exists."

Only a string of DNA?

You are *only* a string of DNA

If this were true, you would have no self, no dignity, no calling, because all you are believed to be is a stream of DNA molecules. Since DNA comprises more than the genes we talked about earlier, it does indeed sound better to be a string of DNA than a bag of genes. As a matter of fact, the one-time idea of DNA holding only genes has been refined by the discovery that protein-coding regions of genes can be interrupted by DNA segments that play more of a *regulatory* role by producing proteins that either activate or repress the activity of "regular" genes. Some of these regulatory genes are actually very short and do not produce proteins at all but short strands of mRNA capable of blocking the mRNA of a "regular" gene from creating its protein; they are called micro-RNA-genes. So, the DNA picture is much more intricate than the gene picture. In addition, genes may be separated by long stretches of DNA that do not seem to be doing much, as far as we know. Some of this "non-coding" DNA is repetitive DNA, usually replicated from regular, coding DNA, and perhaps a rich source from which potentially useful new genes can emerge in evolution.

Because of these discoveries, many people now think that it is DNA that holds the script for a person's entire life, so they would like to know their "personal genomics." The science journal *Nature* listed "Personal Genomics Goes Mainstream" as a top news story of 2008. No wonder one of the DNA pioneers said he could compute the entire organism if he were given its DNA sequence and a large enough computer. And out *you* are—literally! DNA seems to have become the definitive controlling agency behind our lives.

As a matter of fact, the ultimate goal of most geneticists seems to be an explanation of life in terms of DNA. In their view, the "secret of life" is supposed to reside in DNA. From now on, all that counts is DNA. Now that the human genome project is finished, we are supposed to know all there is to know about human beings. Really?

We are *more* than strings of DNA

Is what DNA-gurus are telling us really all there is? Or is there another side to the story? Again, all forms of reductionism reduce the complexity of the whole to the simplicity of its parts, and then claim there is nothing else than those parts—in this case, those DNA molecules. Thus, they curtail our outlook on life by not seeing the forest for the trees.

Scientists who defend the primacy of DNA essentially demote organisms to merely being DNA's way of creating more DNA—a form of "selfish DNA," so they say. The biologist E.O. Wilson even had the audacity to say, "We are DNA's way of making more DNA." What these scientists forget, however, is that DNA in itself is useless, unless it is part of a larger, very intricate system which includes enzymes and other cellular components located in separate compartments of the cell. DNA cannot even replicate itself without an elaborate cell machinery that is made up of proteins. As a result, DNA looks more like an *archive* with instructions, but *what* to use from this archive *when, where,* and *how* is determined somewhere else. DNA on its own is more like a book without readers. Wait for the "readers."

To show how important it is to regulate how and when the genetic instructions are executed, think of the phenomenon of metamorphosis in the world of insects. A butterfly, for instance, goes through dramatic changes in life: from egg to caterpillar, to pupa, and finally to a mature butterfly. This kind of metamorphosis can be found in 80% of our fauna and involves dramatic conversions with regard to physiological changes combined with structural body changes. Yet, during this entire process, the butterfly keeps the same DNA, while different parts of it are either activated or repressed by factors that go in this case ultimately back to one particular hormone, the Juvenile Hormone (JH), which is regulated by one single gene and decreases its level from high, during the first stage of metamorphosis, to low at the end. But this is only the tip of the iceberg—the iceberg being the entire regulatory system. For this does not explain what then is regulating this decrease.

To make a long story short, we cannot possibly compute an organism from its DNA, for the simple reason that an organism doesn't compute itself from its DNA. DNA is only a small link in a complex process of protein synthesis, and this system, in turn, is part of and is regulated by an even larger system—the elaborate system of an organism that switches genes on and off with hormones, and the like. As it turns out, the statement that the secret of life resides in DNA has its mirror image in the following, equally valid, yet less popular statement: Life is as much the secret of DNA as DNA is the secret of life. Think of viruses, which are essentially pure DNA or RNA; their DNA or RNA cannot do anything until it penetrates, like a Trojan horse, the environment of a "living" cell.

Nevertheless, the reductionists' creed says that, after dissecting them, things are much simpler than they appear. But we should ask them next why explanations must always go one way, in the direction of "smaller," "lower," and "simpler" things. If the "smaller" can explain the "larger," why couldn't the "larger" also explain the "smaller" as well? Would it really be "better" to explain the working of DNA in terms of its (smaller) molecular structure than in terms of its (larger) surrounding cellular structure? "Smaller" is not necessarily "simpler."

Then we have an important philosophical question left to ask: Did DNA discover itself? Here is my reason for asking this question: If all we are is DNA, and if we are the ones who discovered DNA, then DNA must have discovered itself! That is like a camera taking a shot of itself (not through mirrors of course!). A copier makes copies, but not copies of itself; a projector can project pictures, but it cannot project itself. In other words, a world-view that portrays us as solely being a DNA chain is as fragile as the DNA structure that presumably generated this world-view; it cannot be worth more than its molecular origin—which is a detrimental outcome.

To put it differently, if we were only a chain of DNA, we have in fact cut off the very branch that even science itself needs to sit on. We would have lost our reason for reasoning and for trusting our own rationality. Hence, we must be "more" than the molecules we are made of. We need something bigger than ourselves—certainly something "higher" than our DNA. We cannot

Chapter 2: You Are Only... 37

pull ourselves up by our own bootstraps. Later in the book, we will get back to this issue.

Only a blob of cells?

You are *only* a blob of cells

There we go again: You have no personality, no morals, no significance, no destiny, for all you are is a bunch of cells. This is another popular present-day slogan! It seems to be backed by the facts of science.

The power of science is that it makes scientific problems soluble by creating a test-tube-like shelter in a laboratory, removed from the complexity of nature, so that the various factors under investigation can be isolated and manipulated on an individual basis. Research is "the art of the soluble" according to Nobel Laureate Peter Medawar. Well, thanks to this artful technique, scientists have been able to *isolate* parts of living organisms so they can study them better. That is how they came across cells (and other entities such as genes and hormones).

A visit to an immunological laboratory, for instance, may show us immune cells (B *lymphocytes*) in test tubes (*in vitro*) attacking so-called antigens by producing antibodies all by themselves. No doubt, the test-tube approach makes things just easier "soluble." But this same observation may also be deceiving and giving us the false impression that the immunity system is really an isolated self-regulating system, until we learn from other research that the immune system interacts extensively with other bodily systems (*in vivo*)—which fact, in turn, makes things much more complicated.

Yet, many scientists often forget, or are just not willing, to place those parts or pieces back into the *whole* they came from.

Therefore, they think we end up being nothing more than a blob of cells. Really?

We are *more* than blobs of cells

Is what cell-biologists are telling us really all there is? There must be more to the story than those blobs of cells! What we stated earlier concerning genes and DNA, we should also say about cells: Most cells do not operate on their own but are embedded in a much wider framework, the framework of an organism. Just as DNA is part of genes, and genes are parts of cells, so are cells typically parts of organisms.

Perhaps philosophy can help us understand this problem better. Bear with me for a moment! Our universe is "stuffed" with *substances* which are endowed with *properties*, and which are mutually connected by *relationships*. In other words, there appear to be three different kinds of entities in this universe. First, we have things (often called *substances*) such as molecules, cells, and stones. Next, we have *properties*, making certain things inorganic and others organic, some heavy and some light, and so on. Finally, we have *relationships* between things, such as the relationship a mother has to her daughter, or football players to their team. When we say, "Joe is tall and single,"—unlike "tall"— "single" is not a property; it is about a (missing) relationship.

Why is this discussion so important for us? Well, it helps us to answer the question as to how we can be more than what we are made of. According to some, the *whole* (say, an organism) is nothing more than the sum total of its *parts* (say, its cells); only the parts are presumably "real," whereas the rest is considered fiction. But others would object to this and claim that a cell is certainly "more" than the collection of its molecules, or that an organism is "more" than the collection of its cells—or more in general, that the whole is "more" than the sum total of its parts. I think these latter people make a good point, but the question is how we should take this "more." If we consider this "more" to be an added, new "thing" or substance, we make the same mistake as those who oppose this view by only focusing on substances and properties, without paying any attention to the *relationships*, the interactions, between all components.

If that is a valid point, then the properties of the "whole" cannot be found in its composing parts alone, but they arise from interrelating or interacting activities *between* the parts, making for some kind of synergism depending on the way the whole is organized. That is why "lower-level" DNA can properly function and do its work, as it is harnessed inside "higher-level" cells, and those cells, for their part, can only function more intricately when they are harnessed inside an organism at a still higher level. That is why the "secret" of DNA is life—as much so as the "secret" of life is DNA, or perhaps even more so.

This explains why the world of cells is a highly interactive world that has developed new properties based on new relationships. St. Paul would put this view in a more down-to-earth way: "The eye cannot say to the hand, 'I have no need of you,' nor again the head to the feet, 'I have no need of you.'" (1 Cor. 12:21). Therefore, I would say, let no one ever fool you by claiming that we are just a blob of isolated cells.

Only a pack of neurons?

You are *only* a pack of neurons

If this were true, you would have no mind, no free-will, no personality. All you are believed to be is a network of neurons. It was the DNA co-discoverer Francis Crick who had the audacity to tell us this—in his own words, "You're nothing but a pack of neurons."

The people who say something like this are basically proclaiming that the mental state of the *mind* is "nothing but" the neural state of the *brain*. In other words, a brain scan can presumably tell you everything about what is going on in your mind. If so, neurologists should be able to read your mind! Are they really? Are their brains really all there is to their minds? It is a "nothing-buttery" claim again—this time, the claim of reducing the mental to the neural.

This flawed idea has been reinforced by the observation that the brain works in the same way as a computer operates. This is thought to be so, because both use a binary code based on "ones" (1) and "zeros" (0). The idea is that neurons either do (1) or do not (0) fire an electric impulse—in the same way as transistors either do (1) or do not (0) conduct an electric current. Therefore, it does appear as if the brain "thinks" like a computer "thinks." Therefore, you are not only a pack of neurons, but also a mere stream of binary code. Poor you!

We are *more* than packs of neurons

Is what Francis Crick is telling us really all there is? Or is he, like many others, just telling us parts of the truth, thereby missing an essential part?

First of all, the mind doesn't go away when we try to explain it away. Picture yourself watching through a mirror how a scientist is studying your opened skull for "brain waves." The philosopher Ludwig Wittgenstein once noted correctly that the scientist is observing just *one* thing, outer brain activities, but the brain-owner is actually observing *two* things—that is, the outer brain activities via the mirror as well as the inner mental processes that no one else has access to. In order for them to make the connection between "inner" *mental* states and "outer" *neural* states, scientists would depend on information that only the "brain-owner" can provide.

My second argument is that there is something wrong with this analogy of a stream of binary code in the brain. True, our thoughts may have a material substrate that works like a binary code, but it would not really matter whether this material substrate works with impulses (like in the brain) or with currents (like in a computer), because such material is only a physical *carrier*, merely a vehicle that carries something else—in the way trains can transport people or goods or the like. One and the same thought can be coded in Morse, Braille, hieroglyphics, impulses, or whatever code language; it doesn't really matter, for these codes are just physical carriers, vehicles, or tools. But thoughts are not something physical.

So, what is it then that sets the thought apart from its carrier? Well, thoughts are more than a binary code; they also have sense and meaning, and that is what the binary code is missing. Thoughts are *about* something else, something mental, which is something beyond themselves. And it is this very "about-ness" that a computer lacks; anything that shows up on a computer monitor remains just an "empty" collection of "ones and zeros," until some kind of human interpretation gives sense and meaning to the code and interprets it as being *about* something.

Therefore, the question is then: Who "reads" and "interprets" the neuron firings that take place in our "pack of neurons"? Could we perhaps say that the *mind* reads, writes, and uses the neurons in the *brain*? I would say so, for something has got to be doing this. If that is true, then we may, someday, be able to fully understand the human *brain*, but that doesn't mean we will ever fully understand the human *mind* as well. The mind can study the brain, but never could the brain study itself! Put in more general terms, the knowing *subject* must be more than the known *object*—for it requires a mind to understand the brain, as it requires a subject to study any object. We will discuss this more extensively later in this book.

Then I have a third objection to the alleged brain-mind equality. If the mind were nothing but the brain, we have lost an entire world of thoughts and truths. That would be a tremendous loss! If the materialism of the brain is true, then we cannot know that it is true—which is absurd. As I said before, thoughts are more than the code that carries them; they also have sense and meaning; we don't just think, we always think something. If indeed the brain merely carries thoughts, but doesn't create them, then it must be our thoughts that "use" the vehicle of the brain.

Then there is a fourth objection. How can thoughts be merely a neural issue? Thoughts can be true or false, but there is no "true or false" in a network of neurons. If the mind were just a brain issue, thoughts could not be right or wrong and true or false, as neural events simply happen and that is it. Just as the brain cannot distinguish between legal and illegal narcotics, neither can the brain tell false thoughts apart from true beliefs. Besides, we are in for a detrimental contradiction: denying the existence of mental activities is in itself a mental activity, which cannot be true by its own verdict.

But if there is indeed a mind in addition to the brain, then that raises the following question: where does the mind come from? I would say the mind cannot come from the brain, but from something or rather Someone transcending all of this. If humans were only a pack of neurons, and if humans are the ones who study neurons, then neurons would be studying themselves. We obviously need something "higher" than neurons—something beyond them, something that transcends them. Even to study the brain, one would need a mind to begin with! If scientists did not have minds, there would be no science.

Only an automated machine?

You are *only* an automated machine

Here we have another form of reductionism: You have no soul, no mind, no free-will, for all you do is in fact controlled by the machinery of your body. This idea is probably best known from the French physician and philosopher Julien de La Mettrie, who wrote a book entitled *Man a Machine* (1748). His ideas became part of another ideology called *mechanicism*. We saw already a hint of this approach when some scientists degraded the working of a brain to the working of a computer.

The doctrine of mechanicism is originally a theory about the nature of the universe, closely linked with the previously discussed version of materialism. Both are based on the extreme simplification of reducing all of reality into matter and its material motions. Its original version holds that the universe is best understood as a completely mechanical system—that is, a system composed entirely of matter in motion under an all-inclusive system of laws of nature. Applied more in particular to human beings, mechanicism became an important philosophical doctrine to declare that even all *living* objects, including human beings, are only and merely machine-like automata, which just follow all the physical laws of the universe.

As a consequence, mechanicism usually denies there is any freedom or free-will in this universe, for everything is determined by its past history, holding everything in the iron grip of *determinism* by working with clockwork precision. In this line of thought, Marvin Minsky, a pioneer in the field of artificial intelligence, described human beings as mere "machines made of meat." According to this form of reductionism, everything about human beings can be completely explained in mechanical terms, with as much certainty as we are certain about the working of clockwork or gasoline engines. Obviously, human freedom has become a mockery.

We are *more* than automated machines

Viewing human beings as merely automated machines leads us into lots of trouble. First of all, when we make truth claims—as we do when claiming that humans are machines—we need freedom of will in order to do so. How can this be compatible with any form of deterministic mechanicism? If this very claim were also predetermined by the machinery, we would be running around in a vicious circle. We cannot freely claim then that free claims do not exist; and we certainly could not convince or persuade everyone else that this is true. A person is more than a robot with a biological algorithm for pattern recognition and stimuli response. I will just leave it at this for now.

Second, there are some nasty philosophical questions emerging: Can machines produce themselves? Can machines put themselves into action? The problem is that the real machines we compare ourselves with are always products of human beings. Then the question emerges as to who or what made these particular "machines" which we call human beings? Did they make themselves? But that wouldn't make sense, for nothing can cause itself. To say that a machine created itself is in fact philosophical nonsense, for such a machine would have to exist before it came into existence. Calling the machine an "animated machine" makes the situation even worse, for where does the "animated" part come from? Calling the machine an "automated" machine evokes the same problem: where does the "automation" part come from?

Third, the machines made by human beings are, curiously enough, always made for a purpose by people who had a certain outcome in mind. So, to use the machine metaphor to claim there is no purpose in this universe is a bit odd, to say the least. The world of technology is per definition based on purposes that designers and engineers have in mind and used for their designs. In a world without purposes, there couldn't be any machines, at least not man-made machines.

Fourth, our bodies make for something so different from our minds that the question forces itself on us as to how a mind can work if it were merely bodily material. The most ancient and simple answer consists of plainly denying that human beings are anything more than mechanical motions of material particles. This materialistic and mechanistic solution is hard to defend, though, partly because of one particular counter-argument advanced by the great German philosopher Leibniz. His idea was to picture the brain so much enlarged that one could walk in it as in a mill. Inside, we would only observe movements of several parts, but never anything like a thought. Hence thoughts and the like must be completely different from simple mechanical movements of parts and particles.

Some philosophers have come up with another reason to defeat mechanicism by calling upon the *incompleteness theorem* phrased by the logician and mathematician Kurt Gödel. He proved in this theorem that no complex mathematical theory can be both consistent and complete; if it is complete, it cannot be consistent; if it is consistent, it cannot be complete, since its consistency cannot be proven within the system. This means that any coherent system is essentially incomplete and needs additional "help" from outside the system.

How does this theorem relate to mechanicism? If the human mind were equivalent to a machine, and if this machine is consistent, then Gödel's incompleteness theorem would apply to it as well. His proof suggests that there must be some higher-level entity, the *mind*, involving concepts which do not appear on lower levels of the *brain*, and that this higher level might explain what cannot be explained on lower levels. If so, the *mind* would escape explanation in terms of mere *brain* components. Gödel himself concluded that the power of the mind exceeds that of any finite machine. As a result, human beings with a spiritual *mind* must be more than automated machines with a physical *brain*. We will delve deeper into this issue later in this book.

Only a glorified animal?

You are *only* a glorified animal

Science, more in particular evolutionary biology, claims that we came forth from the animal world. This means, in translation, that we are merely animals, nothing more and nothing less. Even if we seem to be more than the rest of the animal world, that makes us at best *glorified* animals, albeit overvalued. Charles Darwin made it very clear in *The Descent of Man* that it was his goal "to show that there is no fundamental difference between man and the higher mammals in their mental faculties."

The only characteristic scientists of this form of reductionism are willing to give humans is their high brain volume. True, *Homo sapiens* is a "wise man" who surely has a relatively large brain compared to other mammals. However, brain volume can vary widely among human beings. Besides, brain mass or quantity is not clearly correlated to brain quality, let alone mental capacities. Neanderthals, for instance, score relatively high on a brain volume scale—but so do elephants. We might as well say that there is not much that really sets us apart from the rest of the animal world, not even our brains. We are just one of them. Nothing special.

In line with this approach, humans ought to be *de*graded to former-animals—animals-on-the-way-to-humans, if you will—but definitely animals, and nothing more. Perhaps these scientists are willing to consider humans as "glorified" animals, but that's as far as they want to go. However, they add, when we evaluate some beings as "higher" than others, we are reading our own preferences into reality, but those preferences are not "real"—they are merely feelings. It is like looking at animals with the eyes of humans. This is often called anthropomorphism, which is the tendence to attribute human traits to non-human entities. In this case, we humanize animal behavior and thus upgrade animals to humans-in-the-making, so to speak.

From that point on, the reasoning goes on: if humans have language, animals must have language too; if humans have rationality, animals must have something like it; if humans have moral rights, animals must have them as well; and the list goes on and on—for to think differently is considered an unjustified feeling of superiority. We should never think in terms of superiority—for we are nothing more than modified animals. Nothing gives us the right to feel superiority over the rest of the animal world.

We are more than glorified animals

Even if you don't believe there is evolution, it is worth noting that St. Thomas Aquinas acknowledged that we are *part* of the animal world. This was long before Charles Darwin came along and then went much further than Aquinas by stating that we in fact came *forth* from the animal world. Aquinas, on the other hand, was merely categorizing human beings as animals, because they share all characteristics most animals have—to mention just a few, they all breed, feed, bleed, and excrete. However, St. Thomas Aquinas called a human being not just an "animal" but a "rational animal," thereby stressing a special dimension of being human compared to the animal world: being *rational*.

Aquinas was fully aware of the fact that there are real distinctions in the nature of things—for instance, humans differ from animals, and animals differ from plants. They all exist, but not on the same level. Denying this is another case of reductionism. The nothing-buttery of glorified animals forces one to think that animals have got to be like humans, even when the differences are quite obvious.

In contrast, there is something in our nature that sets us apart from the animal world, in spite of the fact that we do breed, feed, bleed, and excrete like the rest of the animal world. What sets us apart from the rest of the animal world is something not necessarily of a biological nature, namely our faculties of language, rationality, morality, and religion. Let us briefly discuss why those who defend the nothing-buttery of humans as glorified animals are defending a shaky case.

Language? No matter how hard we try to make animals talk, their "talk" is forced upon them and never spontaneous. They may use sounds for communication, but that is not the same as having a conversation. They may utter sounds, especially for courtship or intimidation, but those are signals—not language. Although the chimp Nim, for instance, was forced to learn 125 signs of American Sign Language, he never got beyond memorized two-word combinations without any syntactical structure. After more than 25 years of research on the origin of language in the animal world, even David Premack himself, the "grand old man" of behavioral studies on Primates, had to come to the conclusion that the emergence of human language is "an embarrassment for evolutionary theory."

Rationality? When prey animals flee from a predator, they are not reading the predator's mind, but they just process certain signals. No matter how hard we try to let animals have reasons for their actions like we do, their "reasons" are merely instincts and motives driven by food and sex. Animals treat everything in their surroundings as signals which call for a direct response (association), but they cannot use thoughts to ponder realities beyond their needs for food and sex. Animals drink because they are thirsty—which is not a mental reason but a material cause. Human beings, on the other hand, can drink because they have various kinds of reasons other than quenching their thirst. Also, carnivores in the world of animals are carnivores by nature, but "carnivores" in the human world are carnivores by choice.

Morality? Animals do not have a moral code, and therefore, they cannot be held responsible for their actions. For example, we will never arrange court sessions for grizzly bears that maul hikers, because we know bears are not morally responsible for what they do. Since animals have no moral code, they have no duties, no responsibilities, and consequently no rights. If animals really had moral rights, like we do, other animals would have the moral duty to respect and honor those rights as well. So, when animals seem to do awful things, it is only because we as human beings consider their actions "awful" according to our standards of morality.

Religion? Animals seem to live their lives entirely in the present, without having any thoughts about the past or the future—perhaps memories, but not thoughts. If pets have a pedigree, it is thanks to their owners; if they have birthdays, wish lists, appointments, or schedules, it is because their owners create those; and if they have graves, those were dug by their owners as well.

What a disparity there is between them and us! Only humans are conscious of time; they can study the past, recognize the present, and anticipate the future; they even desire to transcend time, thinking about living forever.

What I conclude from the above arguments is that the human mind keeps standing tall as a unique entity in the world of the living—an entity which cannot be found anywhere other than in the world of human beings. Humans have faculties no other animals have. Some animals may out-see us, out-smell us, out-hear us, out-run us, out-swim us, because their lives depend more upon these special powers than ours do. In contrast, human beings can out-wit them all because humans have the resourcefulness of reason, making them feel at home in many different fields. For one thing, they try to answer the ultimate questions of life. They ask, for example, who am I, why am I here, and the like. Animals, on the other hand, cannot ask such questions, let alone answer them. All they "know" is what their senses tell them.

Just ask yourself the question why some apes are still swinging from trees, whereas humans are able to walk on the moon—something apes can't even think of doing. G. K. Chesterton said it well, "the more we really look at man as an animal, the less he will look like one." We need to face the fact that our inability to let animals be animals has something to do with our inability to let human beings be human beings. People who deny that humans are superior to animals and plants, would say that all of them are equal—that is, they all exist—and that's supposed to be all there is to it. That view is not based on facts but comes from an ideologically biased view. The warped perception of anthropomorphism cannot obliterate the fact that there is an enormous disparity between animals and humans.

Only a member of a colony?

You are *only* a termite in a colony

If it is true that you are only a statistic, an insignificant member of the larger colony, then you have no rights, no individuality, no personality. You would just be a member of the herd. Here is the situation: Sometimes we do feel part of a herd. Each one of us has the feeling of being confronted with some power in society; this power may provoke in us feelings of rejection or acceptance, but there is no easy way of avoiding or ignoring this power. Society often restrains us physically, and also interferes with our thinking and feeling; it stamps even our spiritual lives, at least to some degree.

No wonder then, this has led some to take society as a *substance* in itself. If this were true, there would only be one thing in society, only one substance—which is the *whole* of the colony. The individual members would only be *parts* of this substance, and therefore would not qualify as complete entities. Just like the hand of a person is not complete in itself, but only a part of the whole, the person, it is in a similar way that an individual person is believed by some to be only a part of society—just like worker bees or termites exist only for the sake of the colony.

If it is so that society is the only truly real entity that enjoys full existence—whereas persons are only a part of this entity—then it should be obvious that human beings have no rights of their own. After all, they live their lives as part of society, through the power of society, and for the benefit of society. In this view, the whole, the state or the society, is more "real" than its parts, the individuals. As a consequence, the state is presumably in full control of its individuals; it determines how many children you can have, how much you can earn, how much care you can get, and even how long you can live. Sounds familiar?

The end-result is some kind of collectivism, actually totalitarianism, turning a human being into a mere means for the sole end of advancing the "colony" of human society. The ultimate consequence of this social collectivism is the following mantra: "You do not exist at all." In this view, individual human beings do no longer really exist. They should always be used and relentlessly exploited as a means for accomplishing the purposes of the whole. They are like termites that exist only to make the colony survive. We all know of societies where this view was rigorously enforced and of the suffering this has caused. The only argument used to defend this claim is a bullet.

But even without bullets, this way of thinking has quietly pervaded modern society more than many people like to believe: We have become mere numbers in a vast colony. The influential biologist Garrett Hardin, for instance, used this kind of thinking in his teachings on human ecology: "The real world is a world of quantified entities"—and so are human beings. The more people there are, the more insignificant they become. Consequently, an individual life is "cheap, very cheap," as he calls it, because there is such an abundance of it—in his terms, "a surplus of demanding human flesh." An individual human life would only become *more* significant if there were *fewer* people. This lopsided view explains why he vigorously campaigned for population control.

We are *more* than termites in a colony

Is what Communism and related ideologies are telling us really all there is? Again, there must be another side to the story! Looking around in society, we do not perceive a society but only human beings—individual human beings, that is. So, what to say about the "colony" we are supposed to work for? Is that perhaps just a collective term for all its members? Or is it the other way around—making the colony indeed more real than the individuals, as the totalitarian view wants us to believe?

To answer this question, let's again use the terminology we introduced earlier. If *substances* were the only real entities that exist, then we are facing a dilemma. Either the society is a real substance—with its members being mere fiction without any rights—or its members are the real substances—with the society being a fiction without any rights.

I would say most people see in all clarity that individuals do have their own rights, yet they should also observe some duties toward society. In other words, neither the individuals nor the society are mere fictions. How can this be? The answer is that societies consist of individuals plus their *relationships*, which makes a society more than the sum total of its individuals. This sound philosophical view was widely promoted by the late philosopher Fr. Joseph Bochenski, O.P.

Therefore, we should come to the conclusion that the individuals are the sole full reality in society, but the society, in turn, is more than the sum total of its individuals, because it also includes the real relationships that individuals have with each other and with their common goal. As human nature is social, some of our duties will be social. Consequently, our individuality remains upright; we are a community of persons. You and I are not a quantity or statistic in the colony, but we have a quality—the quality of being made in God's Image. Each one of us was created in God's image and likeness; and that is where our human dignity and human rights stem from—and no society can take those away.

But at the very moment we glorify the society over its members, individuals lose all their rights and become enslaved to the "rights" of the totality—which is pure totalitarianism. The

Church explicitly rejects "the totalitarian and atheistic ideologies associated in modem times with 'communism' or 'socialism'" (CCC 2425). The horrors placed on human beings by totalitarian regimes—in the labor camps run by Nazis, Soviets, Japanese, and Chinese—tell us how ugly this ideology can get. They turned their "citizens" into cattle and "cheap meat."

What is the bottom-line?

What all forms of reductionism have in common is that their claims may not be plainly false, but they are at best *half*-truths. The problem with half-truths is that a partial truth in itself seems to make so much sense that it actually keeps us from seeking the full truth. Let's change course and go for the full truth.

First, as humans, we have been endowed with *rationality*, which goes far beyond what reductionism has come up with. As said before, the knowing subject has got to be more than the known object. Thank rationality for it! Second, as humans, we have been endowed with *morality*, which again goes far beyond what reductionism can discover. Third, both rationality and morality need something—*Someone*—far beyond themselves to lend them a stable footing. The Catechism quotes the early Church Father Tertullian who said, "Alone among all animate beings, man can boast of having been counted worthy to receive a law from God: as an animal endowed with reason, capable of understanding and discernment, he is to govern his conduct by using his freedom and reason, in obedience to the One who has entrusted everything to him" (1951).

If rationality were only based on DNA, we would have no longer any *reason* to trust our own reasoning; we would not be able to distinguish true from false. Albert Einstein was well aware of the fact that, without God, we cannot even explain why nature is comprehensible at all, why nature is so orderly and logically consistent. We will get back to this later in the book.

And the same holds for morality. If morality were only rooted in our genes, we would have no *right* to tell right from wrong. Even the atheist and philosopher Jean Paul Sartre was aware of the fact that, without an eternal Heaven that would make values objective and universal, there can be no absolute or objective standard of right and wrong. That standard would certainly not be rooted in genes. We will delve deeper into this also later in the book.

You might say it is quite something what religion is claiming here! Let's find out in the rest of this book how Catholicism can maintain such claims and how the Church answers to those who deny the validity of these claims.

3.

The God Who Is, the god Who Isn't

What all forms of atheism have in common is that they misunderstand or misinterpret what orthodox Christians mean when they speak about God. There is so much confusion about who God is, and it is this confusion that can lead to endless discussions. Let me quote from the 1987 romantic comedy *The Princess Bride*: "You keep using that word. I do not think it means what you think it means."

Well, the God whom some, especially atheists, call god isn't God, but a strawman. So, the question is then, who is the God who deserves to be called God—the one and only that theism speaks about? Or put differently, who is the god who does *not* deserve to be called God?

- God is not part of the universe
- God is not a physical being
- God is not an absent landlord
- God is not a deity among other deities
- God is not a hypothesis
- God is not a "god of the gaps"
- God is not a dictator
- God is not all there is

God is not a part of the universe

The God of theism is absolutely not a specific entity *inside* the universe. God is not part of the universe. This point was famously made by St. Thomas Aquinas, among others, who used a vital distinction between the "Primary Cause" and all "secondary causes." He calls God a "Primary Cause," and all the causes that nature deals with he considered "secondary causes." The physical causality of nature reigns "inside" the universe, linking causes together in a chain of secondary causes. God, on the other hand, reigns from "outside" the universe as a Primary Cause (or First Cause), thus providing some sort of "point of suspension" for the chain of secondary causes itself, so to speak. Without a Primary Cause, any chain of causes would just be floating in the air, until it finds a "foundation" for it to rest on, or a "beam" for it to hang from.

Thoughts like this have become known as examples of what are called "proofs of the existence of God." These "logical proofs" have often been under heavy attack, but I should mention that they are having a come-back among some contemporary philosophers and logicians—and surprisingly, they came out still alive and kicking. Let us see what St. Thomas Aquinas—known for his *Five Ways* or "proofs of God's existence"—says about them.

Let's begin with the question as to why our universe is the way it is, or why it even exists at all. As a matter of fact, our universe need not be the way it is, and it need not even exist. In other words, our universe is neither necessary nor absolute, but finite and dependent instead; a more philosophical term would be *contingent*—our universe is contingent. This contingency is self-evident, admits no exception, and cannot be denied by anyone in his or her right mind. However, if there is no inherent necessity for the universe to exist, then the universe is not self-explaining and therefore must find an explanation outside itself. Obviously, it cannot be grounded in something else that is also finite and not self-explaining—for that would lead to infinite regress—so it can only derive from an unconditioned, infinite and ultimate ground, which we call God.

Chapter 3: The God Who Is, the god Who Isn't

The so-called *Five Ways* (or "arguments" of God's existence) that St. Thomas Aquinas mentions are basically variations of this one way, the way from contingency. If there are contingent beings, there "must" be a necessary Being. "Contingent" means that they do not have to exist; but since they do exist, there must be a *necessary* Being that causes them to exist. This Being is not a super-being among other beings, but an *absolute* Being. Well, this Being is what we call God, according to St. Thomas.

There is something very peculiar about this Primary Cause. Whereas anything in this universe can cause other things to change, it cannot be the cause of its own existence. What is so special about the Primary Cause is that it needs *no* cause. And what is so special about secondary causes is that they *do* need a cause. The difference between God and the world is not that one has an explanation and the other lacks it, but rather that the former, God, is self-explanatory while the latter is not. That's why the Primary Cause doesn't need to have a cause itself—it's uncaused. This Primary Cause has the power to produce its effects without being caused by something else. It has *inherent* causal power while the secondary causes have only *derived* causal power.

I use the word "Primary" instead of "First," because "first" might suggest it is first in time. The Primary Cause is not a cause before all other causes in a *temporal* order, but it is before them in *causal* power. It's about causal priority, not temporal priority. Therefore, there is no need to go back in time to determine whether there is a Primary Cause, for the Primary Cause is not a spatiotemporal entity that is the starting point of a temporal series of causes. From this follows that Creation is not something that happened long ago, nor is the Creator someone who did something in the distant past, for the Creator does something at all times—by keeping our contingent world in existence. The book of Wisdom (11:25) puts it this way: "How could a thing remain, unless you willed it; or be preserved, had it not been called forth by you?"

Most atheists would counter that all of this is old and outdated philosophy. However, I would like to mention someone who came into this discussion from an entirely different angle rather recently. The famous mathematician Kurt Gödel from Princeton University, whom we mentioned earlier, rigorously and mathematically proved in his so-called *incompleteness theorem* (1931) that no coherent system—not even the system of science—can be completely closed; any coherent system is essentially incomplete and needs additional "help" from outside the system. Gödel even went as far as believing that we cannot give a credible account of reality itself without invoking God. Gödel was said to be very cautious to mention this belief in scientific circles, because he considered it potential dynamite. But what he did tell us is that our capacity to know truth transcends mere formal logic; in other words, there are truths that we cannot "prove." His theorem shows that no system can ever fill its own gaps. To accept the consistency of the system requires an "act of faith."

What makes this insight even more intriguing is that, in the early 1970s, Gödel circulated among his friends at Princeton an elaboration of one of the proofs of God's existence. This is now known as Gödel's ontological proof. Whatever the verdict is about the power of this proof, the key point is that God is transcendent to our systems and to the universe. God is "above" them and not one of them.

Yet, many atheists have been attacking proofs of God's existence which they misinterpreted *before* attacking them. They search for weak arguments in the proofs and then tear them down. They have never taken the time and energy to study the real proofs carefully. Thus, they are in fact attacking a "strawman" that they borrowed from others or from someone who started the misconception. Their favorite candidate is the statement that everything must have a cause. If that were the case, God must have a cause too, so they claim. However, this is something St. Thomas Aquinas never said. He referred exclusively to things that have come into existence. God, on the other hand, does not need a cause to exist, for He is pure existence—the very source of all that came into existence.

What all proofs of God's existence in fact bring across is that the God of theism is not a god who is a part of the universe. Rather, this is the God of whom St. Paul says, "In him we live and move and have our being" (Acts 17:28). Rather than being part of the universe, God is its source, the very origin of all that exists. Without God there would not even be a universe, nor anything in it.

God is not a physical being

Science is often called the study of physical entities—more in general, the study of matter, of all that can be measured, counted, and quantified. Saying that God is not a physical entity leads to a double-edged outcome. On the one hand, this makes people who glorify what I called earlier *scientism* believe that God is a nonentity, a delusion. But as I argued earlier in this book, this point of view is difficult, if not impossible, to defend. On the other hand, for people who reject scientism, this means that God cannot be studied, let alone rejected, by science.

Since I reject scientism—earlier I discussed my reasons why—I conclude from this that God cannot be studied by science. God is beyond the reach of scientific investigation. In contrast, all material, physical entities owe their existence to God. God is the Primary Cause who brings everything in this universe into existence and sustains it. This not only applies to all material, physical entities, but also to matter in general. Matter cannot bring itself into existence all by itself. That's why matter cannot be a first cause, regardless of how "fundamental" its role seems to be in life. Nothing, not even matter, can just pop itself into existence; as we said earlier, it must have a cause, because it does not and cannot have the power to make itself exist.

It is only thanks to the Primary Cause that secondary causes can come into existence and then be causes of their own. Think of secondary causes such as gravity, radioactivity, procreation, metabolism, and mutation. These are secondary causes which depend on the Primary Cause and can only exist thanks to the Primary Cause.

This insight has quite some consequences as to how we think and talk about God. Because God is the Primary Cause, God could never be discovered among the secondary causes of this universe, for God is not one of them. Therefore, God cannot be another physical entity in this universe. No wonder then that God cannot be "seen" through telescopes or microscopes. As God is "everywhere," it only looks as if God is "nowhere." Theism tells us God is all-present, all-knowing, and all-powerful. God is the Creator of "what is seen and unseen," of "what is visible and invisible," in the words of our Creed. We need to look beyond the natural to see the supernatural, beyond the present to see the eternal. We need to become aware of what no eye has seen, no ear has heard. Because God is omnipresent, He may seem to be "nowhere," yet He is only seemingly absent. They say about fish the last thing a fish would discover is water; well, atheists are in a similar predicament as far as God is concerned.

All of these thoughts combined, no matter how profound, still leave the concept of God quite hazy and distant. Some atheists conclude from this that faith in God—if they allow for such a thing—is necessarily "blind," since God is entirely beyond our reach in science, as we have no physical tools to study Go,. not even outside science. They may find some support in terms such as "God's transcendence" and "God's infinity." However, this seems to make the infinite, transcendent God completely inaccessible to the finite human mind.

Many people nowadays have followed them. Even if they do not completely deny God's existence, they consider it so far beyond their reach that they rather remain entirely silent about God. Otherwise, they would have only two options left. The first one is that our talk about God would be considered so open-ended that it becomes completely empty. I would say such a kind of faith comes very close to "blind" faith, and I would point out that blind *belief* is worth as much or as little as blind *unbelief*. The other option is that we can only speak about God in purely negative terms—"God is *not* this… and God is *not* that…" However, the problem with this latter approach is that one cannot merely say that God is not this and not that, without saying anything positive. A negative definition of God proceeds by elimination—it can begin, it can go on indefinitely, but it can never do its job.

This latter solution reminds me of Hinduism. At least, Hinduism does accept the full consequences of the (erroneous) idea that God is entirely unknown and unknowable. Since religious truth is said to transcend all verbal definition, the core of Hinduism does not depend on the existence or non-existence of God, or not even on whether there is one God or many gods. They are right: If you cannot say anything right about God, you cannot say anything wrong either. Seen this way, anything allegedly goes in religion! If one religion is true, then all of them must be true! It leads to the faulty conclusion that all religions supposedly share a "common ground" of being in search of the ground and source of all being, no matter ho elusive. Some hail this as "one faith… but many beliefs."

But how different is faith as it features in Christianity! On the one hand, Christians do realize that God does transcend all our verbal definitions. St. Augustine would say: "If you have understood, then what you have understood is not God." God always surpasses our human knowledge and understanding of Him. That is why any analogy has its limitations: "Our human words always fall short of the mystery of God" (CCC 42). Pope Benedict XVI speaks of the humble admission of ignorance that may be true knowledge.

However, this doesn't mean that our religious concepts and conceptions are empty and useless. If that were the case, we should immediately stop talking about God. Even when we say, "God is beyond our conceptions," we say something meaningful about God. But we should also add that, as human beings, we do need such conceptions. The same St. Augustine we quoted earlier said once about the Holy Trinity that we speak of such things because it is better to speak than to be totally silent.

But once we begin speaking about God, we realize that our understandings of the divine can be very divergent—and that is why religions can be so different. Therefore, religions may share a "common ground" but not necessarily an equally valid path to that common ground, the living God. Truth is truth, even if you don't accept it; and untruth is untruth, even if you claim it. In other words, some religious conceptions may be wrong! Because God's transcendence is a true reality, we cannot just say about God whatever we choose. That's why we have a Creed!

Hence, never take God's transcendence the wrong way. Some soon-to-be atheists stretch God's transcendence so far that they make God completely inaccessible to human knowledge, which makes them claim we cannot possibly know anything about God. When the apostle Paul tuned in to the philosophical mind of his Greek audience in Athens, he did refer to the idea of an unknown

God: "I found also an altar with this inscription, 'To an unknown god.' What therefore you worship as unknown, this I proclaim to you." (Acts 17:23). But St. Paul certainly didn't imply that this unknown God is also unknowable, for he was quick to add, "Now what you worship as something unknown I am going to proclaim to you."

What is the bottom line? The problem is not so much for us to get in touch with God, because God Himself tries constantly to get in touch with us. In that sense, God is not far away from us. The God who is the source of everything on earth also has the power to speak to us through everything on earth.

God is not an absent landlord

Theism is a cornerstone of the Catholic faith. It is very different from deism. The God of deism is a god who once made the world, but he did so as a watch-maker who makes a watch, then abandons it to itself and lets it run its own course—a "hands-off" approach of an absent landlord, so to speak. The God of deism is an aloof, disconnected deity whose benefits we can still enjoy without his presence or interference. If there is anything left of God, it is at best the god who sets the world's machinery in motion. In contrast to deism, theism tells us that the Creator of this world remains actively involved with this world, not only by sustaining and preserving what He has created but also by guiding its course and history directly. Whereas in deism we are in search of God, in theism God is also in search of us.

Cardinal Avery Dulles put it succinctly: "Why should God be capable of creating the world from nothing but incapable of acting within the world he has made?" Or as Pope Benedict XVI put it, "If God does not also have the power over matter, then he simply is not God." St. Thomas Aquinas explained this further:

"God is [related] to the universe as the soul is to the body." Notice that Thomas did not say that God *is* the soul and that the universe *is* the body"—for that would be pantheism. In his statement, Thomas used the analogy of a person—that is, the relationship between soul and body—to portray the relationship between God and world.

Theism gives God a dual "role" in His relationship to the world. On the one hand, God has all the power. If God were to take away for one instant His sustaining power, the entire creation would at once fall back into nothingness. The God of theism preserves and governs the world, so nothing happens without the will or permission of God. On the other hand, theism also acknowledges the "sovereignty" of the universe. The universe has its own laws of nature. They work on their own accord—just as the body does—without direct interference from God. Nature is bound to "obey" its God-given laws of nature. One simple example of this is that God made a universe in which material objects are attracted to each other, which we call the force of gravity. We do not have to wonder about God's will every time a stone falls to the ground, even if it strikes us on the head. God has given us the force of gravity, which is the direct cause of each stone's earthly plummet. It is not God's direct action, but God's indirect doing.

It is like we are dealing here with two sides of the same coin. On the one side, God is "in" the world, and on the other side, He is "beyond" the world. Another way of expressing this is saying that God is involved with everything in this world—which is God's *immanence*—but without being "absorbed" by it—which is God's *transcendence*. Whoever denies one of these two sides detracts from the Judeo-Christian faith. That is why we need the concept of immanence to counterbalance the other pole of God, His transcendence. God is the Infinite Majesty, and yet He is intimately involved with everything and everyone. Pope Benedict XVI speaks of "God, who is as much in this world as he is beyond it—who infinitely transcends our world, but is also totally interior to it."

God's "immanence" adds a vital dimension to God's "transcendence." Although God is invisible, we can *see* God working in this world; although God is inaudible, we can *hear* God speaking in this world. The concept of immanence stresses the fact that God is God throughout the world, not without the world. In what is going on in the world, we *see* God's presence (sometimes called "God's hand") and we *hear* God's presence (often called "God's Word"). In the midst of what is visible, we see what is invisible. In this sense, God is not entirely beyond our reach. Since we were created in His image, we also share "in the light of the divine mind," in the words of Vatican II.

When we call ourselves "only human," we are actually comparing ourselves with our "Model in Heaven," where God's transcendence resides. In doing so, we are referring to Someone who does not have the limitations we experience. In some mysterious way, we are reaching out into the realm of the Absolute, far beyond ourselves. And yet, that is when God makes Himself known. In doing so, the "finite" catches a glimpse of the Infinite. As St. Bonaventure put it, "We cannot rise above ourselves unless a higher power lifts us up."

In short, the God of theism is not a god who is an absent landlord and has left the world behind, abandoned to itself. He is "beyond" the world, and yet is "in" the world.

God is not a deity among other deities

Many have tried to replace God with some other kind of deity. The crudest example is transforming animals into deities: holy cows in India, holy falcons in ancient Egypt, golden calves in Palestine. Psalm 106:20 could not have said it more sneeringly: "They exchanged the glory of God for the image of an ox that eats grass." Obviously, we are dealing here with deities who are physical parts of the universe. So, we are prone to end up with many gods: polytheism.

Believing in many gods doesn't make sense. There cannot be two or more absolutely absolute absolutes. In polytheism, there can be no certain standards for ethics, logic, and science, for they would be relative to the authority of each different god or a group of god's alliance. Even polytheists seem to realize this problem. We almost always find a supreme being among all their deities: one of them is number one, even in Greek mythology. Nevertheless, this belief is still more rooted in superstition than in religion, and therefore an offense to the one true God. St. Paul made this point clear to his listeners in Athens (Acts 17:23-24): "The God who made the world and everything in it, being Lord of heaven and earth, does not live in shrines made by man."

As a matter of fact, the first chapter of the Book of Genesis is an extensive polemic against this kind of superstition—worshiping creatures instead of their Creator. Each "day of creation" in Genesis 1 dismisses one more cluster of pagan deities. On the first day, the pagan gods of light and darkness are dismissed. On the second day, the gods of sky and sea are smashed. On the third day, earth gods and gods of vegetation take their turn. On the fourth day, it is the sun, moon, and star gods that are on their way out. The fifth and sixth days take away any associations with divinity from the animal kingdom (such as sacred falcons, lions, serpents, and golden calves). And finally, even humans (including pharaohs) are emptied of any intrinsic divinity—while at the same time, they are granted a divine likeness.

Nowadays, hardly anyone still adheres to this crude kind of

Chapter 3: The God Who Is, the god Who Isn't

paganism. Instead, we have come up with more sophisticated replacements for God. One of them is "Mother Nature," personified as a creative and controlling force in this universe endowed with "semi-divine" powers. This idea focuses on the life-giving and nurturing powers of nature. A similar one is "Mother Earth," making its believers use semi-religious language such as "connecting more deeply to the earth," which makes only sense for like-minded believers. What is wrong with these conceptions? They "deify" something that is not God. They "edify" Mother Nature or Mother Earth by giving them the status of Primary Cause. They want Creation—renamed as "Mother Nature"—but without the Creator. However, neither one could ever be a Primary Cause in itself, for neither one is pure existence itself—but, instead, they received their existence from somewhere else. Neither one is a necessary, self-explanatory being bearing the reason for its existence within itself. It is at best a collective noun for everything found on earth or happening in nature.

Only a self-explanatory, necessary being, God, can explain why nature is the way it is. Instead of being necessary, the things "Mother Nature" deals with are contingent—which means they could be different, they could either exist or not exist. Water could exist or not exist. Quarks could exist or not exist. Genes could exist or not exist. If any of these were bound to exist, they would be necessary. But nature is not! Without the necessary being of God, the entire world of contingent beings would have no basis at all—it would collapse on the spot.

A more refined kind of deity, especially as used in science, is randomness—or chance and probability in more colloquial terms. What then is wrong with that conception? True, randomness does play a very legitimate role in the sciences, but that does not make it automatically a Primary Cause. Replacing the role of God with the role of randomness basically means replacing God with randomness as being a primary Cause, thus making randomness the ultimate explanation of all other causes. Why can this not be true? Since randomness is the basis for change in the universe, it must be a secondary cause and cannot be itself a first cause, because chance events occur *within* nature, and therefore must be secondary causes. It is just a feature of *created* things, another secondary cause—and therefore cannot be the ultimate explanation of everything else in this universe. That's why it makes no sense to write "chance" with a capital C or "randomness" with a capital R and thus declaring them self-explanatory principles of nature. This forces us to choose God over randomness as an ultimate explanation of the universe we live in. Besides, if everything were simply a matter of chance, how could the universe be so orderly and coherent?

The one and only Primary Cause is God who can use random secondary causes similar to the way we can use dice to determine who wins a game. So, when some event in nature is considered random, that does not tell us that God has nothing to do with it. Even random events are only possible because they depend on a Primary Cause and were created by a Primary Cause, God—otherwise, they could not even exist. This suggests that God and randomness are not in conflict with each other and do not exclude each other. There is no conflict here: the role of randomness concerns the relationship between secondary causes, whereas the "role" of God is about the relationship of secondary causes to the Primary Cause. Therefore, anything that seems to be random from a scientific point of view may very well be related to God at the same time.

What keeps standing is that the Primary Cause is the Source of all being. The Primary Cause, God, is a deity unlike all other deities that people have come up with. It is Pure Existence—with no beginning and no end, with no reality before it and no reality outside of it—in short, a God who is utterly independent of anything else, and who has everything else depend on Him. If there were no God, there couldn't be any creatures at all. Everything in this world is *contingent* and dependent on God; that is why it is so appropriate to call us "creatures." This means God is not a superbeing among other beings, but the *absolute* Source of *all* being. As Pope Benedict XVI put it, "the 'name of God' meant his 'immanence': his presence in the midst of men, in which he is entirely 'there,' while at the same time infinitely surpassing everything human, everything to do with this world."

To put it differently, God is not a super-power among other powers or a super-power that beats all other powers. God's power does not exceed other powers in degree but beyond any comparison. God is an Infinite Power completely unlike our finite powers—not a worldly power raised to the zillionth power, but an "other-worldly" power. God's power does not exceed other powers, but it *transcends* those other powers. His power is of a different kind of magnitude in such a way that other powers could not even exist outside His power. In that particular sense, God is all-powerful, all-knowing, and all-present. He is infinitely greater than all His works (CCC 300). God is "God alone," the "Holy One," so there are no other gods.

Indeed, it is in God that we are grounded—otherwise we couldn't even exist. God provides the "framework" in which "we live and move and have our being," says St. Paul (Acts 17:28). Therefore, God cannot be found *in* science, but He can certainly be found *behind* and *beyond* science—in the "vacuum" or "residue" science necessarily leaves behind, in the questions science has no answers for.

God is not a hypothesis

Science is known for working with *hypotheses*. Most scientific discoveries start with a hypothesis that leads to certain test implications which can then be tested in the lab or in the field. If the test implications come true, we receive confirmation; but if a test implication is *not* confirmed, we speak of falsification. That's how science typically advances. Scientific research is like a game of questioning and answering, of searching and testing, of trial and error, by falling over and picking oneself up again. It is like a dialogue between subject and object: the subject (the scientist) asks a question couched in a hypothesis, and then the object (nature) gives an answer phrased in terms of test results.

When we want to "tackle the question of God's existence," could this procedure perhaps offer us a solution for the "problem" of God's existence, too? Could God perhaps be some kind of working hypothesis? Yes, this may sound attractive, but there are several reasons why the existence of God cannot be treated as a hypothesis.

The first reason is that we could never call God a hypothesis that we stumbled upon or used in our "search for God." God should never be considered a hypothesis in the sense of an explanation we adopt until a better one might come along. Hypotheses are always open to refutation and thus should only be tentatively held. God, on the other hand, is not a hypothesis that we are supposed to hold on to tentatively and provisionally until more evidence for or against it emerges.

Second, God could never be called a working hypothesis because God is not another secondary cause. Hypotheses may be great tools for studying secondary cases. In that respect, the legendary French astronomer Pierre-Simon Laplace was right, as we mentioned earlier. When given a copy of his latest book, Napoleon Bonaparte asked him why he never even mentioned the Creator. Laplace answered Napoleon bluntly, "I had no need of that hypothesis." However, the fact that there is no need for God in science as a hypothesis cannot be a reason for people such as The New Atheist Richard Dawkins to claim there is no place for God at all. Dawkins' belief that God is a scientific hypothesis is at best a misconception that obscures the real God. Therefore, it makes no longer sense to maintain, as Dawkins does, that "[R]eligions still make claims about the world that on analysis turn out to be scientific claims."

Third, if God is indeed the Primary Cause, then God cannot be degraded to a secondary cause. What works for studying secondary causes may not work at all for the Primary Cause. The question "Does God exist?" is not like "Do neutrinos exist?" God cannot be "trapped" by some kind of ingenious experiment. God resides on a level different from scientific issues—not measurable, quantifiable, or touchable—which means experimental proofs are clearly out of the question. God cannot be made visible with microscopes or telescopes, as we said earlier. There is no way to prove God's existence merely based on a hypothesis.

Fourth, denigrating God to a hypothesis takes away the element of trust that usually comes with faith in God. Instead, the "god hypothesis" approaches faith in God with a critical or skeptical attitude. There is no trust involved—no trust that God exists and that God is in charge of the world and our lives. People with that kind of attitude do not have the guts to place their entire lives in God's hands, not even when the end nears. It is a form of unbelief steeped in skepticism. It accepts God for the sake of argument, but then examines whether this belief can be pulled down. What we often see in the lives of agnostics and atheists, as we found out earlier, is a disconnect between what they know and what they choose to know.

St. Thomas Aquinas was very aware of this disconnect: "Whereas unbelief is in the intellect, the cause of unbelief is in the will." Skepticism makes it look like we are dealing with an intellectual activity by declaring God a hypothesis. But that is a disguise. In reality, it is a reluctance that is not willing to accept God as the source of all that exists in this universe. Blaise Pascal once said there are three kinds of people: those who have sought God and found Him, those who are seeking and have not yet found, and those who neither seek nor find. The first are reasonable and happy, the second are reasonable and unhappy, and the third are both unreasonable and unhappy.

Why can skepticism never lead us to God? Skeptics deny the validity of nearly all aspects of knowledge, because skeptics find a flaw in every truth claimed. They just do not have enough trust to believe in anything at all. As a consequence, skepticism makes for a very restrained view on the world. However, in doing so, skeptics turn things the wrong way. We often do need to eliminate errors to get to the truth; yet our ultimate goal is not to avoid *errors* but to gain *truth*. We want to know, not to know what we do *not* know. Skeptics, on the other hand, make it their final goal to avoid errors, in denial of the fact that eliminating errors is only a means to gaining truth—so they end up with an empty shell of complete mistrust in anything on earth, but also in the Maker of everything on earth whom they had declared a mere hypothesis.

We must conclude from this that the God of theism is not a god who is a hypothesis the way it functions in science. God is above and beyond any kind of hypothesis.

God is not "a god of the gaps"

For centuries, it has been a serious temptation to have God

Chapter 3: The God Who Is, the god Who Isn't

directly interfere in the physical part of the universe each time science has problems left which it cannot explain in scientific terms. Couldn't God be the one to fill those "gaps"? Even Isaac Newton did fall for this timeless temptation of having God keep a "divine foot" in the door, when he called upon God's active intervention to periodically reform the solar system from increasing irregularities, and to prevent the stars from falling in on each other, and perhaps even in preventing the amount of motion in the universe from decaying due to viscosity and friction. Today, we know God does not have to make these interventions in Newton's universe, because science can now explain them with the proper laws (which are God's laws anyway).

This is also the Achilles' heel of making God a "god of the gaps." When Newton called on special interventions by the Creator in the working of the universe, the German philosopher Gottfried Leibniz quipped, "God Almighty wants to wind up his watch from time to time; otherwise, it would cease to move. He had not, it seems, sufficient foresight to make it a perpetual motion." A century earlier, around 1600, the great scholastic theologian Francisco Suárez had expressed something similar in Aquinian terms, "God does not intervene directly in the natural order where secondary causes suffice to produce the intended effect."

But there is more trouble for this approach, expressed even in circles of theologians. In the late Victorian period, the Scottish evangelist Henry Drummond raised concerns about this search for gaps, when he said, "There are reverent minds who ceaselessly scan the fields of Nature and the books of Science in search of gaps—gaps which they fill up with God. As if God lived in gaps!" More recently, the Protestant theologian Dietrich Bonhoeffer famously put it this way, "We are to find God in what we know, not in what we don't know." During his 1954 McNair Lecture at the University of North Carolina, the late chemist Charles Coulson said something comparable: "Either God is in the whole of Nature, with no gaps, or He's not there at all."

Perhaps the most troubling outcome of making God a "god of the gaps" is that this kind of god repeatedly turns out to be a fleeting illusion. Why is that? Well, when the frontiers of science are being pushed back—and they usually are—this kind of god would be pushed back with them as well. Seen this way, God becomes a stand-in god who gets hauled in to explain effects in the world when no better cause seems to be available, at least not yet. In that particular sense, Richard Dawkins was right to say that religious claims may on analysis turn out to be scientific claims. But he was wrong stating that this is the fate of *all* religious claims. He was only right for cases in which we treat God as a "god of the gaps" who helps and supplements science with divine interventions.

However, rejecting a "god of the gaps" may be a wise and sound "strategy" for religion, but it could come with a heavy price: blocking God from *any* intervention in this world. Now it looks like God has been taken hostage by His own laws of nature, thus giving the universe its own independent "sovereignty." Why could that be a problem? Well, it raises new questions: Does this mean God has given His sovereignty away? What about God's governing this world with His providence? What about miracles? Is all of that gone? The answer is, no, no, no.

Here is my first No: God has not given His sovereignty away. First of all, it's God Himself who created the laws of nature according to what would be best for this universe. Take, for instance, the law that things on earth are subject to gravity. Thus, gravitation explains and predicts that things on earth fall towards the center of the earth, thus preventing that they fall away from the earth. But that law also makes sure that planets revolve around the Sun in elliptical orbits. Without gravity, our earth would be in a chaotic state.

Put differently, the laws of nature are God's gift to the world. They are, so to speak, the "backbone" of the world we live in. Without them, we could not predict anything. It would be hard, if not impossible, to live in a world that is unpredictable. Science, for one thing, would not be possible. In biblical terms, they are part of God's *covenant* with us. Laws like these are, in the words of the Catechism, "the sign and pledge of the unshaken-able faithfulness of God's covenant" (CCC 346). God did not give anything "away," but He gave us a "promise."

Here is my second No: God is still governing what He created. God is still able to direct and steer the laws of nature. I like to use the following analogy to make my point. When golfers or baseball players hit a ball, they apply somehow the laws of physics—that is, they use a specific force at a certain angle with a specific impact, leading to a cascade of physical causes and effects. Yet, much more goes on in this process—these players have a specific intention in mind, which eludes and transcends the laws of science. Do they go against the laws of nature? Of course not, but they do go beyond those laws—they use and steer those laws for a specific purpose. People who can't look beyond those physical laws and causes completely miss out on what the game is all about. We can steer the laws of nature in a direction of our own choosing—for instance, when we catch something that is falling. So, I ask you: Why could we not say something similar about God? God can direct the laws of nature for a certain purpose and steer them in a certain direction. That's how God can govern the world.

Here is my third No: God can still work miracles. Miracles play a significant role in Catholic Faith. They are at the core of the Christian message: the incarnation of Jesus, His birth from the Virgin Mary, His resurrection from the dead, and His ascension into heaven. Miracles like these appear frequently in the Book of Scripture. Miracles also play a significant role in the lives of many Saints. So, the question arises why some see a conflict here with what science tells us. The stock argument that skeptic philosophers such as David Hume use is that miracles are violations of the laws of nature. Do they have a point? To answer that question, we need a more concise definition of "miracle." C. S. Lewis provides this one: "I use the word Miracle to mean an interference with Nature by supernatural power." The word supernatural is key here.

Well, then, how do miracles deal with the laws of nature? Here is my main point: the laws of nature manifest themselves only when certain conditions are met; put more technically, they come with a clause of *ceteris paribus* (all things being equal). A law of nature states what happens if, and only if, all other factors are held constant. For instance, the law of gravity makes things fall to the ground, unless we catch them. If that is a valid intervening factor for the law of gravity, then we could also include supernatural factors based on God's interference. Those would obviously also be intervening factors, but now of the supernatural kind. That's basically the point Lewis is making by interpreting miracles as interventions of the supernatural world in the natural world. He argues that miracles go beyond natural law, yet they are still consistent with nature.

There is no way science can eliminate supernatural factors ahead of time. Speaking of miracles simply indicates that we accept the existence of supernatural causes, based on religious faith, in addition to and beyond the natural causes, based on scientific laws of nature. One can only conclude that miracles are impossible on the presumption ahead of time that the supernatural world cannot or does not exist—which is a presupposition not based on scientific tests, but that is in fact based on a flawed logic by assuming already what you want to prove. In other words, rather than breaking laws of nature, God allows His miracles to transcend them.

Pope Benedict XVI went even further when he rejected the modern notion that God is "allowed" to act only in the spiritual realm, but not in the material domain. In his own words, "God is God, and he does not operate merely on the level of ideas…. If God does not also have the power over matter, then he simply is not God." This God is not a "god of the gaps," but a God in charge of the world.

God is not a dictator

We have seen several times that God's power is the Source and Origin that all other causal powers depend on and derive from; those other powers are not "next" to God but "under" God. They would not have any power if God did not give them some power. Somehow, they share in God's power.

God being all-powerful is indeed a nice thought, but it has made some people reject God's creatorship and governance as a form of tyranny. They think that believing in God is believing in a sort of "benevolent dictatorship," as they call it. Probably the best known representative of such a view is the French philosopher and atheist Jean-Paul Sartre. He took it that an almighty God does not leave any room for free human beings, whereas free human beings do not leave room for an almighty God. In Sartre's eyes, there is no room for both God and Man in this world. He opted in favor of human freedom over divine omnipotence and thus became an atheist (until just before he died). Does Sartre have a point here?

No, he does not—for at least three reasons. The first reason is that Sartre's dilemma puts God and Man on an equal level, whereas they certainly are at very different levels. God is not one of the persons among other persons, just as He is not a cause among other causes. There is no power battle between God and His creatures. Therefore, submitting ourselves to God, the Maker of Heaven and Earth, is not like submitting ourselves to a dictator, who is just another person in our midst. Yet, many atheists keep struggling with this problem. They also mention the problem of evil in their attack of God's omnipotence: How does an all-powerful God get away with the evil in the world? If God is not able to take evil away, God cannot be all-powerful. We will get back to this in a later chapter.

My second reason for rejecting Sartre's dilemma is that God's omnipotence does not take our freedom and free-will away. An almighty God does not make humans powerless, for God's power is not a blind brute force like the forces we are familiar with, but a power far beyond our comprehension. As a matter of fact, God decided in His omnipotence to make human beings "participants" and "co-workers" in His creation, in accordance with His image. He chose in His own freedom to endow us too with freedom, as a reflection of His own freedom. Consequently, creation did not spring forth complete from the hands of the Creator. God gave us also the dignity of acting on our own, and thus of cooperating in the accomplishment of His plan, by enabling us to be intelligent and free causes of our own so as to complete the work of creation. More on this later.

My third reason for rejecting Sartre's dilemma is that "human freedom" would remain hanging in the air if there were no God. We have nothing to base it on, other than God who gave it to us. It certainly cannot be based on genetics. Theoretically, there could indeed be a gene in our DNA that allows us to make choices, but if this gene, or any additional genes, would also determine the outcome of these choices, then we cannot really make free choices and have basically lost the free-will we thought we had. If we want to claim human freedom, then we need Someone from whom this freedom derives—a Creator God. So there is no dilemma of "God or freedom," but the only reasonable option is their unison—"both God and freedom."

In other words, there can definitely be human freedom and free-will under an all-powerful God. Dictators may take human freedom away, but God made us in His image and thus He created us, not as marionettes, but as beings endowed with freedom as well. Therefore, we cannot just be marionettes or automata. God gave us freedom in His infinite, selfless love. Because we are rational beings, made in God's image, we have been created with free-will. In other words, the right to choose is ours. God lets the actors on the world stage be free actors, who may not act the way the Author of the "play" would like them to act. So, we are master over our acts, despite the fact that they will be misused over and over again in error and sin.

So far, the discussion about human freedom has been focused on an all-*mighty* God. But it could also be focused on an all-*demanding* God. People who like to turn the discussion in this direction tell you that Christianity is a religion of many commandments. The Catholic Church has been called the Church of No's: no abortion, no euthanasia, no divorce, no blasphemy, no perjury, and the list goes on. They consider these commandments another attack on human freedom. Do they have a point?

No, commandments like these are not strictly enforced like the mask mandates during the COVID epidemic. True, eight of the Ten Commandments begin with "You shall *not*..." No wonder then that many people think God has taken our freedom away. But God hasn't. Quite to the contrary, God's commandments are needed because we do have a free-will to follow them or not. Why should we follow them then? Because God, as the

Creator of this world, knows best what is best for us to live in this world. It is like with parents, who usually know best what is best for their children. We all know that our acts have consequences. God teaches us to choose those actions that have good consequences. Later in this book, we will delve deeper into this issue.

Let's bring this section to a conclusion. The God of theism is not a god who is a dictator, who suffocates human freedom either by His power or by His commandments. He gave us the power to either follow or reject His commandments.

God is not all there is

Earlier we quoted St Thomas Aquinas who said: "God is [related] to the universe as the soul is to the body." We also remarked that Thomas did not say, "God *is* the soul, and the universe *is* the body"—for that would be *pantheism*, equating God with "all there is." If God were indeed everything and if everything is god, as most forms of pantheism proclaim, then everything and everyone is part of god. That idea comes close to the "Mother Nature" ideology, which we discussed earlier. They both share the same difficulties.

Another problem is that the god of pantheism must be evil as well as good at the same time, for both are seen as part of God. If that were true; then god must have a good side as well as a bad side—half-evil and half-good, so to speak. That is a price almost everyone will find hard to pay. Referring to God as the source of all good, St. Thomas Aquinas famously stated, "Good can exist without evil, whereas evil cannot exist without good." We know of "evil" because we have an idea of "good" and of what things should be like if everything were "good"—that is, the way God intends them to be, before humanity dissented.

Besides, because pantheism states that "all is one, and everything is god," the pantheistic god cannot be distinguished from everything and everyone in the universe, as everything and everyone is identical to god. He is "diffused" throughout the universe, no longer separate and different from his creation. Thus, it obscures the distinction between the Creator and His creation. In pantheism, god is absolutely and solely immanent in his creation, but without remaining fully transcendent to it. It is exactly because the Creator is distinguished from His creation that God is divine and that His creation is *not* divine. Even when pantheists say they are grateful for everything they can enjoy in life, we should ask them. "Grateful to whom?" In pantheism, there is no one to be grateful to for all that we enjoy.

In contrast, Christianity says about God that there is indeed not a single grain of dust, not a single subatomic particle in all the universe, which does not belong to God and in which God is not wholly present. As we said earlier. God is fully immanent in His creation. Yet, on the other hand, God is also fully transcendent to His creation, so He can never be fully identified with what He created. Obviously, that is very different from saying that god is everything and that everything is god or part of god. When St. Paul says (Ephes. 4:6) that there is "one God and Father of all, who is over all and through all and in all," he is referring to God's immanence in the world, not His identity with the world.

But the problems for pantheism do not end here. Declaring God identical to the universe, as most forms of pantheism do, makes the idea or concept of god quite needless—it only adds to the world an allure of divinity, whatever that might be. By identifying the Creator with His creation, pantheism collapses an important distinction and thus obscures an essential characteristic of God, being the Maker of Heaven and earth. It makes god fully redundant. In contrast, the God of theism adds an essential role to God as the world's Creator. We will go deeper into this issue in a later chapter.

For now, I will bring this chapter to an end by just repeating that there are many misconceptions about God. They conceal for us who God really is. Hence, they can also be easily used to reject God Himself—but for the wrong reasons.

4.

Do We Really Have a Free-will?

So far, we mentioned several times that human beings were given a free-will. But can that really be true? The idea of free-will has come under heavy attack from various angles. Probably the most serious attack has come from *determinism*.

Determinism is the doctrine that all events are completely determined by previously existing causes, and that all human actions too are completely determined by causes external to the human will. Some philosophers have taken this position even farther by claiming that human beings have no free-will at all and cannot be held morally responsible for their actions. These are quite extravagant claims with wide implications. So, we need to investigate whether determinism can be true. If so, that would be the end of this book. If not, we have a difficult task ahead of us to argue against determinism. The core question is: Do we really have a free-will?

Genetics: perhaps we do have a free-will

Genetics is usually taken as one of the most important obstacles to the proclamation of human freedom and free-will, because it seems to entail that our individual future is in the iron grip of our genes and DNA.

In its simplest version, the story goes like this: DNA makes RNA makes protein. The step from DNA to protein involves another molecule called RNA, very similar to DNA. To begin with, the DNA of a gene makes a matching RNA version of its code, and then the RNA string determines which amino acids are being strung together into a protein. This way, DNA is indirectly in control of the proteins that a cell produces, but also of the way cells work together to create an organism. Applied to human beings, at the end of this proces is a human person. Everything seems to unfold in an entirely predetermined fashion. This idea gave DNA the aura of being "the secret of life"—not only the "secret" of life, but also the one and only determining factor of all forms of life. It is indeed a powerful scenario of genetic determinism.

Over-confident geneticists have been broadcasting this idea for a while. Sidney Brenner, one of the DNA pioneers, said not too long ago he could compute an entire organism, humans included, if he were given its DNA sequence and a large enough computer. With a like mind, the American molecular biologist Walter Gilbert had the audacity to claim that "when we have the complete sequence of the human genome we will know what it is to be human." That is genetic determinism in full glory, with DNA holding the script for a person's entire life!

How much determining power does DNA have?

We seem to have a clear dilemma here: If we are fully determined, or predetermined, by genetic factors, there would be no space left for a free-will which some still believe steers how we grow up and mature. On the other hand, if we do have a free-will, we cannot be fully determined by genes and DNA. Is there a way out of this dilemma, or is it a false dilemma?

There is no doubt that genes and their DNA do determine certain things. All human beings carry 23 pairs of chromosomes—of which one pair, by the way, is an "unmatched" pair in males (XY), but a "real" pair of sex chromosomes (XX) in females. All genes are located on these chromosomes, so they come in pairs as well. During conception, both parents each contribute only a half set of their chromosomes, one of each pair, so their child ends up again with 23 pairs. Depending on whether the father passed on his X- or his Y-chromosome, the child will be either male (XY) or female (XX). There is a gene on the Y chromosome that acts as a master switch and is responsible for the development of an unborn baby into a male by initiating the testes development (whereas other genes on the Y chromosome are mainly important for male fertility). In this case, the power of genes and their DNA is quite determining and controlling.

As a matter of fact, an XY person is going to be a male, whether he likes it or not. And an XX person is going to be a female, whether she likes it or not. Those are facts that cannot be changed, regardless of what we would like the facts to be. The free-will is only coming is to accept or reject this fact, but it cannot change that fact. As a consequence, a person whose biological identity is male cannot have a female identity; if he still thinks he does, it is only in his head as an imitation of the other sex. We do not have the freedom to be either, or both, or neither, depending on our mood.

In other words, sexual orientation is not a social construction but a biological one that is essential to our identity. But you don't need to be a biologist to know that boys are different from girls, as little as you would need to be a veterinarian to know that cats are different from dogs. It is a physical, empirically verifiable reality that does not change simply because our beliefs or desires do. One can surgically change the genitalia and gonads one was born with, but not one's sex. The physician Carl Elliott once remarked that cultural and historical conditions have not just revealed transsexuals but may in fact be creating them. This may explain why the so-called gender-identity disorder is on the rise; it seems to be spreading like wildfire. Because of an increasing number of broken families and same-sex parents, a child may not have the right parent to identify with, and therefore its gender may not have a chance to line up with the appropriate sex. As the lawyer Joseph Backholm said about gender ideologists, "The irony is that a sex change itself reinforces the gender stereotypes they claim to be rejecting."

Something similar can be said about skin color, which is also strongly regulated by genes. Just as transgendered men do not become women, or vice versa—for our sex is part of who we are, even genetically—in a similar way do transracial individuals not become members of another race by perception, because their skin color, too, is a part of who they are and what they were born with. A white woman declaring that she is "in fact" black is just as odd as a woman declaring that she is in fact a man. Desires cannot change facts, no matter what our free-will tells us.

The determining role of genes and their DNA does not end here. Certain genes are very regulating and controlling. For one thing, they regulate all the important metabolic pathways through the enzymes they produce. Without those enzymes and the genes that code for them, no metabolic pathways would be possible. That's why we share many of them with the animal world. We have no say on this, thank God. They do their work without us knowing much about them. And thus, they keep us alive and kicking. The free-will has no role to play here.

This also is the case for many other genetic features we have. If you carry the genetic code for colorblindness, for instance, there is not much you can do about it. If you have the genetic code for blood type AB, you will have that blood type for the rest of your life, whether you like it or not. That's not a matter of free-will. And the same holds for many other genes and alleles—unfortunately also the ones that cause diseases.

Apparently, the power of having a free-will is very limited here, albeit not entirely useless. People who were born with alleles that cause a disease may have the free choice to accept their disease or rather ignore it. They may also have the free choice to counteract the effects of these diseases with diets and other treatments, if possible. For instance, persons who carry an allele that causes increased levels of the amino acid phenylalanine in their body can decide to follow a diet that limits the intake of phenylalanine. Not easy to do, but that's where the free-will must play a role. A more serious case is a person who has the genetic code for hemophilia, caused by some missing or low-level blood clotting factors. There is no simple solution to combat this disease, even if we are determined to search for a cure. We will just leave it at that for now, without going into more examples.

Genes, and their DNA, are not fully autonomous

There is no doubt that genes and their DNA do have power. But how far does their power go? We get constantly bombarded with an ideology of complete genetic determinism. We are supposedly the mere product of our genes. Genetic determinism says that the *genotype* completely determines the *phenotype*—that is, the genes completely determine what an organism turns out to be. We could also call this view "puppet determinism," because we are supposed to dance entirely on the strings of our genes. The simplest form of genetic determinism holds that the genes of parents inevitably determine the characteristics of their children. If so, our next generation has already been fully predestined. If that were true, there wouldn't be much freedom left, if any.

The case for human freedom and free-will looks completely lost, unless you know a bit more about those genes. A few decades ago, the general estimate for the number of human genes was thought to be well over 100,000. However, the number of protein-coding genes has gradually been lowered to around 21,000 genes—which is only a little bit more than the 20,470 genes a tiny roundworm needs in order to manufacture its utter simplicity. And we have only 300 unique genes not found in mice. No wonder that the president of Celera, a bio-corporation, said about this surprising finding "This tells me genes cannot possibly explain all of what makes us what we are." At least, we have a first indication here that genes are not as "almighty" as some tend to think.

Whereas simple genetic disorders like albinism follow a simple rule of being determined by one single gene, most cases do not belong to this category. The vast majority of human diseases and other genetic traits are *multi*-factorial, influenced by many genes interacting with one another as well as by a vast array of signals from the environment of each cell (nutrient supply, hormones, electrical signals from other cells, etc.). All of these together will reflect the external world of the organism as a whole (upbringing, learning, experience, culture, religion). Thus, the same mutation in a specific gene may produce very different results, depending on their surrounding background as well as their genetic background (all other interacting genes), as each human being has a background that is in essence unique. No two persons are completely identical, not even when they have the same genome as is the case in identical twins. Identical twins don't even have identical fingerprints!

Here is another nail in the coffin of simple genetic determinism. DNA on its own does usually not produce anything, not even proteins! The role of DNA is to provide a specification as to how amino acids are to be strung together into proteins by some synthetic machinery. But this string of amino acids is not even yet a protein. To become a protein with the proper physiological and structural functions, it must be folded into a three-dimensional configuration that is only partly based on its amino acid sequence; it is also determined by the cellular environment and by special

Chapter 4: Do We Really Have a Free-will?

processing proteins. Insulin for diabetics makes a case in point. Recently, the DNA coding sequence for human insulin was inserted into bacteria, which are then grown in large fermenters until a protein with the amino acid sequence of human insulin can be extracted. But amino acid sequence does not determine the shape of a protein. The first proteins harvested through this process did have the correct sequence but were physiologically inactive. Imagine what had happened: The bacterial cell had folded the protein incorrectly!

Another new development is the role of DNA methylation and histone modification, each of which alters how genes are expressed without altering the underlying DNA sequence of the genome. They can turn a gene off, resulting in the inability of genetic information to be read from DNA—so removing the methyl tag could turn the gene back on. The study of such phenomena is called epigenetics. It is the study of heritable changes in gene activity which are not genetic—that is, not caused by changes in the genotype.

All of this means that there is no simple pathway from genotype to phenotype. In general, it is not only the genes that shape our behavior, but everything that we see and hear around us, plus all the dreams, hopes, plans, and expectations we foster in our minds. All of these have an impact on the way we develop ourselves. Obviously, this is where the free-will can play a significant role. What seems to be "in-born" may in fact very well be "in-printed" or even "self-taught." This issue has become known as the nature-nurture debate in genetics.

Brainwashed by the ideology of genetic determinism, some geneticists still think there is a gene for *everything* we find in human beings. Possible candidates are plenty: homosexuality, bisexuality, schizophrenia, alcoholism, kleptomania, pedophilia, even religion. But we should realize that many of these gene candidates are still in the stage of invention while awaiting the stage of discovery. In science, discoveries always start as inventions—typically called hypotheses. However, not all inventions lead to discoveries. To use an analogy, the person who invented "Atlantis" did not discover Atlantis; it remains a legendary island until further notice. The same in science: Most inventions do not lead to discoveries. Yet some scientists think they have made a discovery when all they have in mind is an invention, a hypothesis. As a result, we have been bombarded with new genes for almost everything you might think of.

Apparently, there are geneticists who claim a genetic basis for something that may not be genetic. Perhaps alcoholism is not genetic but rather something acquired at home or in the womb or in a group of peers. Perhaps pedophilia is not genetic but a form of rape. Perhaps addictions can be healed better by religious conversion than by medication. Perhaps child abuse can be better cured with self-discipline than with sedatives. Perhaps sexual abuse of children is not based on a pedophilia gene but on sinful behavior—another form of rape that requires self-discipline rather than genetic analysis. It could very well be that a guilt complex doesn't require a shrink session but the therapy of the confessional. By reducing sinfulness to sickness, we can get rid of its moral and religious dimension. Instead, we need to constantly remind ourselves that there is more to life than genes. Genes do not provide us easy alibis. Only people who swear by genetic determinism think there must be a gene for everything—which must also include a gene for believing in determinism. That's how we get trapped in a vicious circle.

Don't take me wrong, I am not declaring all the above inventions bogus. Let me also make clear that I am not against the thought that many human features *may* have a genetic cause, but I reject that they *must* have a genetic cause. I have seen too many of them come and go in genetics. To put it differently, there certainly isn't a gene for everything. There's no "chip gene" for people with an addiction to potato chips, no "chocolate gene" for chocoholics, no "spending gene" for big spenders, etc. I could even come up with a gene that makes one believe in genetic determinism!

What can we learn from all of this? Well, genetic determinism fails to take into account human freedom and free-will ahead of time—a priori, that is, by mere definition. It excludes these beforehand, not based on scientific evidence but on mere assumption. I know that most of us would choose not to kill or to be killed, but determinists would claim also that our choice to be killed or not to kill is itself already a predetermined effect. In essence, the acceptance of determinism makes each one of us into a mechanical, automated entity without the power to deliberate how to act or how to change our direction in life. If that were true, we wouldn't be responsible for whatever we do in life.

Neuroscience: perhaps we do have a free-will

People who swear by science want science to prove or disprove there is a free-will. That's quite a claim. Is science capable of doing that? The only way to find out is analyzing what science has come up with so far.

Can science prove there is a free-will?

Well, there seems to be some recent experimental evidence that "free-will" is just an illusion. I am referring here to Benjamin Libet's famous experiments, done in the 80's, which appear to demonstrate that so-called conscious decisions are already settled before we become aware of them. How did Libet come to this conclusion?

Earlier research had already indicated that consciously chosen actions are preceded by a pattern of activity known as a Readiness Potential (RP). RP is a measurable electrical change in the brain that that is supposed to precede an act that we choose to make. This would make RP a good marker for a decision. Well, it turned out that the reported time of each decision that the people in Libet's experiment made was always a short period (some tenths of a second) *after* the RP appeared. This outcome seems to prove that the supposedly conscious decisions are in fact determined unconsciously beforehand.

What are we to make of all of this? There are many problems with this experiment. I won't go into all the details but just raise a few pertinent questions. To begin with, we should question whether the Readiness Potential really is a signal that a decision has been made. In these experiments, the experimental subjects were required to get into a frame of mind where they were ready to make a decision any moment. Perhaps the RP merely signals a quickening of attention, rather than a moment of decision!

Second, one might argue that these experiments were based more on training than on conscious intervention. It is very well possible that the experiment only measured a trained reaction time. Perhaps simple decisions like pressing a button do not require much mental intervention by reasoning or other mental activities. Experiments such as these do not seem to represent normal decision making, for we do not typically make random decisions at a random moment of our choosing. Libet asked his subjects to "let the urge [to move] appear on its own at any time without any pre-planning or concentration on when to act." However, one cannot passively wait for an urge to occur while at the same time being the one who is consciously bringing it about.

Third, being aware of the decision one has made is one thing, being aware of that awareness is another—the latter of which might require more time to develop. The delay between decision and awareness does not mean the decision was not ours, any more than the short delay before we hear our own voice means we didn't intend to say what we said.

Fourth, the most ironic part of Benjamin Libet's experiment is that on a specific day in the 1980s he personally decided—or at least he thought he did—that he would set up an experiment to find out whether human beings are in fact able to make conscious decisions. Should we then deduce from his experiment that this very decision to study the problem of free-will in an experimental setting had already been settled before Libet became aware of the fact that he wanted to set up such an experiment? Did he really make such a decision, or had all of this already been decided for him before he made the decision to study this issue? In the latter case, his experiment could work like a boomerang. Based on his own conclusion, one could very well argue that Libet must have had already a deterministic "impulse" before he consciously started his experiment.

Let's leave it at that. Where do we go from here? I would respond to all of this that we don't really need complicated experiments like Libet's to demonstrate the existence of free-will, or more in particular the existence of conscious decisions. One of the pioneers in neurosurgery, Wilder Penfield, made a compelling case about the difference between neural events and free-will activity when, during open-brain surgery, he asked one of his patients to try to resist the movement of his left arm, which Penfield was about to make move by stimulating the motor cortex in the right hemisphere of the patient's brain. The patient grabbed his left arm with his right hand in order to restrict the movement Penfield was inducing. As Penfield described this, "Behind the brain action of one hemisphere was the patient's mind. Behind the action of the other hemisphere was the electrode." In other words, one action had a physical, neural cause, whereas the other action had a non-neural, free-will cause. Therefore, he concluded that the physical cause and the mental cause had a different origin and were of a different nature.

From this follows, as the neurologist Viktor Frankl put it, that while the brain does condition the mind and its free-will, it does not give rise to it. This was also confirmed by The Nobel prize winner and neurophysiologist John Eccles who concluded from experiments such as Penfield's, "Voluntary movements can be freely initiated independently of any determining influences within the neuronal machinery of the brain itself." The cognitive scientist Jerry Fodor put it most vividly and dramatically: "If it isn't literally true that my wanting is causally responsible for my reaching, and my itching is causally responsible for my scratching, and my believing is causally responsible for my saying ... if none of that is literally true, then practically everything I believe about anything is false and it's the end of the world."

What the brain cannot do

You might be surprised to hear how I answer the question of what it is that the brain—and therefore, neuroscience—cannot do. Here is my answer: what the brain cannot do is *thinking*. I know that is hard to accept for many of us who have been brainwashed by neuroscientists into believing that the "mind" is a very nebulous concept, whereas the "brain" is something tangible for everyone and is more accessible to scientific tools and therefore more acceptable in science. That's why many neuroscientists have done away with the mind and replaced it with the brain. Each time they use the word "mind," you can just swap it with the word "brain." Well, my response would be that neuroscientists

Chapter 4: Do We Really Have a Free-will? 97

do indeed study the brain, but then I must ask next: can they study the mind as well?

At first sight, you would think so. When we are thinking, we think with our brains, not our stomach. Neuroscience has shown us that it is the brain that produces and manages our thoughts. But upon closer inspection, there is something strange going on here. Charles Darwin wrote in an early notebook that "thought" is a "secretion of the brain." It may indeed look like the brain secretes thoughts the way the pancreas secretes insulin, but thoughts are non-material entities. As mentioned earlier, the German philosopher and mathematician Gottfried Leibniz used a striking analogy, picturing the brain so much enlarged that one could walk in it as in a mill. Inside the mill, we could see movements of several parts, but never anything like a thought. Hence thoughts and the like must be completely different from simple mechanical movements of parts and particles. His analogy is quite compelling, even when we replace mechanical movements with the chemical cascades and electrical pathways that neuroscience speaks of today.

As a matter of fact, there is something very peculiar about thoughts: they have something that we do not find in material things. Unlike material entities, thoughts are not large or small, light or heavy, hard or soft—but instead, they are true or false, right or wrong, clear or unclear. Thoughts have no mass, no size, no color. In the world of molecules and neurons, on the other hand, there is no true of false. Therefore, the brain cannot tell false thoughts apart from true beliefs.

But there is at least one more peculiarity that we find in thoughts. Whereas something like pain, for instance, can be induced in a physical way, there is no evidence that experimental stimulation of specific neuronal areas is able to produce a specific mental state, let alone a specific thought. Again, the brain is not an organ that secretes thoughts similar to the way the hypothalamus secretes hormones. The presumed jump from physical matter to "thinking matter" appears to be enormous, perhaps even unbridgeable. There must be something more to bridge this gap—the mind, I would say.

You might think that a thought is merely made up of words, but there is much more to it. What gives thinking and having thoughts the power they have is not just words, but *concepts*. What, then, makes these activities so powerful? Well, thinking by using a concept such as "circle" requires *universality*, whereas sensory information is about particulars only. We can talk about specific circles, but the concept "circle" is about all and any kind of circles. We can even conceptualize what we cannot visualize—a circle with four dimensions, for instance—which must be something mental then, not neural. All of this would be possible only if the mind is not identical to the brain. In fact, the mind is necessary to come up with generalizations and abstractions such as the law of gravity, for instance. Newton's mind was able to see beyond the sensory impression of a particular falling apple. He "saw" gravity as the connection between falling objects on earth and planets moving around the sun in elliptical orbits. This has got to be more than a brain issue. Put differently, the law of gravity didn't come from Newton's brain, but from his mind.

Claiming that concepts are merely the product of neural activity, as some neuroscientists have tried to broadcast, is not going to save their case. They say, for instance, that thoughts are nothing but neurons firing in the brain. However, the problem is that they get trapped in a vicious circle, because the claim that thoughts or concepts are merely neurons firing would then also be nothing but neurons firing. If neuroscientists want to claim that their denying of anything immaterial is true, then they should realize this very thought must be more than a certain pattern of

Chapter 4: Do We Really Have a Free-will?

electrical activity in their brain cells—otherwise, they are undermining their very own foundation, making their claim self-destructive. The conclusion is clear: thoughts must be more than neural entities.

Neuroscientists may not give up too easily on their claim of brain-mind identity. They use, for instance, so-called localization studies to make their case. When a certain kind of mental activity occurs, certain parts of the brain do display increased blood flow and increased electrical activity. They will point out that certain mental phenomena, such as thoughts, are associated with certain neural phenomena, such as brain waves. This correlation makes them conclude that mental activity is only a brain issue.

However, they cannot conclude from this that these mental phenomena were *caused* by neural phenomena. Correlation doesn't automatically imply causation, as we learned already in high school. There is, for instance, a statistical correlation between the sales of ice cream and the sales of sunglasses, but that does not mean one causes the other. In a similar way, the fact that regions light up during functional magnetic resonance imaging (fMRI) does not tell us whether this lit-up state is causing a certain mental state, or rather just reflecting it. The fact remains that the brain is governed by laws of physics, chemistry, and biology, whereas thoughts are not. Thoughts come from the mind and are immaterial entities, whereas brainwaves come from the brain and are material entities—unlike thoughts, they can have different frequencies, for instance. The mind's dependence on the brain is one thing, but identity between mind and brain quite another. In short, neuroscientists may be able to read a person's brain, but not a person's mind.

When we want to understand the problems we encounter here, the brain may fail us terribly. It is indeed true that we cannot understand things without using our brains, but it does not follow that our brains are doing the understanding. Understanding is the result of an intellectual, and therefore immaterial, activity that cannot be achieved by any material organ, not even the brain. St. Thomas Aquinas stressed that already long ago. Many believe that if one makes the brain responsible for thinking, then it somehow becomes the principal agent of thinking. However, that idea is as dubious as assuming that if one makes the hand responsible for grasping, then it must be the principal agent of grasping. In fact, the hand is not the agent of grasping, but merely an organ or tool of grasping.

Nevertheless, it remains tempting for neuroscientists to make the brain responsible for everything the mind does. This is also obvious when they equate the working of the mind to the working of a machine such as a computer—thus making the computer a popular model for the brain nowadays. However, computers require a human maker with a mind and would still need a human subject to give their informational output some meaning or sense. Without human subjects, computers just cannot "think." This means computers cannot explain the human mind, but they must presume its existence. Computers do not create thoughts, but they may carry thoughts that were created by the mind of a human subject—namely, the programmer of the computer. This makes it hard to use the computer analogy to fully understand and explain the human mind, for without the human mind, there would be no computers. Hence, we end up being trapped again in a form of circular reasoning from which there is no way out.

Of course, new questions arise. If the mind is indeed different from the brain, you may want to ask how those two are related. I would say, one of the best analogies to explain how mind and brain can work together is comparing this with a news report on radio coming to us from a receiver through its antenna, transistors, and speakers. The radio does indeed help transmit the news, but the receiver is certainly not the origin of the news and does not determine the content of the news that it broadcasts. In a similar way, one might say that the mind somehow uses and needs the brain just like a radio station uses and needs the receiver. Think of the following case. We may use our eyes or fingers to count things; however, it is not the eyes or fingers that do the counting, neither does the brain—the mind does.

Something similar can be said about thoughts. The brain acts as the physical carrier for the mind's immaterial thoughts, comparable to the way thoughts can be expressed on paper. The thoughts come from the mind, not the brain; the brain just communicates them. On the other hand, when something is broken in the carrier—the brain, that is—this does not mean there is something broken in the mind too. When the receiver breaks down, the news broadcast is still there.

I still think there are more fundamental problems for those who replace the mind with the brain. Earlier in this book, we identified this view as a form of reductionism and scientism. That means there are serious problems with this view. One of them is the following. If the mind were just the brain, then its thoughts would be as fragile as the molecules they are supposedly based on. Our thoughts would be sitting on a "swamp of molecules," unable to pull themselves up by their own bootstraps. In order to make any claims, even more so in science, we must validate them; otherwise, they are worth nothing. If Watson and Crick, Planck and Einstein, Darwin and Dawkins, or any other scientists, were nothing but their neurons, then their scientific theories would be as fragile as the molecules within their neurons, leading to self-destruction.

It is actually quite ironic that this leads to contradictions besides—for example, the contradiction that one cannot deny the mental without affirming it. Scholars such as J.B.S. Haldane and

C.S. Lewis have worded this paradox along the following lines: If I believe that my thoughts are determined fully by the motions of atoms in my brain, I have no reason to suppose that this belief is indeed true, and hence I have no reason for accepting that they are fully determined by atoms. This paradox leads to the conclusion that mental activities must be different from neural activities. To explain the mind in terms of physics (atoms) or biology (neurons) obscures the fact that one would still need to have a mind first before one could even have physics or biology.

This leads to an even more general conclusion: the physical world can never be studied by something purely physical. Obviously, science can study the human brain, but I doubt whether it could ever study the human mind. Even when scientists pretend that they do have the capacity to study the human mind, they enter a mind-boggling situation. Why is that? To study the human mind, science needs to start from the very minds of those scientists. Scientists may be able to comprehend the brain, but not the mind, for they need a mind to begin with so they can study the brain. We have a simple truth here: the brain cannot be studied without the minds of neuroscientists.

Hence, we end up with the assertion that the mind is not the same as the brain. The brain needs a mind so it can deal with thoughts. It could very well be the mind that gives us what the brain and neuroscience may not be able to give us. That would also be true of the free-will. We are back again where we started.

The free-will is hard to deny

Commonsense tells us we do have a free-will and can make free decisions. G. K. Chesterton, for instance, once said in a rather direct and simple way as is characteristic for him: if the world is fully determined, it makes no sense to say "thank you" to the waiter for bringing the mustard. To give thanks implies that something that did happen need not have happened. Chesterton's observation is even backed by some advanced-thinking scientists. One of them is the Nobel-laureate and physicist Arthur Compton (known for the Compton Effect) who used to say: "If the laws of physics ever should come to contradict my conviction that I can move my little finger at will, then all the laws of physics should be revised and reformulated."

As we mentioned earlier, Wilder Penfield gave some experimental backing for this conviction. Let's give Penfield's experiment a more philosophical background. It is *I*, as a person and subject, who makes rational and moral decisions. We have a fascinating situation here: I-as-a-subject (I-now) can reflect on I-as-an-object (I-past). As a subject, I may investigate I-as-an-object and then realize, for instance, that I-as-an-object made a mistake. Call it *self-examination*, if you want. Because I-now is always a pace ahead of I-past, I can never blame my "glands" or my genes or my neurons for what I did wrong. All decisions are *my* decisions—no matter whether they are rational and moral, or irrational and immoral. Whenever I reflect on myself as an object, I determine who I want to be in life.

Because "I-now" is always a pace ahead of "I-past"—thus leaving open what the next step of "I-now" will be—my past is part of my future but doesn't determine who I am now or will be in the future. That is why I am also responsible for my future—including all the rational and moral decisions which I am about to make. The existence of the free-will defies determinism, thus allowing us to make free choices and decisions in life based on *rationality* and *morality*. Go for a version of yourself, not someone else's—which is called self-determination. To be self-determined, you cannot be fully pre-determined!

I would conclude that the free-will remains standing, in spite of what science may tell us. Science is just not able to prove or disprove the existence of a free-will, because science is about material things, whereas the free-will is a non-material entity. Why, then, is it so hard for neuroscientists to acknowledge that there is a free-will? Probably their main reason is that when they study the brain, they think they are also studying the mind. So, if the brain doesn't show free-will activity, then the mind cannot either. However, this argument is based on the assumption that the mind is identical to the brain. As we argued earlier, this assumption might very well be a form of reductionism, even scientism. Could it be that the free-will is part of the mind, but not necessarily of the brain?

Philosophy: yes, we do have a free-will

If science cannot prove definitively that we have a free-will, perhaps philosophy can. I take philosophy here in its broad sense, including the application of logic and math—taken after its original meaning, "the love of wisdom," in the sense of thinking about thinking. Let's try to think about our thinking in terms of a free-will.

Can determinism be defeated?

There is this classic technique for proving that a system or theory is deficient by demonstrating that it creates contradictions or inconsistencies—and therefore, cannot be true. The philosopher and physicist Karl Popper used this technique to show that the notion of overall determinism is inherently wrong. He achieved his point as follows. First suppose we have a huge computer that can predict the future based on data regarding all initial conditions and all the laws needed to derive effects from causes.

The machine gives answers by turning a lamp on in case of "no" and off in case of "yes." Now we feed and ask the computer to predict whether the lamp will be on or off after ninety nine years. After going through numerous calculations, the computer predicts that the lamp will be on by actually switching the lamp off (or reversed)—which makes either prediction wrong. This result demonstrates that there is something wrong with the assumption of complete determinism.

Here are some possible explanations why determinism may be wrong: not all necessary data and/or laws can be specified; prediction is inherently different from explanation; a computer with enough computational power does not exist; prediction-before-the-fact always takes so much time that it becomes explanation-after-the-fact; or determinism is just not an all-pervasive phenomenon. Personally, I would go for the last explanation: determinism is not an all-pervasive phenomenon. It is only true in limited, demarcated areas. That should leave us space for what is called "free-will."

Therefore, I would like to make a distinction between *methodological* determinism and *ontological* (or metaphysical) determinism. Methodological determinism is a harmless yet powerful technique used in science; it applies the law of cause-and-effect to a simplified version of the object under investigation. It is a handy tool to study things in the "test-tube-like" shelter of a model, which acts as a simplified replica of the original—that is, with a limited scope and under specific boundary conditions. But once we go outside the model and export its findings to other territories, methodological determinism becomes ontological determinism—a "hard-core" kind of determinism, basically a world-view that claims that what holds for the model also holds for the entire world.

Methodological determinism is very attractive, especially so for scientists, as we found out. Think of the solar system, which is very predictable—in fact, a system with no surprises. The situation becomes a bit more ambiguous when we try to forecast the weather, but it is nevertheless of a deterministic nature as well. Today's weather depends on what happened yesterday, and so will tomorrow's weather depend on today's. If meteorologists give us a faulty forecast, they can always blame something else—the inaccuracy of the data, the complexity of the calculations, and so on—but never will they give up the idea of determinism. Science would not be possible if it did not assume that like causes have like effects and that the future depends on the past. In other words, the orderliness of this universe is in fact a prerequisite for all science's endeavors.

No wonder then, that we end up with the doctrine of complete causal determinism, in its ontological version, which the French astronomer Pierre Simon Laplace described emphatically in these terms: "We may regard the present state of the universe as the effect of its past and as the cause of its future." Science seems to confirm this over and over again: The future is completely determined by the past. Period!

Some might object that determinism in its all-pervading version is outdated and has forever been defeated by the physicist Niels Bohr and his followers. According to Werner Heisenberg, one of them, it is impossible to determine simultaneously the position and momentum of a particle with any great degree of certainty; the more precisely one property is known, the less precisely the other can be known. Without having exact values, the behavior of atoms and subatomic particles can presumably no longer be predicted until measured. There is serious discussion among scientists how to interpret all of this. But no matter what, a simple, or simplistic, version of determinism might be on its way out.

In classical physics, we were still able to predict the exact location of particles from moment to moment, but in quantum physics, we can only calculate the *probabilities* that the particle will be found in various places. These probabilities are expressed in the so-called "wave function" of a particle. Therefore, in quantum theory, one does not calculate what is bound to happen, but what might happen based on probabilities. Apparently, in addition to deterministic laws, there are now also probabilistic laws in physics. Is this the end of the determinism debate?

Not really. We still have a crucial point left. In the real world, things do happen or do not happen—there is no in-between. This step requires measurements or observations of what does happen in reality, so we can bring probability and reality back together. That step requires an "observer," the physicist, who intervenes in the physical system as an "outsider" to determine which possibility has become reality. The observer cannot be *within* the physical system, and at the same time, observe that physical system from the outside. What the actual outcome of the observation is cannot be determined by quantum theory alone but must be determined by an observer. The role of the observer is to find out which possibility did occur, and which probabilities did not. This amounts to making a judgment, which can only be done by the human mind of the observer and its intellect. Lo and behold, we are back again to the elusiveness of the human mind and its free-will.

But the fight is not over yet. It probably does not come as a surprise that the free-will has been explained by using the quantum interpretation of probability. That might be in fact a desperate move to defend our free-will in terms that physics can provide. However, such a move would reduce the free-will to a merely and entirely physical phenomenon, which is a despicable form of reductionism and scientism. I think I have said enough against that idea.

Another attack on free-will

Another surprise might come from a completely unexpected corner. St. Thomas Aquinas, of all people, has sometimes been accused of denying the existence of the free-will because of his proofs for the existence of God. If God is the Primary Cause, so the reasoning goes, then human beings are merely secondary causes, and therefore must be merely God's puppets. However, these misinformed accusers think of God's activities as some kind of secondary cause, situated at the same level as our own free decisions. We think, for instance, that God creatively wills that I decide to do something, and His willing then causes me to make a decision. In this scenario, God's creative fiat would be an event independent of my decision, which would indeed rob me of my autonomy. I would no longer be a free agent, but rather a puppet in the hands of God. In other words, whatever I believe to be doing on my own is in fact God's doing.

Where do these accusers go wrong? According to Aquinas, God as a Primary Cause works in such a way that we are not acted upon as if God were a secondary cause, but instead exercise our own free-will as a secondary cause of our own decisions and actions. God is not the direct cause of my decisions—I am—but He is the indirect cause that lets me be the cause of my own decisions. Seen in this light, our human freedom and free-will need not be in conflict with an all-knowing God at all. God is the complete and Primary Cause of a free act, whereas the human agent is its complete secondary cause. God's willing that I decide as I do does not make my decision God's. God's willing does not take away from me the operations of my free-will, or the actions founded upon them; they remain my own. In short, God is not the direct cause of my decisions—I am. Thomas Aquinas worded this in his own characteristic way: "Free-will is the cause of its own movement because by his free-will man moves himself to act."

But there might be another problem lurking for the human free-will. It is God's omniscience, including His fore-knowledge of all that happens. This means that God knows infallibly and from eternity what a certain person, in the exercise of free-will, will do in any given circumstances, and what he or she might or would actually have done in different circumstances. God does not have to wait on the contingent and temporal event of a person's free choice to know what that person's action will be—He knows it from eternity. However, God's infallible knowledge of our future does not mean He has some kind of secret knowledge that makes our free choices not really free but already chosen for us. "Eternity" describes something outside our experience of time. Again, St. Thomas argues that God's infallible knowledge of our future is not some secret predictive power because there is no such thing as the future for God. Rather, in God's transcendent eternity, which is outside the flow of time, all events from any time are present to God's knowledge in one eternal now. But seen from our "temporary now" perspective, we are still free actors who freely decide to cause things to happen.

Is there a way in which we, with our limited intellect, can picture this? The best I can come up with myself is something like this. Picture yourself watching a video of certain events in your past life. You may get the impression that these actions were in fact predetermined and preordained, and yet you know that most of them were freely decided upon when they were taking place. Your knowing and seeing that they happened does not mean they were predetermined—they were still rooted in your free-will. However, what is definitely wrong in this analogy is that it might suggest God's fore-knowledge is the result of God watching what happens as history unfolds. God doesn't need to watch how things happen in order to know that they happen. God knows everything by virtue of being the Primary Cause of everything that happens. God's knowledge is outside the flow of time. Hence, we do not have a conflict here with the human free-will.

The conclusion after all these detours is obvious: if we do not have a free-will, all the chapters to follow in this book would make no sense at all. Since we do have a free-will, we need to explore further.

5.

Science and Faith Reunited

So far, we have seen many cases where religious claims are being blocked by scientific claims. They often seem to be in a constant combative confrontation with each other. As we discussed already, nowadays there is even a breed of scientists and semi-scientists who are very vocal atheists, promoting their new "religion" with extremely popular books and preaching their "gospel" in media and academia. No wonder the faithful feel personally attacked. Although Christians did launch some counterattacks, they mostly retreated to their new catacombs, the church pews.

It is about time to face the challenge head-on: are science and religion really hostile to each other? Is there truly an inevitable conflict between science and religion? For centuries, the "age of religion," was the old normal that has now systematically been replaced by a new normal, the "age of science." What many people do not realize is that the conflict theory is a quite recent invention—a myth, born during the Enlightenment era. It's an ideology that denies the simple fact that many scientists are still religious, and that many Christians are scientists.

Apparently, science and faith are not in conflict with each other. To put it in a catchphrase, when I say that I come from God, I am not denying that I came here through my parents. There is nothing wrong with saying that children come from their parents, and yet at the same time, that children come from God—there is no contradiction here, no conflict, no inconsistency between the two, unless you decide ahead of time that this has got to be an either-or issue.

Of course, there is much more to it. That's why we will spend an entire chapter on this issue.

Galileo stoked the fire

Ask any audience, even an audience of Catholics, whose name they associate with the Catholic Church and her dealings with science. They will most likely shout, almost in unison, "Galileo!" This is a short reference to the "Galileo affair," which they take as a serious conflict between science and religion. It is a case that many nowadays see through the lens of the Enlightenment.

I admit, there were mistakes made on both sides of the conflict at the time, but I maintain also there was no inherent conflict here between science and religion. The point I am making is that the perceived conflict that so many talk about is in essence a myth to make the sweeping claim that religion—and the Catholic Church in particular—has always obstructed science from doing its work. Many see the Galileo affair as prima facie evidence that the free pursuit of truth became possible only after science had "liberated" itself from the religious and theological shackles of the Middle Ages. I am not so sure this is a fair characterization of what went on between Galileo's science and the Church. The case is a bit more complicated than it looks at first glance. Let's see why.

The Galileo case has in fact spawned a whole conglomerate of myths—at least ten—with each and every one being a fabrication. This cloud of myths obscures the real facts about the Galileo affair. Although conventional wisdom asserts that the controversy was simply a clash between Galileo's heliocentric theory and the traditional outdated view of the Sun revolving around Earth, there was a lot more going on than simply a disagreement about astronomy. Here is what is wrong with those myths.

Myth 1: Galileo discovered that the earth is round. Galileo did not. Many had done so already long before Galileo was even born. Columbus faced trouble going west not because his sailors thought they would sail off the edge of the world but because they rightly thought that the distance between Europe and the East Indies was much greater than Columbus did. Pythagoras and others had already assumed in the 4th century BC that the earth was a sphere. Although St. Basil the Great, in the 4th century AD, declared it a matter of no interest to us whether the earth is a sphere or a cylinder or a disk, or concave in the middle like a fan, influential Christian thinkers such as St. Clement, Origen, St. Ambrose, St. Augustine, and St. Thomas Aquinas all accepted that the earth was a globe. They did not have to wait for Galileo to come along to tell them that.

Myth 2: Galileo invented the telescope. Galileo did not. When he heard about the invention of the "telescope" in Holland—called a "spyglass" there—he immediately built one for himself, characteristically taking full credit for the invention. But his telescope was still rather primitive. Soon the Jesuit Christopher Clavius of the Roman College used an improved telescope, until Fr. Christoph Grienberger invented a telescope in 1620 that rotated on an axis parallel to the Earth's. Notice they were both dedicated Catholics.

The rather primitive features of Galileo's telescope partially explain why even Galileo himself had to concede in a letter to Johannes Kepler that many people were unable to see what they were "supposed" to see through his telescope. When Galileo demonstrated his simple telescope to a group of professors in Bologna in 1610, all admitted the instrument seemed to deceive, with some fixed stars actually seen double. Of course, this also raises the question of how reliable Galileo's observations were. Optical illusions are not uncommon in science. For instance, the founder of the Lowell Observatory, Percival Lowell, believed, based on what he called "careful scientific observation," that there were Martian-made canals on Planet Mars.

Myth 3: Galileo was the first to advance heliocentrism. Galileo was not. Nicolaus Copernicus (1473-1543) was in fact the first astronomer after the Middle Ages to publish the idea of a heliocentric model, suggesting that the earth orbited the Sun. In 1543, Copernicus had published *On the Revolution of the Celestial Orbs*, in which he supported heliocentricity—which was almost a century before Galileo "launched" his heliocentrism. So, there was nothing really new "under the sun" when Galileo made his claim. In fact, as early as the 3rd century BC, Aristarchus of Samos proposed a serious model of a heliocentric solar system.

Myth 4: Galileo proved heliocentrism to be true. Galileo did not. What he badly needed for his theory was what he could not provide—proof that his theory was true. The proof he came up with was in fact nonsense. In desperation, Galileo fabricated his theory of the tides, which purported to show that the tides are caused by the rotation of the earth. Even some of Galileo's friends could see that this was highly problematic, but Galileo plainly rejected the idea that the moon was a causal factor here.

On the other hand, Galileo could not solve the most serious problem heliocentrism was facing: an argument that had been made nearly two thousand years earlier by Aristotle himself. If the Earth did orbit the Sun, the philosopher wrote, then there would be a shift in the position of a star observed from the Earth when on one side of the Sun, and then six months later seen from the other side—the so-called stellar parallaxes. True, given the technology of Galileo's time, no such shifts in their positions could possibly be observed at the time, as it would require more sensitive measuring equipment that was not available until 1838. But the problem was still there, yet basically ignored by Galileo.

Myth 5: Galileo was an impartial scientist. Galileo was not. He consistently ignored that thee were other alternative theories for what he tried to defend. He completely neglected the heliocentric model of Johannes Kepler who had the planets move in ellipses instead of circles—which would turn out to be more accurate than Galileo's model. Besides, Galileo's model with its circular orbits—instead of the more accurate elliptical orbits of Kepler—would still need the so despised epicycles of the Ptolemaic model to correct for its own inaccuracy.

Second, there was also the geocentric model of Tycho Brahe. Brahe had the Moon and the Sun revolve around the Earth (geocentrism), but the other planets (Mercury, Venus, Mars, Jupiter, and Saturn) revolve around the Sun (heliocentrism); so, he had the Sun with those planets together revolve around the Earth. Interestingly enough, Tycho's system did fit all the prevailing data and was mathematically identical to Galileo's system for all observations available at the time. Yet, Galileo was intent to ignore Tycho's system; he never mentioned it in any of his writings. But the Jesuits of the Roman College did not and could not ignore Tycho's model—they even favored it as a halfway solution, but this did not mean they plainly rejected Galileo's model.

Myth 6: Galileo was silenced by anti-scientists. Galileo was not. Even his closest colleagues were not as convinced as he was about the validity of his heliocentrism. One can't even say that the Church condemned his theory. The Church and her Inquisition do not deal with disputes in science—only with controversies in theology, about matters of orthodoxy and heresy. Because the inquisitors in the case were very aware of their incompetence in evaluating the scientific case, they decided in 1615 to further consult their own experts for an opinion on the status of heliocentrism. They followed proper procedure by requesting professional opinions on the matter. Had the scientific experts been unanimous in their support of Galileo's model, perhaps the theologians would have bowed to their authority. But the scientific community was divided herself—Tycho, Galileo, or Kepler? The scientific case was far from settled at the time.

Myth 7: Galileo had an open mind. Galileo did not. We mentioned already how he kept silent about competing astronomical theories, but he also was not willing to listen to wise advice. The main Inquisitor, Jesuit Cardinal St. Robert Bellarmine, had pointed out to Galileo that it is perfectly acceptable to maintain Copernican's model, and thus Galileo's model, as a working hypothesis, but not necessarily as a theory about reality. But Galileo was not willing to accept Bellarmine's suggestion. He refused to present his theory as merely a hypothesis rather than established truth. He refused the reasonable alternative that heliocentrism might be considered a hypothesis until further proof could be given. On the contrary, Galileo was intent on ramming heliocentrism down the throat of Christendom.

Myth 8: Galileo muttered, "And yet it moves"—referring to a revolving earth—after he was sentenced by the Inquisition to keep silent on the subject for the rest of his life. It is among the most famous phrases attributed to Galileo, but history tells us he did not mutter this one-liner. The earliest biography of Galileo does not mention this phrase, Galileo's letters do not use the quote, and records of his trial do not cite it. In short, there is no historical evidence that Galileo did mutter this line. As with many legends, it's probably too good to be true. It is rather a fabrication that suddenly popped up in a book written by Giuseppe Baretti, more than 120 years after Galileo's death. It gave at least a dramatic twist to the Galileo case that would live on for centuries to come. Myths can live a long life.

Myth 9: Galileo was burnt at the stake, tortured, and incarcerated. Galileo was not. Voltaire's line that Galileo "groaned away his days in the dungeons of the Inquisition" is a complete fabrication made up by an anti-Catholic. In fact, Galileo never was tortured, he never was sentenced to death, and he never was imprisoned. After a period of staying with his friend Ascanio Piccolomini, the Archbishop of Siena, Galileo was allowed to return to his villa at Arcetri near Florence in 1634, where he spent the last eight years of his life under house arrest. As the late Harvard mathematician and philosopher Alfred North Whitehead put it, "In a generation which saw the Thirty Year's War and remembered Alva in the Netherlands, the worst that happened to men of science was that Galileo suffered an honorable detention and a mild reproof, before dying peacefully in his bed."

Myth 10: Galileo was condemned by the Church for his astronomy. Galileo was not. He was condemned for promoting a theory that seemingly contradicts Scripture as if it were certain, true, and proven, while failing to offer sufficient scientific evidence or mentioning any alternatives. To paint him as a "martyr" for science requires quite some imagination. May we consider the case closed? It is interesting to note that St. Thomas Aquinas had thought about this problem as early as four centuries before Galileo. He astutely noticed that the appearance of the visible motions of the celestial bodies "are produced either by the motion of the object seen or by the motion of the observer... it makes no difference which one is moving." In other words, either the sun could be moving, or we on earth could be moving. How profound are these words, coming from the mouth of a religious scholar whom many scientists nowadays would call outdated!

Myth 11: Galileo was an unbiased scientist. Galileo was not, at least not in his case against the Church. He became highly embroiled in various controversies with Jesuit astronomers. One dispute was with the eminent Jesuit mathematician and astronomer Fr. Horazio Grassi over the nature of comets. Although we now know that Galileo was on the wrong side of the argument, his irony and wit took their toll on his opponents. Another dispute was with Fr. Christopher Scheiner, over the priority of the discovery of sunspots. (Scholars now believe that neither man was the first.) Undoubtedly, controversies like these helped cement the Jesuits' opposition to Galileo. Initially, he had powerful friends among Cardinals, Jesuits, and even Popes, but in time, he would lose their support—not so much as a result of scientific disputes, but mostly because of the frequency and acidity of his attacks. All these factors played an important role in causing many Jesuits to withdraw their support of Galileo—which he later would need so badly. What irked Church officials was not so much *what* Galileo was saying, but *how* he was saying it.

Myth 12: Galileo was a genuine scientist in this dispute. Galileo was not. He deliberately ventured into theological territory, when certain theologians objected that his theory seemed contrary to Scripture. In response, he entered, with no real expertise, into a theological discussion on the proper mode of interpreting Scripture. In those days, if you argued a new scientific theory, you would get the Church's attention and even support, because so many high-ranking churchmen were also men of science, so you would be arguing on equal footing. But if you ventured to argue a new scriptural interpretation, you immediately got the whole Church on her feet, and you would no longer be arguing on equal footing.

At the time, there was little elasticity in Catholic biblical theology, because the Church had just gone through the bruising battles of the Protestant Reformation. Times had changed: whereas Copernicus, almost a century earlier, had hardly received any negative response from the Church, Galileo published his books at a time when the Church was facing theological turbulence. One of the chief quarrels with the Protestants was over the private interpretation of Scripture—and here was another private interpretation by a scientist. Theologians were not prepared to entertain the heliocentric theory based on a layman's interpretation of Scripture. As to be expected, he was asking for more trouble. His friend Cardinal Dini had already warned him that he could write freely so long as he "kept out of the sacristy." But Galileo had his mind set.

I think we may conclude from all the above, that Galileo was not massacred by the Church, nor did religion suffer defeat during the Galileo trial. In this trial, it was not science that was condemned by the Church but rather that part of Galileo that was more of an ideologue than a scientist during this dispute. He was an early instance of that very modern type: the cultural, political, and activist scientist. Galileo was a passionately driven man with a new, sacred mission: all of Europe, starting with the Church, had to buy into the heliocentric model of Copernicus. And he wanted the Church to back that mission—but that is not the Church's mission. It led him to proclaiming himself an expert in theological matters and promoting a theory that seemingly contradicts Scripture as certain, true, and proven, but without sufficient scientific evidence.

Born in the cradle of religion

As we found out, the "Galileo affair" does not support the idea that there is a conflict between science and faith. On the contrary, the conflict theory is at best a presupposition some people like to advocate before starting the discussion. I am going even one step further than saying there is no conflict between the two by claiming that science was in fact born in the cradle of Christianity—which amounts to saying that there might not have been any science without the Judeo-Christian tradition.

What is this idea based on? The main argument for this claim is that the Judeo-Christian God is a reliable God—not confined inside the Aristotelian box, not capricious like the Olympians in ancient Greece, and not entirely beyond human comprehension like in Islam. The world depends on the laws that God has laid down in creation. That is where the order of the universe ultimately comes from. And the only way to find out what this order looks like is to "interrogate" the universe by investigation, exploration, and experiment. That means science was on its way. Through experiments we can "read" God's mind, so to speak. Even the nuclear physicist J. Robert Oppenheimer, who was not a Christian himself, was ready to acknowledge this very fact when he said, "Christianity was needed to give birth to modern science."

It is this very Judeo-Christian concept of a Creator God that makes science possible. Belief in a Creator God entails that nature is not a divine but a created entity. Nature is not divine in itself, only its Maker is—which opens the door for scientific exploration. A created world is other than God, and in that very otherness, scientists find their freedom to act. Without this belief, one would not be allowed to even "touch" the divine. A rational God has created a universe that we can rely on with our rational minds, made in likeness of God's mind. The Book of Wisdom (11:20) says about God, "You have arranged all things by measure and number and weight." Hence the only way to find out what the Creator has actually done in His creation is to go out, look, and measure—which opens the door for scientific exploration. It requires the "humility" of scientists to wait for and subject themselves to the outcome of their experiments.

In contrast, nature remains an enigma when it is ruled by whimsical deities, chaotic powers, or by man-made philosophical decrees and regulations. The late physicist Fr. Stanley L. Jaki used the phrase "stillbirths of science" in reference to the ancient cultures of Egypt, China, India, Babylon, Greece, and Arabia. Jaki claimed that science—as a universal discipline by which laws of physics and systems of laws were established—was born of Christianity, and nowhere else. In his own words, "Within the biblical world view it was ultimately possible to assume that the heavens and the earth are ruled by the same laws. But it was not possible to do this within the world vision that dominated all other ancient cultures. In all of them the heavens were divine." Jaki again: "Within the Greek ambiance it was impossible, in fact it would have been a sacrilege, to assume that the motion of the moon and the fall of an apple were governed by the same law. It was, however, possible for Newton, because he was the beneficiary of the age-old Christian faith."

Is this idea far-fetched? The idea that Christianity gave rise to science may indeed surprise many, as it did to Alfred North Whitehead's Harvard audience in 1925. When this famous mathematician and philosopher told them that modern science was a product of Christianity, they were shocked, probably out of mere ignorance. Currently, this claim of giving such an exclusive role to Christianity for the rise of science is receiving more traction. More and more scholars have come to realize that Christianity was indeed a fertile ground for the birth of science. The sociologist Rodney Stark, for instance, argues that the reason why science arose in Europe, and nowhere else, is because of Catholicism: "It is instructive that China, Islam, India, ancient Greece, and Rome all had a highly developed alchemy. But only in Europe did alchemy develop into chemistry. By the same token, many societies developed elaborate systems of astrology, but only in Europe did astrology lead to astronomy." Stark had to come to the conclusion, "Science was not the work of western secularists or even deists; it was entirely the work of devout believers in an active, conscious, creator God."

Even the atheist and biologist E. O. Wilson had to say about Chinese scholars, "No rational Author of Nature existed in their universe; consequently the objects they meticulously described did not follow universal principles." This explains why the first Jesuits, when they went to China, were amazed at the Asians' lack of progress in their understanding of the world and the heavens. These cultures contributed talent and ingenuity, but scientific enterprise never came along. Other scholars have come to similar conclusions. As I mentioned already, the nuclear physicist J. Robert Oppenheimer had to acknowledge, "Christianity was needed to give birth to modern science." Even someone like the philosopher of science Thomas Kuhn—without identifying its Judeo-Christian core, though—had to say about Europe, "No other place and time has supported that very special community from with scientific productivity comes."

But there are still many people who are not aware of the fact that science was born in the cradle of Christianity. I believe it is quite obvious that Christianity was a sufficient condition for the rise of science. But was it also a necessary condition? That is obviously impossible to prove. We should point out, though, that we did not see science arise in Asia or Africa, neither did we in ancient Greece, which might indicate a necessary condition was missing. Aristotle may have done quite accurate observations on the embryology of chickens, but that was not real science. He merely used tools not to experiment but to remove what obstructs a scholar's view. Experiments were out of the question for him and for his contemporaries because they were believed to disturb the delicate harmony of nature through unnatural interventions from without. The only exception might be found in Alexandria where Egyptian technicians and Greek theoreticians worked together. Archimedes comes to mind. He was first of all a mathematician, but he was also a genius in applying mathematics

Chapter 5: Science and Faith Reunited

to the natural world. However, he and others had to wait for people such as the Franciscan Friar Roger Bacon who introduced the distinction between "passive observation" and "experimental intervention," which started a unique, revolutionary conception of science in the 1200s.

As said earlier, only in Christian Europe did astrology develop into astronomy, and alchemy into chemistry. Is this proof for my claim? Probably not, but it makes my claim very likely. The historian of science Edward Grant is arguably right in stating that the gift from the Latin Middle Ages to the modern world "is a gift that may never be acknowledged. Perhaps it will always retain the status it has had for the past four centuries as the best-kept secret of Western civilization." Why does this elude so many modern minds, including those of scientists? The reason is probably that they have been brainwashed by ideas from the Enlightenment and the ideology of scientism. Yet, some are honest enough to thank the Catholic Church for her support.

Support for the claim that religious faith was conducive to the rise of science comes also from a different angle. Science cannot be done without certain assumptions. Without those assumptions, science has no base to rest on. Science cannot take credit for its own starting point. Think of the following. Without the assumption that there is an objectively real world, science would not be possible. Without the assumption that there is order in nature, science would not be possible. Without the assumption that like causes have like effects, science would not be possible. Without the assumption that the world is comprehensible, science would not be possible. However, what science cannot do is proving its own assumptions, as it cannot attempt to justify them without arguing in a circle. Yet, these assumptions are needed for science to get started and do what it can do. In other words, what science can do is possible only if it realizes what it cannot do—

testing and proving its own assumptions.

So, where do those assumptions then come from and what are they based on? Since science itself cannot prove or explain them, religious faith may provide the help and support science needs but cannot provide on its own. It is faith in God, especially in line with the Judeo-Christian tradition, that makes these assumptions rational and understandable. The God of Christianity is the best, and perhaps only, explanation for these assumptions, which science can only assume but never prove.

What we have here is a faith that makes you think. It creates a cradle in which science can be born. To say it more strongly, it is only in such a cradle that science could have been born. Put in another way, all scientists—whether they like it or not—are still living off Judeo-Christian capital, no matter how "independent" they think they are.

Science, a Judeo-Christian project

Science, as a Judeo-Christian project, is based on what the Bible and the Church teach us—namely, that the universe was created by a rational intellect and can be rationally interrogated, even by using experiments. Is there any historical evidence to confirm that Christianity did provide this insight?

One of the first to be aware of the Catholic roots of science during the Middle Ages was the French physicist Pierre Duhem (1861-1916). When he studied the works of Catholic medieval mathematicians and philosophers such as John Buridan, Nicholas of Oresme, and Roger Bacon, their sophistication took him by surprise. He consequently came to regard them as the founders of modern science, as they had in his view anticipated many of the discoveries of Galileo and later scientists. Duhem had to come to the conclusion that "the mechanics and physics of which

Chapter 5: Science and Faith Reunited 125

modern times are justifiably proud [came] from doctrines professed in the heart of the medieval schools." And those schools were undeniably Catholic.

Pierre Duhem did in fact path-breaking work in the history of science when he showed that the doctrines of the Church have been a permanent ally of, rather than an obstacle to, the success of the scientific enterprise in the West. He opened many eyes for the fact that it was indeed the—so often despised—metaphysical framework of medieval Catholicism that made modern science possible. Many historians of science and other scholars would later follow his lead.

The facts are quite clear. Just as the Catholic Church patronized the arts, so did she vigorously support scientific research. We find this support as early as in the Middle Ages. Many nowadays still have the wrong impression about the Middle Ages, thinking they were "dark" ages that did not have any scientific activities. Nowadays it is common to distinguish the "Dark Ages" (ca 500 – ca 1000) from the "Middle Ages" (ca 1000 – ca 1500). The "Dark Ages" were certainly not "dark" because of the Catholic Church, but rather because of invading vandals. The only reason any science at all made it through these "dark" ages was because the Catholic Church was hiding all her textbooks from the rampaging and pillaging Huns, Vandals, Visigoths, and Vikings. Had it not been for the Catholic Church, all schools of learning would have died during these "Dark Ages."

Even during the "Dark Ages," monasteries of that era were diligent in the study of sciences such as medicine. As early as 633, the Council of Toledo required the establishment of a school in every diocese, teaching every branch of knowledge, including medicine. Then, around 800, King Charlemagne decreed that each monastery and cathedral chapter establish a school, and in these schools, medicine was commonly taught. It was at one such school that the future Pope Sylvester II taught medicine. Clergy were also active at the School of Salerno, the oldest medical school in Western Europe. Famous physicians and medical researchers included the Abbot of Monte Cassino (Bertharius), the Abbot of Reichenau (Walafrid Strabo), and the Bishop of Rennes (Marbodus of Angers). And last but not least, Hildegard of Bingen (1098-1179), a Doctor of the Church, is among the most distinguished of Medieval Catholic women scientists. Hildegard wrote a text on the natural sciences [*Physica*], as well as a text on "Causes and Cures" [*Causae et Curae*].

It is becoming more and more evident—and has been accepted by a growing contingent of historians—that science was indeed born in the Catholic cradle of the Middle Ages. Just look at the following list of some of its pioneer crafters. As early as the 7th century, the English Benedictine monk Bede studied the sea's tidal currents. At the end of the first millennium, Pope Sylvester II had already used advanced instruments of astronomical observation, driven by a passion for understanding the order of the universe. He also endorsed and promoted study of arithmetic, mathematics, and astronomy.

It was also during this time that Bishop Robert Grosseteste introduced the scientific method, including the concept of falsification, while the Franciscan friar Roger Bacon established concepts such as hypothesis, experimentation, and verification. In other words, the scientific project, even the scientific method itself, was and is an invention of these Catholic pioneers. Had it not been for the Catholic Church, the Scientific Revolution would probably never have happened. After all, science did not take root in South America, Africa, the Middle East, or Asia—it took place in Christian Europe.

The currently rather popular idea that classic Greek texts had been lost in Europe during the Middle Ages and then were given back to Europe by Muslims ignores the fact that they had been preserved and transmitted by Catholic scholars such as Boethius, the monks of Mont Saint-Michel, William of Moerbeke, and Catholic Greeks in the Eastern part of the Empire. It was also during the Middle Ages that the first universities arose. The Middle Ages were obviously Catholic, so these first universities of the world were Catholic universities. They were the hotbed for a period of great technological and scientific advancements, as well as achievements in nearly all other fields.

After the Middle Ages, the Catholic Church got even more involved with the sciences, especially through the work of Jesuits. The historian Jonathan Wright mentions the breadth of Jesuit involvement in the sciences. He says about them:

> *[The Jesuits] contributed to the development of pendulum clocks, pantographs, barometers, reflecting telescopes and microscopes, to scientific fields as various as magnetism, optics and electricity. They observed, in some cases before anyone else, the colored bands on Jupiter's surface, the Andromeda nebula and Saturn's rings. They theorized about the circulation of the blood (independently of Harvey), the theoretical possibility of flight, the way the moon effected the tides, and the wave-like nature of light.*

In the centuries to follow, things would be moving ahead even more quickly, but still with the continuous support of the Catholic Church. In the words of Bishop Robert Barron,

> *The great founders of modern science—Copernicus, Galileo, Tycho Brahe, Descartes, Pascal, etc.—were formed in church-sponsored universities where they learned their mathematics, astronomy, and physics. Moreover, in those same universities, all of the founders would have imbibed the two fundamentally theological assumptions that made the modern sciences possible, namely, that the world is not divine—and hence can be experimented upon rather*

than worshiped—and that the world is imbued with intelligibility—and hence can be understood.

There is also growing empirical evidence that the "scientific revolution" in the 15th and 16th century had its roots more in the Christian Middle Ages than in the world of ancient Greeks such as Aristotle or of Islamic scholars such as Avicenna. The latter may have been masters in geometry and mathematics, where pure reason reigns, but this made them think they could generate scientific results deductively from passive observation, which would make those conclusions seem logically necessary. I admit that the Greek and Muslim traditions of logic and mathematics did provide the tools that science would also badly need for its ascent, but do not confuse these tools with science itself. There was a different environment needed for applying these tools in a scientific context—and that environment was the Judeo-Christian concept of Creation and a Creator God.

And more was coming! It is in fact revealing that the "scientific revolution" of the 17th century coincided with the period when Christian faith was at its strongest. It was in God that these scientists found reason to investigate nature and trust their own scientific reasoning. Copernicus' achievements were in fact based on his religious belief that nothing was easier for God than to have the earth move, if He so wished: "To know the mighty works of God, to comprehend His wisdom and majesty and power ... surely all this must be a pleasing and acceptable mode of worship to the Most High, to whom ignorance cannot be more grateful than knowledge." And Kepler's Christian faith told him God would not tolerate the inaccuracy of circular models of planetary movements in astronomy, so he replaced circular orbits with elliptical orbits —which made him exclaim, "through my effort God is being celebrated in astronomy."

Curiously enough, it was in God that these scientists found reason to investigate nature and trust their own scientific reasoning. No conflict here between science and faith! The founder of quantum physics, Max Planck, put it well: "It was not by accident that the greatest thinkers of all ages were deeply religious souls." Scientists who come to mind are Johannes Kepler, Isaac Newton, Blaise Pascal, Fr. Gregor Mendel, Louis Pasteur, Fr. George Lemaître, and so many others. Obviously, the Catholic Church has no problem with science, to put it mildly. All of this reinforces the idea that science at the time was a Judeo-Christian project. The evolutionary anthropologist and science writer Loren Eiseley summarizes this well: "It is surely one of the curious paradoxes of history that science, which professionally has little to do with faith, owes its origins to an act of faith that the universe can be rationally interpreted, and that science today is sustained by that assumption." Indeed, it is faith that makes you think.

God is the author of both

It was Galileo, of all people, who made a distinction between the Book of Nature and the Book of Scripture. It was a smart move on his part, for it placed astronomy, not under theology, but next to theology, and thus elevated the status of astronomy to a science which, like theology, dealt with the decoding of "divine speech"—the speech that had authored both Nature and Scripture. With his characteristic audacity, not only did Galileo declare himself an authority in interpreting the Book of Nature, but an equal authority in interpreting the Book of Scripture.

The distinction between the Two Books was not Galileo's own invention but had been around for centuries in the Catholic Church. Its origin can be traced back to these words of Augustine: "It is the divine page that you must listen to; it is the book of the universe that you must observe." This conviction was a belief shared in the past by many other Christian thinkers: from early Apologists and Fathers to St. Basil; from St. Gregory of Nyssa to St. Augustine, from St. Albert the Great to St. Thomas Aquinas, from Roger Bacon to William of Ockham.

Since both "books" come from the same "Author," God, they can never be in conflict with each other. Standing within this strong and solid tradition, the Ecumenical Council of Vatican II declared that "if methodical investigation within every branch of learning is carried out in a genuinely scientific manner and in accord with moral norms, it never truly conflicts with faith, for earthly matters and the concerns of faith derive from the same God." Pope Benedict XVI used the same distinction to see "nature as a book whose author is God in the same way that Scripture has God as its author."

However, there is an important caveat based on this distinction: we should never read the Book of Scripture as if it were the Book of Nature, or vice-versa. St. Augustine made this very clear when he warned us that it is "dangerous to have an infidel hear a Christian … talking nonsense." Since there are truths of science as well as truths of faith—which can never contradict each other—it cannot be that the earth is flat according to faith and religion, but at the same time spherical according to reason and science, for that would create a contradiction. You cannot have it both ways. In a similar way, if science tells us that the earth circles the sun, it cannot be that faith has the sun circle the earth. We need both "books" to understand nature better and faith better. As it turns out, science in itself is incomplete, and religion on its own is insufficient. Therefore, we need to "read both books." By the way, that's something scientism refuses to do.

Put in more general terms, the Catholic Church strongly affirms that what we know through *reason* can never be in conflict

Chapter 5: Science and Faith Reunited 131

with what we know through *faith*. As a matter of fact, the Catholic Church has a long history of asserting that faith and reason can never contradict each other. It was actually St. Thomas Aquinas who stressed that faith and reason can never arrive at a conclusion in opposition to each other, because it is the God of our faith who created the reasoning mind. Although faith is above reason, there can never be any real discrepancy between faith and reason (CCC 159). That is why we can speak of "faith that makes you think" in the title of this book.

The First Vatican Council clearly condemned the doctrine that faith is irrational; it insisted that faith is always in harmony with reason. St. Augustine could not have said it better when he warned us that it is "dangerous to have an infidel hear a Christian... talking nonsense." Nonsense is a form of irrationality, which may include blind faith. It is a rejection of reason. Then in 1879, Pope Leo XIII issued the encyclical *Aeterni Patris*, in which he reaffirmed a central principle of the Catholic intellectual tradition: the harmony of faith and reason. Nevertheless, some people still think that when we begin to use reason, we have no choice but to abandon faith; conversely, they think that if we have faith, we cannot use reason. The Church teaches differently: discovering the truth through reason can never destroy faith. Pope John Paul II even wrote an encyclical on this very issue (*Fides et Ratio*); and Pope Benedict relentlessly followed in his footsteps—actually the Church's footsteps. Therefore, when we search for truth, we can and must have the confidence that its discovery will not destroy our faith.

Because science is a specific form of using reason, based on a specific methodology, we could say something similar about the relationship between faith and science. Good research in all branches of knowledge can never conflict with the faith, because the things of the world and the things of faith derive from the same God (CCC 159). That is why Catholicism doesn't see any conflict between faith and science, while many Protestant denominations still do. Discovering the truth through reason, even when done through strict scientific procedures, can never destroy faith. It is faith that makes us understand and it is reason that helps us to believe. But we do need to put science in its place, as we also should put faith in its place.

Going back to the distinction between the Book of Scripture and the Book of Nature, many might object to what I said so far by pointing out that in fact these two books have sometimes been in contradiction to each other. Take, for instance, the Big Bang Theory according to the Book of Nature versus the Creation account according to the Book of Scripture. They seem to be in contradiction to each other. But not so on further inspection. The Big Bang account is about how events are related *to each other*, whereas the Creation account is about how events are related *to God*. Something similar can be said about other seeming contradictions, such as the heliocentrism of the Book of Nature versus the geocentrism of the Book of Scripture. The former is about "how the heavens go," whereas the latter is about "how to go to Heaven." Another example is the seeming conflict between the Creation account versus the theory of evolution. On further analysis, these two turn out not to be in conflict with each other either. Cardinal John Henry Newman wrote in an 1868 letter, "I do not [see] that 'the accidental evolution of organic beings' is inconsistent with divine design—it is accidental to us, not to God."

In all these cases, we must keep in mind that the Book of Scripture cannot be read as if it were the Book of Nature. We just need to "read" them correctly. If we do find a seeming contradiction between the two "books," we have not correctly understood either the Book of Scripture, or the Book of Nature, or both. The question is, of course, how we read them correctly, especially when it comes to the Book of Scripture.

How to read the Book of Scripture?

Let's make clear from the outset again that the Book of Scripture cannot be read as if it were the Book of Nature. That's one important rule. But another one is that not everything in the Bible can be read as a historical, let alone scientific, report. It is important to note that the Catholic Church does not enforce a literal reading of all parts of the Bible. The Scriptures have many types of texts: prayers (Psalms), visions (Revelation), debates (Job), parables (Gospels), letters (St. Paul), and of course, historical reports (Acts). This means you cannot read all sections of the Bible in the same manner. For instance, you cannot read the creation account as a historical record; neither can you read parables as historical reports.

Apparently, the texts of Scripture are open to various interpretations. Any text—so also a text in Scripture—can have multiple interpretations. Hence Scripture cannot be interpreted by itself. As St. Thomas Aquinas used to say, "[It] is the task of the good interpreter to look, not at the words, but at the meaning." *Interpretation* is key here. Even Jesus himself often demonstrated how the Scribes and Pharisees used incorrect interpretations, and hence He had to correct them by properly interpreting Scripture, thus demonstrating that the Scriptures do not interpret themselves.

The Church is very aware of this. As early as the first century, the first pope, St. Peter (2 Peter 3:16) said about the Epistles of St. Paul, "There are some things in them hard to understand, which the ignorant and unstable twist to their own destruction, as they do the other Scriptures." St. Augustine confirmed this in a different way: "We find in Holy Scripture passages which can be interpreted in very different ways without prejudice to the faith we have received." Even the Protestant Reformer Martin Luther—who once told his followers that everyone is able to understand what they are reading—realized that there are as many theologies as there are heads. How right he was: Soon there would be over 300 Protestant denominations with each having their own distinct beliefs about how to interpret Scripture.

How then should we read the Bible? Who or what tells us what the right interpretation is? We need guidance! Where does this guidance come from? There is only one sensible answer: from the Church. We find this already in the early Church. According to Acts 8:30-31, the apostle Philip ran to the Ethiopian eunuch in his chariot, "and heard him reading Isaiah the prophet and said, 'Do you understand what you are reading?' He replied, 'How can I, unless someone instructs me?'" And he invited Philip to come up and sit with him. Philip acted as a representative of the Church here. Although Scripture is a vital authority in Christianity, it cannot be that authority without the Tradition of the Church, for Scripture on its own cannot determine how to read and interpret Scripture.

Of course, this means also we cannot read the Book of Scripture as if it were the Book of Nature. Writing more than a century ago, Pope Leo XIII (1878–1903) quoted St. Augustine when he said:

> *[T]he sacred writers, or to speak more accurately, the Holy Ghost Who spoke by them, did not intend to teach men these things (that is to say, the essential nature of the things of the visible universe), things in no way profitable unto salvation.' Hence they did not seek to penetrate the secrets of nature, but rather described and dealt with things in more or less figurative language, or in terms which were commonly used at the time and which in many instances are in daily use at this day, even by the most eminent men of science.*

Let me illustrate this point further with one of the most controversial texts in the Bible: the Creation account. There are in fact *two* creation accounts: one is described in the first chapter of the Book of Genesis; the second one starts all over again in the second chapter, as though nothing had happened yet in the first chapter. So, the question arises as to how to read and interpret these two accounts.

Let me start with the first Creation account, which unfolds in a series of seven days. I indicated already that this account cannot be interpreted literally, let alone scientifically. Reading the first chapter of Genesis, you might easily think it gives us a chronology of seven days. But that cannot be true, for the simple reason that creation cannot follow a timeline, as time itself is also a product of creation. Our *universe* has a beginning and a timeline, but *creation* itself doesn't have a beginning or a timeline. It is very hard to interpret creation as a step-by-step process unfolding in a temporal order, for "creation at the beginning of time" is impossible, since there is no time until time has been created. Creating time "at a certain time" is tough to do! For us creatures, creation had a beginning, but God Himself is time-less. Creation isn't something that happened long ago in time, and neither is the Creator someone who did something in the distant past, but the Creator is "creating" at all times—by bringing a contingent world into existence and keeping it in existence.

Consequently, it is hard to take the creation account as a *chronological* description of the initial stages of this world, for without creation, there wouldn't be any world at all. Therefore, creation may create chronology, but it cannot become part of chronology, nor can chronology be the framework of creation. In other words, creation is not exclusively focused on the *beginning* of this world, but more so on the *origin* of this world. Creation is both giving a beginning to all that exists and sustaining in being all that exists (CCC 290). In other words, the first chapter in the Book of Genesis is not about what happened *at* the beginning, but about what everything is based on to begin with—that is, *in* the beginning, so to speak.

The Catechism (337) explains it this way: "Scripture presents the work of the Creator symbolically as a succession of six days of divine 'work,' concluded by the 'rest' of the seventh day." This is sometimes called a *structural* approach, to distinguish it from a literal one. The structural approach is not some new, modern idea. For many centuries, it has been recognized that the first six days of creation are divided into two sets of three. In the first set, God separates one thing from another: On day one, he separates the light and the darkness (thus giving rise to night and day); on day two, he separates the waters above from the waters below (thus giving rise to the sky and the sea); and on day three, he separates the waters below from each other (thus giving rise to dry land in-between the waters). Classically, this section is known as describing the work of *division*.

In the second set of three days, God goes back over the realms he produced by division during the first three days, and then populates, or "adorns," them. On day four, he adorns the day and the night with the sun, moon, and stars. On day five, he populates the sky and sea with birds and fish. And on day six, he populates the land (between the divided waters) with animals and humankind. Classically, this is known as describing the work of *adornment*.

That this twofold process is not a modern invention but does indeed represent the ordering principle of Genesis 1 is also indicated at the beginning and end of the account. At the beginning, we are told that "the earth was a formless void" (Gen 1:2). The work of division cures the "formless" problem, whereas the work of adornment fixes the "void" problem. Likewise, at the end of the account we are told "the heavens and the earth were finished [i.e., by division], and all their multitude [i.e., by adornment]" (Gen. 2:1). The Church has recognized for centuries that these are the ordering principles at work in Genesis 1. We find this interpretation also in the writings of St. Thomas Aquinas many centuries ago.

It is through this structure that Genesis 1 proclaims its core message: a radical and imperative affirmation of a monotheistic belief in opposition to pagan beliefs. Each day dismisses an additional cluster of pagan deities: on the first day, the gods of light and darkness; on the second day, the gods of sky and sea; on the third day, earth gods and gods of vegetation; on the fourth day, sun, moon, and star gods (including astrology); on the fifth and sixth days, gods from the animal kingdom (such as sacred falcons, lions, serpents, and golden calves). Finally, even human beings are emptied of any intrinsic divinity, although they are granted a divine likeness.

Apparently, each day of creation shows us how another set of idols is being smashed. Nothing on earth is god, but everything comes from God. Obviously, the issue at stake in Genesis 1 is idolatry, not science; mythology, not natural history; theology, not chronology. Genesis proclaims monotheism, not a scientific theory of origin. It concludes that God's Creation is good, very good, but it is certainly not divine. The main message is this: God is the Creator of everything, and there are no other gods or deities beside Him.

After the six-day creation account in Genesis 1, followed by a day of rest, there is the creation account from Genesis 2—which indicates already we cannot take either one literally. It is almost as if the Bible starts all over again in this second chapter, but now with roles reversed. Whereas Genesis 1 paints an immense world with abundant water, carrying a tiny human being who appears at the eleventh hour after everything else had been prepared for his coming, Genesis 2 describes a mirror image: a tiny world with a shortage of water, in which a human being stalks about like a giant and nothing starts working until this being is around. In Genesis 2, everything is on hold until humankind arrives; all the earth is thirsty until a human being begins to cultivate it; the animals do not have names until this human being gives them names.

In comparison, the second creation story is much more "down to earth" than the first one. God works here more in an immanent way than in a transcendent way. He "formed man of dust from the ground, and breathed into his nostrils the breath of life; and man became a living being" (Gen. 2:7). Then, "The Lord God took the man and put him in the garden of Eden to till it and keep it" (Gen. 2:15). Next, God takes one of his "sides" to create the woman. It is in paradise, called the "garden of Eden," that they sin against God and lose their original dignity. That starts the Original Sin in human history. Although these two accounts seem very different, they are in fact two sides of the same coin. To put it in the most general terms, they are both about the power of God and of God's relationship to His people. The first account focuses on the "role" of God, the second one more explicitly on the role of humanity. Of course, there is much more to it.

Science and faith back together again

It was the well-known mathematician, philosopher, and scientist Gottfried Leibniz who challenged us in 1714 with the following probing question: "Why is there something rather than nothing?" Or more simplified, "Why is there anything?" His point was that there must be an explanation of why there is something, as there could very well have been nothing. The question as to why there is something rather than nothing applies to anything that has come into existence, whether it is the universe itself or anything else ranging from organisms to cells to subatomic particles.

Of course, we can ignore the question, but that does not make the question go away. It stubbornly keeps calling on us for an answer. For people with a contemporary mind, this question may seem quite odd. They can easily accept that there is something—they see it all around them. But how could they accept that there might have been nothing at all? Plenty of nothing is still nothing. Even if we claim that the universe is eternal—that is, having no beginning and no end, as Albert Einstein believed at one point in his life—we still need to acknowledge that the universe could have been different from the universe we live in and might not even have existed at all. As we said before, the universe is contingent.

So, the question keeps echoing: why is there something rather than nothing? As mentioned earlier, the reason for this is quite basic and fundamental: nothing can make itself exist. Or put differently: everything needs a cause for it to come into existence. Or perhaps even better and more accurate: everything that comes into existence must have a cause. Let me say it again: nothing, not even an eternal universe, can just pop itself into existence; it must have a cause, because it does not and cannot have the power to make itself exist. Nothing can generate itself, just like children cannot generate themselves.

Science and religion alike have come up with their own answers to this nagging question. Science will typically do so in terms of secondary causes, whereas religion will do so in terms of the Primary Cause, God, and His presence in the world. Do we really need both? Or is science able to explain everything on its own, without religion?

Well, science has certainly tried to be "self-sufficient" in its explanations. A popular move is to point at the laws of nature, which regulate how the universe works and brings things into existence. As mentioned earlier, these laws can be deterministic or probabilistic. Deterministic laws of nature predict one specific effect or outcome. A few examples are the law of Archimedes, the law of gravitation, Kepler's laws, Newton's three laws of motion, the ideal-gas laws, Ohm's law, Boyle's law, Joule's first law, and the laws of thermodynamics. In these laws, the outcome is specifically determined. In addition, there are also probabilistic laws, which state that, on average, a certain fraction of cases displaying a given condition will display a certain other condition as well. Examples are the law of radioactive decay, Mendel's law of segregation, the law of natural selection, or a quantum law that expresses the probability that a particle will be found at a certain location.

The laws of nature are essential to this world. They are vital for our existence and work with a high "reliability." The physicist Paul Davies once expressed the constancy of such laws with these words: "You've got to believe that these laws won't fail, that we won't wake up tomorrow to find heat flowing from cold to hot, or the speed of light changing by the hour." However, do they also explain why there is something rather than nothing? Not really. These laws in themselves are already "something"! They may explain why the universe operates the way it does, but they do not explain how the universe came to be.

The problem is that the universe itself cannot be the explanation of its own existence. First of all, a law of nature such as the law of gravity cannot do the trick, for the laws of nature come with this universe and are ultimately the set of laws which govern the existing universe. When someone like Stephen Hawking still speaks in terms of a "spontaneous creation," he is committing a form of circular reasoning by saying: "Because there is a law such as gravity, the universe can and will create itself from nothing. Spontaneous creation is the reason there is something rather than nothing." The problem is, though, that the laws of nature cannot be used to explain the existence of the universe, because they presuppose the very existence of the universe they are supposed to explain. So, this is not an answer to Leibniz' question.

Second, how could the universe "create" itself from nothing—let alone cause itself? That is philosophically impossible, so we said earlier, for a cause just cannot cause itself; it would have to exist before it came into existence. When Hawking tells us that gravity would be able to create the universe, I would counter that the law of gravity would have to exist before there was gravity. Albert Einstein hit the nail right on the head when he said: "the man of science is a poor philosopher." And Hawking is not the only one. The physical chemist Peter Atkins, for instance, has the audacity to state that "there is hope for a scientific elucidation of creation from nothing" after he had said earlier that science has a limitless power and must even be able to account for the "emergence of everything from absolutely nothing." That answer is an offense to Leibniz' question as to why there is something rather than nothing!

Third, the laws of nature could have been other than they are—they could exist or not exist, they could be this or that. It is easy to think, for instance, about possible worlds in which the laws of nature are radically different from those that are operational right here and now in our universe. Besides, the universe could have been as much as "law-less." Physicist Paul C. Davies is right: "There are endless ways in which the universe might have been totally chaotic. It might have had no laws at all, or merely an incoherent jumble of laws that caused matter to behave in disorderly or unstable ways." Instead, we find in this universe a very specific law and order. Why are the laws of nature the way they are? When John Stuart Mill said, "It is a law that every event depends on some law," he just shifted the problem and never wondered where that law itself then came from (other than from himself).

This means that the laws of nature cannot explain the existence of the universe. But that seems to have eluded those scientists who have fallen into the trap of arguing that the Big Bang has replaced what we call creation. They were so "stone-deaf" that the physicist Carl Sagan still dared to exclaim, in the preface of one of Hawking's books, that such a cosmological model "left nothing for a creator to do." Others, such as the cosmologist Lee Smolin, made sure there is no space for a Creator left by proclaiming that "by definition the universe is all there is, and there can be nothing outside it." Isn't that a cheap strategy? The laws of nature are important when used in science, but they are irrelevant outside that domain.

Something similar can be said about the so-called *physical constants*. What are these constants? As Stephen Hawking has rightly noted, "The laws of science, as we know them at present, contain many fundamental numbers." In fact, those numbers are constants that come with our universe. They have a fixed value that physicists are feverously trying to explain by connecting each value to some law of nature. However, their trials have not been very successful—at least not yet, or perhaps never. Examples are the speed of light, the gravitational constant, the cosmological constant, the constants of electromagnetism, weak nuclear interactions, and strong nuclear interactions. The values of these constants are both universal in nature and have a value that doesn't change in time. Besides, their specific values are very crucial: a small change in their magnitude could have dramatic consequences for the operation of the universe and the possibility of life on Planet Earth.

We must conclude from this that the laws of nature as well as the existence of physical constants cannot explain how the universe itself came into existence. So, they must have come from somewhere else, from something beyond the universe itself. Science has reached its limits here and has no further answers. Religion, on the other hand, does have answers as to why there is something rather than nothing. It speaks of a Divine Lawgiver as being the Primary Cause of all that exists, including the laws of nature and the existence of physical constants. As to the physical constants, the Book of Wisdom (11:20) says about God, "You have arranged all things by measure and number and weight." In a way, religion complements science when science has reached its own limits.

It should not come as a surprise, though, that science has not given up the fight easily. There are still scientists who try to prove that science can replace religion by attacking one of religion's key beliefs—creation out of nothing. The religious doctrine of "creation out of nothing" [*creatio ex nihilo*] dates back to at least 1215 when the Fourth Lateran Council officially taught that, at the beginning of time, the universe was "created out of nothing." What the Council meant by this statement is that God made the universe without making it out of anything else—and certainly not out of pre-existing matter, as some religions and Platonic philosophers have suggested. Creation has everything to do with the philosophical and theological question as to what makes things exist at all. Without God's creation, the universe could *not* even exist. Existence is received, comes from God, and requires God's creation and preservation. That is the centuries-old Judeo-Christian belief.

How, then, could science ever come up with a scientific explanation of this religious belief? Well, some scientists—for instance, Stephen Hawking, Carl Sagan, and Alexander Vilenkin, to name just a few—claim that they have a scientific version of "creation out of nothing." They do so by referring to what is called "quantum tunneling from nothing," which makes subatomic particles emerge and disappear spontaneously in vacuums in laboratories. They seem to have the facts on their side. When an "empty" space is filled with an electric field, but without particles, there is a chance that suddenly an electron-positron pair will pop out of empty space. On the other hand, the reverse can occur as well: when an electron and a positron collide, they can "annihil-ate" each other and thus change into "nothing" [*nihil*]. This "void" or "nothing" can be described in mathematical terms with a wave function—which is considered the quantum gravity equivalent of the quantum vacuum in quantum field theory. This makes these scientists postulate that the Big Bang could also be the result of a random quantum fluctuation in a vacuum—a spaceless and timeless void. In translation: the universe came "out of nothing."

The problem of this scientific solution is that the term "nothing" in religion is very different from "nothing" in science. They both use the same word for two quite different concepts. When religion and faith speak of "nothing" during creation, they mean literally "nothing"—a no-thing. It is not a highly unusual kind of exotic "stuff" that is more difficult to observe or measure than other things; it is not some kind of element that has not found a position yet in science's Periodic System; it is in no way a material thing that can change into something else, but it is in fact the *absence* of anything.

In science, on the other hand, the situation is entirely different. When scientists speak of "nothing" in their supposedly scien-

Chapter 5: Science and Faith Reunited

tific version of "creation out of nothing," they are not really speaking of "nothing" in the literal sense as philosophy and religion do. When an electron and a positron collide in the lab, they can indeed "an-nihil-ate" and thus change into "nothing," but this "nothing" is not really nothing in the literal sense. What really happens is this: when these particles annihilate, they emit a burst of energetic photons—which is certainly not "nothing" in a philosophical or religious sense.

To put it differently, "quantum tunneling" causes a "system" to change from one "state" (an electric field without particles) into another "state" (a changed electric field with two particles), or reversed. These two states are different "states," but of the same "system." However, it must be realized that a pair of particles does not suddenly appear out of literally "nothing," but rather out of an electric field of an existing "system." To explain the idea of different states, the particle-physicist Stephen Barr uses the striking analogy of having a bank account. Even when we have "nothing" in the bank, we still have a bank account, with all that comes with it, but it happens to be in a "no-money state" for us. Obviously, this kind of "nothing" is different from having no bank account at all.

In this example, science cannot replace or annihilate religion. They are very different from each other. When the Church speaks of creation out of nothing (CCC 296), it is not talking science. Science is about producing something from something else, whereas creation is about creating something from nothing. Science is about changes in this universe, but creation is certainly not a change; it is not a change from "nothing" to "something." Creation has everything to do with the question as to why things exist at all—that is, before they can even undergo change. Unlike the Big Bang, creation is the reason why there is something rather than nothing (including something such as the law of gravity).

Apparently, if we do not distinguish scientific questions from religious questions, we would be in for a real mix-up. But when we take them correctly, they can complement one another from two different perspectives. Thus, the Book of Nature and the Book of Scripture can enrich one another and make our lives worth living. Otherwise, we will be robbed of many things that count in life but cannot be counted. Thank God, the Catholic religion comes with a faith that makes you think.

6.

Made in God's Image

As we discussed in the previous chapter, the first creation account tells us we were made "in God's image and likeness" (Gen1:26-27). That sets us apart from the animal world. The second account adds another detail: God "breathed into [man's] nostrils the breath of life; and man became a living being" (Gen.2:7). This "breath of life" is probably best interpreted as our human *soul*—which is something else that sets us apart from the animal world.

So, we end up as unique beings in this world. That's where our grandeur comes from. However, the second creation account has more to say about this grandeur: it was tarnished by sinning in Paradise. Those are again two sides of the same coin: grandeur and degradation. What does that mean?

The soul has two parts

It is important to stress that it is the soul of human beings, made in God's image and likeness, that sets humans apart from the rest of the animal world. When did human souls emerge in evolution or in the course of history? Science cannot answer this question, for the soul is a non-material entity. As astronomer Owen Gingerich pithily puts it, "the transition to a spiritual being... does not fossilize." Yet, the human soul makes humans unique in the living world.

What then is so unique about the human soul? The human soul comes with two essential parts: an *intellectual* part, the mind, as well as a *voluntary* part, the will. The intellectual part enables human beings to have thoughts and to think properly. We talked about that earlier and found out that science fails to tell us much more about that part. The voluntary part enables human beings to have intentions and to act freely. We talked about that, too, and argued that human beings do have a will to act freely. Now we need to delve a bit deeper into what all of this entails.

In classical philosophy, going back to Aristotle and St. Thomas Aquinas, the soul is the "form" of the body. The body may come from genes and the like, but it is the soul that makes us human. The soul is God's breath of life, which "forms" us in God's image and likeness. This soul has an intellectual part, the mind, which endows us with rationality, and a voluntary part, the will, which endows us with morality. Without those two, we would be mere bodies, "brutes" like the rest of the animal world.

Rationality, the intellectual part of the soul, makes each one of us an "animal rationale," so that our thoughts can be judged as true or false. *Morality,* the voluntary part of the soul, makes us beings who live by a moral code, so that our actions can be judged as good or bad. Without a soul, human beings would no longer be rational beings, nor would they be moral beings; they would not be able to have thoughts and intentions.

In other words, our rationality and morality are part of our grandeur that we were given in Paradise. As the French philosopher Blaise Pascal once put it so succinctly, "It is dangerous to show man in how many respects he resembles the lower animals, without pointing out his grandeur." But then he adds, "It is also dangerous to direct his attention to his grandeur, without keeping him aware of his degradation." So, it is not all good news here. Because of the Original Sin, we are prone to making errors in our rational judgments and in our moral decisions. That means we are often guided by a darkened mind and a corrupted will. The ironic thing is that those affected by false ideologies often believe they themselves are free from sin and able to take us to a better place.

The mind is the intellectual part of the soul

It is the mind that gives us the ability to determine what is true and what is false. We do that with rationality, which is an amazing faculty we have been endowed with. Th mind is the "soul's eye," so to speak. But again, because of our history in Paradise, this faculty can be darkened, so we may claim as true what is in fact false. This tendency has often been the cause and origin of false ideologies or doctrines.

There are many false doctrines around that try to change and mold our minds—doctrines such as relativism and secularism, to name just a few. They are rather dictatorial and don't allow for any other views than their own. Doctrines portray to be very reliable and solid, but in fact they may turn out to be floating and fleeting opinions that have no foot to stand on. They are shaky ideologies disguised as solid doctrines. It's their disguise that lures us in. One of these doctrines is relativism. Cardinal Joseph Ratzinger, during a homily just before he became Pope Benedict XVI, spoke of the dictatorship of relativism as "the greatest problem of our time."

The pontiff did not invent this idea on his own. St. Paul was already eager to warn us against false doctrines when he says, "For the time is coming when people will not endure sound teaching, but having itching ears they will accumulate for themselves teachers to suit their own likings, and will turn away from listening to the truth and wander into myths" (2 Tim. 4:3-4). Relativism is a clear case in point.

Attacks on what is true: relativism

People who put their faith in relativism—let's call them dedicated "relativists"—claim that there is no absolute truth—there are only *opinions* about what is true, depending on one's point of view. Relativism denies, or perhaps just doesn't want to acknowledge, that there is something like absolute, objective truth—truth that cannot be denied or declined by anyone. This doctrine of relativism is promoted, for instance, by the late philosopher Richard M. Rorty: "Truth is what your contemporaries let you get away with." But he is certainly not alone.

Hence, we end up with this allegedly "democratic" idea: whatever is true for me may be false for you; whatever is right for me may be wrong for someone else. It is basically the idea of "anything goes." Even mutually opposed viewpoints are considered equally legitimate. Taken to its extreme, this would entail that gravity, for instance, may be true for you but not for me. In other words, relativism promotes a sort of democratic ideal in matters of truth and knowledge. But this seemingly "democratic" ideal turns out to be "auto-cratic."

There are many reasons why relativism cannot be true. First of all, relativism replaces truth claims with opinions and feelings. Truth is no longer a matter of facts but of opinions, convictions, and feelings. This doctrine tells us that all that we have left in matters of truth is our own personal opinions—the freedom to believe whatever we like, including nonsense. This amounts to claiming some kind of "freedom from reality." What's wrong with that? Well, because relatives have genetic ties, someone's opposing opinion that they are connected by blood ties cannot be true. Or because the world is round, someone's opposing opinion will not make it flat. Opinions don't trump truths. Truth is truth, even if you do not accept it; and untruth is untruth, even if you claim it. Truth is not something we create or invent, but something that we try to "capture" in the real world. Truth is the conformity of mind and reality—a match between thoughts and reality. This entails that truth is truth—for everyone, anywhere, at any time. G. K. Chesterton once firmly asserted "that truth exists whether we like it or not, and that it is for us to accommodate ourselves to it." Relativism, on the other hand, disconnects us from reality.

Another problem of relativism is that it contradicts itself. Claiming that "There is no such a thing as objective truth" claims in fact to be objectively true. We cannot make such a sweeping assertion without also asserting, implicitly, that there is such a thing as objective truth after all. Denying that there is objective truth means you are insisting in your denial that such a statement is objectively true, which cannot be true by its own verdict. You cannot have it both ways. Apparently, this position leaves us with only one objective truth—the objective truth of relativism itself.

Not surprisingly, relativists have tried to make an exception for their own absolute claim of relativism, so that the problem of contradiction might disappear. However, when claiming that all truths are relative except the one of relativism, we should ask these relativists: what is it that entitles them to make this exception? Their strategy is to argue that no universal statement can ever refer to itself. Applied to the doctrine of relativism, this would mean that the universal statement of "all truth is relative" supposedly cannot refer to this statement itself. However, the rule of excluding self-reference is an easy way out and cannot be right. Just consider the word "word" and ask whether it refers to itself. Of course, it does. The word "word" is a word. Excluding or forbidding self-reference is not a viable way to follow, not even to defend relativism.

But there is more wrong with relativism. Whereas absolutism claims some of us may be wrong, relativism claims everyone is right. We cannot have it both ways. Either there is a real right and a real wrong or there is nothing wrong with being an absolutist, and nothing right with being a relativist. Peter Kreeft then comes to a powerful conclusion, "Relativism is not rational, it is rationalization. It is not the conclusion of a rational argument. It is the rationalization of a prior action." As a matter of fact, relativism has lost contact with objective reality. It entitles us to claim whatever we want to claim, for there is no final benchmark or yardstick that everyone has access to. There would no longer be any facts, which would also be the end of science.

Given the above arguments, we should wonder why there are still relativists left. Although the idea of relativism may have a long history, it was never popular or widespread, but nowadays it is receiving more and more traction. Somehow, relativism has invaded, as a Trojan horse, the mind of many nowadays, blinding them to the truth. That's what has happened to the beauty of the human mind. Relativism is one of those devastating ideologies that came forth from a darkened mind.

The powers of the intellect

Thanks to the *intellect*, we are "rational beings." Rationality includes not only the power of conceptual understanding—the ability to understand the meanings of concepts—but also the power of conceptual reasoning—the ability to judge the adequacy of these concepts and of the propositions containing them. In other words, the intellect makes it possible for us to deal with truths as well as abstract ideas. These are in fact two different powers, so let's discuss them separately.

Conceptual understanding

Conceptual understanding means that we understand things with the help of concepts. What is a concept? It is more than just a word like "yes" or "no." A concept is the result of abstraction

Chapter 6: Made in God's Image 153

from what we have experienced through the senses. To be sure, all we know about the world does come through our physical senses, but this is then processed by the human intellect that extracts from sensory experiences that which is *intelligible* in conceptual terms.

For instance, we have seen several round objects and then we abstract from this the concept of "circle." This concept is abstract—in this case even highly abstract. It is very unlikely that we will ever encounter a perfect circle in this world, which means we do not literally or physically see a circle. Besides, the concept of circle does not include any specific size, whereas the "circular" objects around us do. True, we can visualize a circle without imagining any specific size, but concepts have a universality that images can never possess. Therefore, the concept "circle" can be used for any specific circular object regardless of its size and its imperfections. That's what concepts can do for us.

In addition, a concept has an intricate web of connections with other concepts—in case of a circle, for instance, with concepts such as "radius" and "diameter." As a result, concepts go far beyond what the senses provide—they transform "things" of the world into "objects" of knowledge, thus enabling us to see with our "mental eyes" what no physical eyes could ever see before. Thanks to our intellect, we can understand abstract concepts. The intellect can make the step from singular entities to universal entities, from concrete entities to abstract entities. That's how it can use the concept of gravity to see what falling objects on earth and orbiting planets in the solar system have in common.

What is central to all concepts is that they have a *meaning*—sometimes a simple meaning, such as in the concept "snow," sometimes a complicated, sophisticated meaning, such as in the concept "quantum" or "gene." Always does a concept carry a certain meaning. But not always does a concept refer to something in the real world. Sometimes the relation of reference is merely hoped for (e.g., the "Higgs boson") or is imaginary (e.g., "centaur") or is stipulated (e.g., an irrational number such as π). In other words, concepts don't create reality—they only try to capture it, and they may succeed or fail. Anyone can understand what a unicorn or mermaid is, and yet we know these do not exist in reality. Reality "determines" what is fiction and what is nonfiction.

The main point I want to make is that concepts are abstract entities that depend on the ability of the human intellect to understand the meanings of concepts. Of course, I can explain what the word "red" means by pointing at a red tulip. But that gesture is still very ambiguous. Perhaps someone else thinks "red" stands for a tulip, or for a flower, or whatever else might come to mind in connection with pointing at a red tulip. The word "red" is based on an abstraction of what we perceive—a concept, that is. Without that concept, it doesn't refer to anything. Besides, for many concepts there is nothing to point at. To explain the concept of "tomorrow," there is nothing to point at (other than on a calendar). And for the concept of "pi" (π), there will never be anything we can point at.

St. Thomas Aquinas' famous motto is that "nothing is in the intellect that is not first in the senses." But concepts do not come through the senses, they come through the immaterial intellect which extracts from sensory experiences that which is intelligible. Well, it is the rationality of our intellect that makes the world intelligible and understandable, all of which is done with the help of concepts. Science has many of them: electron, atom, enzyme, cell, gene, neuron, radiation, gravity, and so many more. They make us "see" what we could not "see" without them. For people who don't know what these concepts stand for, it is hard, if not im-

Chapter 6: Made in God's Image

possible, to understand what science tells them.

Concepts in science may go through a long process of growth. Let me use one example: cells in biology. Cells were not known as cells until the concept "cell" had been developed. In the beginning the concept had hardly any content. What Robert Hooke saw through his microscope in 1665 was more of dead or lifeless cell-walls of plants than real, living cells. He coined the term cell, because the structure of plants seen through his microscope reminded him of honeycomb cells. It was through Schleiden and Schwann that the cell became a structural unit (1839); and since Virchow it is also a functional unit (1855). It was Virchow who interpreted the organism as a "cell state," composed of physiologically interdependent cell units. But soon, Virchow's anatomical building-block cell theory had to yield to the biological unity of the cell. Ever since, the cell has been viewed as the seat of the morphological and physiological unity of the body of animals and plants. Thus, the cell had become the very unit of life. As frequently occurs, a great conceptual battle won is often a new scientific phase begun. The theory of cells has now become a central, basic science, cell-biology, from which many other areas of research derive.

Like science, religion also uses concepts. Examples are concepts such as sin, purgatory, incarnation, resurrection, revelation, salvation, redemption, grace, providence, sacrifice, transubstantiation, trinity, and so many more. Let me just use one example to show how these concepts may have developed over time. The first Christians learned that the concept "God" or "Lord" had to be revised. It remained having a reference to the one God of monotheism, but from now on it referred to a *triune* God—one God in three Persons: the Father, the Son, and the Holy spirit. St. Augustine, for instance, made sure we understand the concept of the Holy Trinity properly:

> *they are not three Gods, but one God: although the Father has begotten the Son, and so He who is the Father is not the Son; and the Son is begotten by the Father, and so He who is the Son is not the Father; and the Holy Spirit is neither the Father nor the Son, but only the Spirit of the Father and of the Son, Himself also co-equal with the Father and the Son, and pertaining to the unity of the Trinity.*

This concept tells us in essence that the Father is not the Son; the Son is not the Father, and the Spirit is neither Father nor Son. They are all "one" precisely by not being each other—one in being, God, but diverse in Persons, three of them. It is certainly not an easy concept, and it took the Christian community a while to learn how to deal with it correctly. But a concept it is. Whether it is also true—that is, in reference to the real world—is for conceptual reasoning to find out.

Conceptual reasoning

How do we know something is true? Pontius Pilate was right, in a way, when he asked: what is truth? As we saw, relativism would answer, "anything you believe or like to be true." But that is an argument-stopper, the end of all discussion. Science, for one thing, would have never made any progress if that were true—for progress means coming closer to the truth. Truth is a nonnegotiable absolute. We may not have reached the full truth yet, but it's the ultimate goal of all our seeking.

How is it possible for the mind, with its intellect, to have access to reality and to its truths? This is only possible if we do have access to the reality that we live in. Only then can we determine whether something is true or false. It is the intellect that has the ability to make such an assessment—it's called reasoning. But, again, this requires that we do have access to that reality.

Some philosophers have blocked this access by trying to disconnect and detach the mind from reality. They do so by driving a wedge between you and the world, between your mind and reality, between *subject* and *object*, between the *knowing* subject and the *known* object. If that were the case, the subject doesn't really know, and the object is not really known. A famous representative of such misleading thoughts is Immanuel Kant. He argued that we have no access to the "thing-in-itself" (*Ding an sich*), distinct from the appearances we discover through the senses. Thus he makes every object in essence "unknowable." The ideology of relativism is an offshoot of such flawed trials. Therefore, we end up being strangers in our own world. Only when the mind and its intellect have been reconnected with reality, does it make sense again to talk about what is true and untrue. True, our grasp of reality is limited by our senses—by what we can see, hear, touch, smell, and taste. However, there is also an "outside" to the envelope of our natural senses that humans can only accept in faith. It is the faith that there is an external, objective reality surrounding us.

Can we search for the truth again once this connection has been reestablished? It may not be as easy as it sounds. Let me make clear from the outset that truths are not *material* entities like stones that you stumble across on your way. Truths are not something we can touch or smell or locate in space and time. They are not the rock-solid pieces of this world that you can "kick" at. They are not just "there" waiting for us to open our eyes. They are *mental* entities, instead. They require a mind with the ability to form concepts!

And yet, truths are about what is surrounding us in this universe. How can we unite the truths of the mind with the reality of the world around us? Put differently, how are truths about the world around us related to the reality around us? There must be some kind of connection. The ancient Greek philosophers believed that truths "correspond" with an objective reality, which makes them objective truths. Aristotle, for instance, wrote in his *Metaphysics*, "To say ... of what is that it is, and of what is not that it is not, is true." St. Thomas Aquinas restates Aristotle rather elegantly, saying simply, "Truth is the conformity of the intellect to the things." Aquinas speaks of a correspondence between reality and intellect [*adequatio intellectus et rei*].

This may sound trivial, but it basically asserts that any true understanding of reality must correspond to that reality. So, truths are the outcome of what St. Thomas Aquinas calls a correspondence or conformity between reality and intellect. Objective reality is independent of us and not under control of our minds; it goes far beyond personal experiences. We cannot create reality with our thoughts. The sun and the moon, for instance, are there even when they are obstructed by clouds. In short, reality does not depend on our thoughts; instead, our thoughts should be checked against reality, otherwise they are fictitious and illusionary. No wonder, Albert Einstein always vehemently defended the role of objective reality of an "external" world, especially in science, when he said, "The belief in an external world independent of the perceiving subject is the basis of all natural science." Nevertheless, the concept of an objective reality has been replaced by some with something called the "plasticity of reality," the faulty view that something only becomes what it is when we determine it.

Obviously, if there is no real, objective world to understand, there is no science. But how does science find truths about the physical world? Many people believe that science is only based on experiments, without any reasoning. However, scientists also need reasoning so as to design the right experiments and they need reasoning again to come to conclusions based on these ex-

Chapter 6: Made in God's Image

periments. Science needs reasoning and thinking both before and after observations and experiments come into play. Observations and experiments can only do their job thanks to reasoning. Reasoning is our gateway to truth.

As a matter of fact, the findings science has come up with are usually more based on reasoning than on observation. Think of these cases: William Harvey did not *see* the capillaries he needed for a closed blood circulation; Galileo did not *see* the much needed shift in position for a star observed from the earth on one side of the Sun, and then six months later from the other side; Louis Pasteur did not *see* the germs he needed for his theory of fermentation and contamination; Urbain Le Verrier did not *see* the planet Neptune he needed to explain the strange motion of Uranus. All of these became only visible after they had been captured in hypotheses and concepts. As the late Father Joseph Canavan, SJ puts it, "Science depends on minds that can judge what is a fact, which facts constitute evidence, and when the evidence leads to a firm conclusion."

There are many ways of reasoning in science. I won't go into that issue here. But I do want to mention one particular case. Albert Einstein used conceptual reasoning to prove the truth of his general relativity theory. He couldn't have said it better: "No amount of experimentation can ever prove me right." He needed reasoning to come up with a good test implication. The testable proposition for Einstein's general relativity was that light, like any material object, should bend when passing through the gravitational field of a massive body such as the sun. For verification of this conjecture, Einstein proposed that photographs taken of stars bordering the sun during a full solar eclipse be compared with those same stars made at another time. Einstein staked his entire theory of general relativity on such a test. During the total solar eclipse of May 29, 1919, photographs were taken to measure the light deflection, if any. Well, the photographs confirmed the deflection of the starlight in the gravitational field of the sun! His theory had passed the truth test. Kudos to Einstein.

Another great case of conceptual reasoning came from Aristotle. It is a much simpler case than Einstein's, but it does show the power of reasoning in finding the truth. He used the following argument based on lunar eclipses: Since it is the interposition of the earth that causes the eclipse, the form of this line will be caused by the form of the earth's surface, which is therefore spherical—and not flat. He did not need experiments but just observation and reasoning to come to this conclusion. In most other cases in science, experiments are needed in addition.

You might think the situation is different in religion. However, religion also has truths that need support gained through reasoning. Even if they are truths that God has revealed to us, we still must do our part to understand them by using the God-given power of human reasoning. Here are a few examples of how truths can be assessed in religion:

1. A proof of God's existence: all things that have come into existence need a cause that makes them exist. As mentioned earlier, such things are *contingent*, which means they could have been different and could easily not have existed. Here is a summarized, simplified version of this argument for God's existence. Premise 1: contingent beings must have a cause that explains their existence | Premise 2: even a sequence of causes needs a cause that explains this very sequence itself | Conclusion: there must be a Primary Cause, a Necessary Being, who needs no cause to explain its existence, but is existence itself. In short, reasoning gets us to the truth.

2. St. Thomas Aquinas gives us a good summary of what reason can and must do for faith. He says that reason prepares the mind for faith, explains the truths of faith, and defends the truths of faith. Again, it is reasoning that gets us to the truth. Even faith is not immune to reasoning.
3. St. Paul says about the Christians in Thessalonica; "they received the word with all eagerness, examining the Scriptures daily to see if these things were so" (Acts 17:11). They wanted to see whether things they were told are true. Paul also says, "Test everything; hold fast what is good" (1 Thess. 5:21). It is reasoning again, through testing, that gets us to the truth.
4. St. Paul even mentions truths found in Creation (Rom. 1: 21-3): "Ever since the creation of the world, [God's] invisible attributes of eternal power and divinity have been able to be understood and perceived in what he has made. As a result, [non-believers] have no excuse; for although they knew God, they did not accord him glory as God or give him thanks." Reasoning gets us to the truth.
5. Pascal's Wager uses reasoning to prove that faith in God is your "safest bet" for we are all bound to die. Faith in God is either true or false. If it is true, you gain everything and lose nothing. If it is false, you gain nothing, but you also lose nothing. Therefore, your best bet is faith in God.
6. Reasoning basically made Fyodor Dostoyevsky make his famous statement, "without God, everything is permissible." Jean-Paul Sartre said something similar when he argued that there can be no absolute and objective standards of right and wrong, if there were no eternal Heaven that would make moral laws and values objective and universal. Although, he rejected the existence of God and

Heaven, he affirmed that we cannot have objective standards of right and wrong without God.
7. St. Augustine said it quite clearly: "Believers are also thinkers: in believing, they think and in thinking, they believe.... If faith does not think, it is nothing." This means faith is not blind but needs to be backed by reasoning. The Bible has actually a proverb against blind faith: "A simple man believes anything, but a prudent man gives thoughts to his steps" (Proverbs 14:15). It is reasoning again that gets us to the truth. That's why the title of this book is *Faith that Makes You Think*.
8. To explain why the doctrine of Original Sin is so pivotal in Catholic Faith, the reasoning goes as follows: If there is no Original Sin, then there is no need for redemption; if there is no need for redemption, then Jesus' Cross is a hoax; and if there is no Cross, then the whole economy of salvation through the Incarnation is up for grabs. To avoid this outcome, we need the doctrine of Original Sin.

In all the above cases—which could be expanded with many more—we see that reasoning gets us to the truth—not only in daily life or science but also in religion. Reasoning shows us the enormous power of the human intellect. Through the intellect, we can discover truths about the universe as well as about Creation. We may be so used to this that we easily lose sight of the fact that this is quite amazing and calls for an explanation.

The mystery of the match

We discussed earlier that truth is based on a correspondence between intellect and reality, or more accurately, between thoughts of the intellect and the related facts in reality. But the

Chapter 6: Made in God's Image

question remains how such a correspondence (or conformity or match) is possible. The mystery we have here is the fact that something in the intellect matches something in reality. To give this "something" more body, we could also say that there is rationality in the intellect and there must also be some kind of rationality in the real world. Now we can rephrase what we just said: the rationality present in our minds matches the rationality we find in the world. How so?

It would be easy to explain this correspondence by stating that we merely project our rationality into the world, but that belies the fact that we constantly need to adjust the "speculations" in our minds to the "data" of reality. St. Thomas Aquinas would remark that we cannot just mold our sensorial experiences to our reason-seeking will, as the phenomena we encounter resist our attempts to bend them to our prior expectations. Hence, there must be another explanation for this mysterious conformity between the rationality of our minds and the rationality found around us.

The apparent harmony of thought and being, or truth and reality, calls for an explanation. The best, and arguably only, solution for this conformity runs like this: they both derive from the rationality we find in the Intellect of the One who created all of this. That's exactly the solution religion gives us: we were created in God's image and likeness. In other words, the human intellect is a reflection of the Divine Intellect. In the words of Vatican II (*Gaudium et Spes*, 15), "Man judges rightly that by his intellect he surpasses the material universe, for he shares in the light of the divine mind." Only this can explain the power of reason both in the physical world and in the human intellect. The encyclical *Fides et Ratio* puts it this way, "It is the one and the same God who establishes and guarantees the intelligibility and reasonableness of the natural order of things upon which scientists confidently depend." This opens the way for the intellect to get in touch with the real world and its truths.

Truth has obviously something to do with *facts*. But "facts" are not so easy to come by as you might think at first sight. Please bear with me for this short, rather technical analysis of what a fact stands for.

- Facts are not the *events* we see happening around us. Things and events may seem attractive candidates to offer us a rock-solid foundation for our facts, but they cannot really fulfill their promise, for facts and events are very different from each other. Unlike facts, events are dated, tied to space and time, whereas facts are detached from space and time. It is even considered a fact that certain events did not occur at all—for instance, it is a fact that Darwin did not have a copy of Mendel's 1866 article in his collection of papers and books. Apparently, a fact is not the same as an event; the best we can say is that a fact is a *description* of an event, but not the event itself—which makes quite a difference.

- But if facts are indeed different from events, things, situations, and processes, then this might suggest that facts must be merely *thoughts*, existing only in our minds. However, thoughts cannot be equated to facts either. Thoughts can have some peculiar characteristics such as being imaginary, illogical, confused, time-consuming, and so on—whereas facts cannot. Facts, on the other hand, deal with what the events actually are, and not with what they might be. Facts are true, even if some people have never thought about them. Therefore, a fact is not just a thought, but it may be the *object* of a thought.

- Not surprisingly, some have claimed that facts are identical to what people say about them—that is, identical to (true) *statements*. However, if that were the case, there would be as many facts as there are statements (for instance, facts would be different in English and Dutch). However, facts must be clearly distinguished from statements. Statements can be hypothetical, inaccurate, exaggerated, long-winded, and difficult to understand, and so forth. Facts, on the other hand, cannot be any of these; a fact may be hard to accept, but never hard to understand; it is never hypothetical or half-true. There are even facts which everyone has forgotten, or which were never thought of yet, or which were never expressed yet in a statement. So, we must come to the conclusion that a fact is not a statement, but it may be the *content* of a statement.

- From this analysis follows that we are facing here a rather intricate situation: If facts are neither events nor thoughts nor statements, what then are they? Well, facts actually feature as a focus point at the intersection of those three other elements: A fact is the description of an event, the object of a thought, and the content of a statement—and all of these at once. This means that facts are closely connected to these three other elements through the process of abstraction and interpretation. It is through interpretation that thoughts and statements transform events into facts. Facts need events so they can be tested; they need thoughts so they can be understood; and they need statements so they can be communicated.

The mind has access to natural truths

Although we know the world through sensations or sense impressions, they are just the media that give us access to reality. The Scottish philosopher John Haldane put it well when he said, "One only knows about cats and dogs through sensations, but they are not themselves sensations, any more than the players in a televised football game are color patterns on a flat screen." Knowledge does rest on sensation, but that doesn't mean it is confined to it. It is about objective reality, and this reality sometimes forces us to revise what we thought we knew as true but didn't. Let me use an example from genetics. There are people who can taste PTC as bitter but there are also people who do not taste the bitterness. However, different tastes or impressions do not obliterate that PTC is the "real" thing, not how we perceive it.

The search for the truth can be a tedious job. Let me just mention the telling story of what happened to Gregor Mendel's genes. Most of us learned in school that Mendel had been working with genes—for instance, with two forms of the gene for seed shape, one that produced round peas and another one that produced wrinkled peas. Well, that is not quite the case. Mendel never mentioned the word "gene," but used the word "element" instead. That was in 1865. Even at the beginning of the 1900s—when Mendel had been "rediscovered"—it was still unclear what the nature of these "elements" was. They were entities of a rather hypothetical nature. Finally, what Mendel had referred to as "elements" was named "genes" in 1909 by Wilhelm Johannsen, but they were still taken as some sort of accounting or calculating unit.

Things began to change when geneticists discovered that two or more pairs of genes may not always separate independently as Mendel had suggested. Sometimes genes seem to be linked to each other. Interestingly enough, the geneticist Walter Sutton had already noticed that genes always occur in pairs and that chromosomes also occur in pairs. Was this mere coincidence? Or could it be that genes and chromosomes are connected, and that genes are actually located in chromosomes? Nevertheless, acceptance of chromosomes as carriers of genes remained controversial. Ironically, the famous geneticist Thomas Hunt Morgan rejected the chromosome theory of heredity, but then in his classic 1910 paper in the journal *Science*, embraced it wholeheartedly. At last,

Mendel's hypothetical elements had found a material basis.

Well, the search for the material basis of genetics has never stopped since. It is the ongoing story of dramatic changes: Starting as an element (1865), turning into a gene as a unit of transmission (1909), becoming part of a chromosome (1915), with a specific order of DNA bases (1953), contributing to the production of enzymes (1940), or of polypeptides in general (1957), and having either a structural or regulatory function (1961). As a result, the gene has moved far away from what Mendel had envisioned. The search took many decades—and is far from over. At each step in the process, the geneticists involved used their intellect, their power of reasoning, and their experiments to get closer and closer to the truth.

Something similar to what we said about the search of truth in genetics can also be said about truths in religion. Let's take the example of God's revelation to humanity through the Old and the New Testament. More than any of his predecessors, Abraham was given a fuller knowledge of God, and a greater intimacy with Him, than God had given to anyone else since the Fall. Then, God revealed himself even more to Moses in the burning bush. He gave Moses a yet fuller revelation of the divine Name, which had been withheld from mankind until then. Further revelations came through the Messianic prophecies in the Old Testament, which prepared the human mind for the coming of the Messiah. When the Messiah did come, God's revelation did not end. Through the minds of the apostles and Gospel writers, and the help of the Holy Spirit, our knowledge about God became even more specific and detailed. That's how we came closer and closer to the truth.

The mind has access to supernatural truths.

If you think it is absurd to believe that a child can be born of a virgin, or that a man can rise from the dead, or that Jesus can be present in what appears to be bread and wine during the Eucharist, you have probably many people on your side. Why? Because they think there is no place for supernatural truths in this world. True, these truths cannot be tested by experiment—the sacred cow of science—but that does not mean they cannot be tested by reason. As a matter of fact, what goes against reason cannot be true, for God is the Author of reason. Nonsense does not pass the test of reason. Reason offers us a "litmus test" that all beliefs must go through.

You may think that the test of reason cannot work in religion. Perhaps the best example to counter this misperception is the following. If God is indeed all-powerful, then God must be able to do whatever He wants—including what is logically contradictory, you might think. Based on reason, St. Thomas Aquinas argues strongly against this idea. He gives many examples of what God is *not* able to do: God cannot create square circles; God cannot create triangles with four sides; God cannot make anyone blind and not-blind at the same time; God cannot declare true what is false; God cannot declare right what is wrong; God cannot undo something that happened in the past; God does not even have the power to make a stone so heavy that He Himself cannot lift it—that would indeed be contradictory, and therefore against reason, and therefore impossible. Aquinas concludes from this, "Hence it is better to say that such things cannot be done, than that God cannot do them."

Why can God *not* go against reason? Doesn't that limit His omnipotence? Aquinas is very definite in defending that even an almighty God cannot act against reason. When something is against reason, God cannot create it. Aquinas is so adamant on this issue because God is reason Himself, so He cannot act against His own nature by doing what is contradictory. God is absolutely free, but His freedom is not arbitrary, so He cannot go against what is true and right. How do we know this? Because our own power of reason is rooted in creation and thus participates in God's power of reason. St. Augustine famously said, "*All truth is God's truth.*"

Therefore, even in religion, we cannot just believe anything we want. The slogan "Don't think, just believe" gives agnostics a powerful weapon: "Don't believe, just think." The key question is: Why should we believe something? Because others believe it? Not so! Because religion says it? Not so! Because it feels good? Not so! The only reason is this: because it is *true*. What supernatural truths have in common with natural truths is that they, too, are true and deal with *facts*. If they are false, then the facts we thought we had turned out *not* to be facts.

Example 1: God is *Triune*, or He is not—that's a fact, not a matter of opinion (although it's a fact we could not have known without God's revelation). If God is not Triune, then what we thought is a fact may turn out to *not* be a fact. Our faith was wrong. Faith in a triune God cannot change the facts as little as a belief in a flat earth can make the earth flat. It is a factual issue of a yes-or-no nature.

Example 2: God is *Incarnate*, or He is not—that's a fact, not a matter of opinion (although it's a fact we could not have known without God's revelation). If God is not Incarnate, then what we thought is a fact may turn out to *not* be a fact. Our faith was wrong. Faith in an incarnate God cannot change the facts as little as believing that the Sun orbits the earth can make the Sun orbiting the earth. It is a factual issue of a yes-or-no nature.

A triune God—is that possible?

Doesn't the Jewish Shema Yisrael say, "Hear, O Israel: The Lord is our God, the Lord is *one*"? Doesn't this imply God is not *three*? Not really. It's not quite clear as to how the last part of the Shema should be translated—either as "the Lord is one" or rather as "the Lord alone." In the former version, it seems to stress the monotheistic essence of Judaism, but not so in the latter version. One puts the emphasis on the oneness of God and the other on the sole worship of God to the exclusion of other gods. Both translations are possible, for the Hebrew word *echad* used here means "one," but sometimes it should be translated with "alone" or "only" (as is the case in Joshua 22:20, 1 Chron. 29:1, Isaiah 51:2). However, translating it as "the Lord *alone*" seems to be more in line with the permanent Jewish battle against the idols and false deities they were exposed to in their surroundings.

Not surprisingly, the most common objection against a Triune God is that it violates monotheism. But does it? People who think there is a logical or mathematical inconsistency here might consider the following analogy: the Trinity does not represent $1+1+1=3$, which could amount to polytheism, but rather $1 \times 1 \times 1 = 1^3 = 1$, which is in accord with monotheism. Or, with the help of a geometric analogy: the fact that we distinguish three dimensions does not mean that we can separate those three dimensions. In a similar, analogous way, the Trinity is like the three "dimensions" of the same and one reality, God. Or think of a triangle: it has three lines forming three angles, yet it's only one figure. St. Patrick famously explained the doctrine of the Holy Trinity to his flock in Ireland by using the three leaves of the shamrock: each leaf represents one of the three Persons, but yet it is still only one shamrock.

St. Augustine used another analogy to help us understand

Chapter 6: Made in God's Image

how you can have relational distinctions within one Being, when he said, "I cannot love love [sic] unless I love a lover; for there is no love where nothing is loved. So there are three things: the lover [Father], the loved [Son], and the love [Holy Spirit]." Augustine's analogy is particularly striking when we realize that God's attribute of being all-loving even extends to the very inner being of the Holy Trinity. God is a triad of love: a going out in love, a return in love, and thus love itself. God is all-loving, a perfect love—which requires three!

To further articulate the dogma of the Trinity, the Church had to use reason more than ever to develop her own terminology with the help of certain notions of philosophical origin—notions such as "substance," "person" or "hypostasis", "relation" and so on. With the help of these concepts, the Church could make clear she does not confess three Gods, but one God in three Persons, the "consubstantial Trinity." Each of the three Persons in the Godhead possesses the same eternal and infinite divine nature; thus, they are not "three Gods," but the one, true God in essence or nature. The classic formula, articulated by the theologian Tertullian around 200, has been "one Substance, three Persons."

St. Hilary of Poitiers, one of the early Church Fathers, puts it quite paradoxically around the year 350: "Each Divine Person is in the Unity, yet no Person is the One God." In short, there is one God, but in three Persons. Because the three Persons are all "one" in Being, they share the same divine attributes: each Person in the Trinity is all-perfect, all-powerful, all-present, all-knowing, and all-good.

An incarnate God—is that possible?

The doctrine of the Incarnation—an infinite God becoming a

finite Man in Jesus of Nazareth—speaks of an *incarnate* God, which is probably even more of a mystery than a *triune* God. The truth of Jesus being the Son of God is a key supernatural truth on which everything else hinges in the New Testament. That key truth was the main reason why Jesus was crucified. The Gospel of St. John (19:7) had the Jews say, "We have a law, and by that law he ought to die, because he has made himself the Son of God."

How do we know this key truth to be true? Not because Jesus or John or the Jews tell us so—that would be circular reasoning. Confirmation came from what Jesus said and did. But the best and final confirmation came from God, the Father, Himself—it was the Resurrection. Evidence for the Resurrection did not come from an empty tomb—someone, even thieves, could have done that, which was also acknowledged in the Bible, when Mary Magdalen said to Peter, "They have taken the Lord out of the tomb, and we do not know where they have laid him" (John 20:2). The real evidence comes from the quite detailed resurrection reports. They convinced even non-believers such as Saul, the later apostle Paul.

The Incarnation of the God-man Jesus is somehow tightly connected with God's attribute of being all-loving. St. John expresses this emphatically, "For God so loved the world that he gave his only Son, so that everyone who believes in him might not perish but might have eternal life" (John 3:16). Love is the keyword here; it's the love of an all-good, all-loving God. God so loved what God had made—all of creation, all of us—that God came down in his Son Jesus to redeem all of us. This explains how our death penalty can be commuted into eternal life.

Yet the question remains as to how we *know* Jesus is God? That Jesus is the Son of God cannot be tested by experiment— by shouting, "Let him come down now from the cross, and we

Chapter 6: Made in God's Image

will believe in him" (Mat. 27:42). Instead, it should be tested by reason, to make sure it is not *against* reason. The Church has tried to do this for centuries, as it professes a faith that makes you think. Perhaps a good example of such an attempt is St. Anselm's book *Why the God-man?* [*Cur Deus Homo*], written around 1095. It is a rational defense of the necessity of the Incarnation in light of the atonement and reparation. The question for Anselm was how both God's love and God's justice can be interpreted given the grave reality of human sin. The idea of atonement interprets Jesus' death on the cross as a sacrifice that brings us back into relationship with God. In the atonement, we see that God both manifests His gracious love towards us and yet at the same time, manifests a commitment to His own righteousness and justice. Justice is served by the work of Christ who satisfies what God's righteousness demands, by giving to us a Substitute who stands in our place. Only Jesus Christ as the divine-human mediator can render to God the positive honor He is due; only He can bear the negative consequences of humanity's failure to honor God's justice. "For an adequate satisfaction," says St. Thomas Aquinas, "it is necessary that the act of him who satisfies should possess an infinite value and proceed from one who is both God and Man." No mere man can take away all the sins of the world— only a God-Man can.

Yet the question keeps coming back: how do we *know* Jesus is God? Again, we can't just say Jesus is God because Jesus says so. Most people who say they are God end up in an asylum, as do people who claim to be Jesus. Ironically, the main reason for Jesus's crucifixion was His blasphemous claim of being God. It was a claim with a death sentence. Therefore, denying that Jesus is God has very serious consequences. If Jesus is not God but merely a human being, then His words and actions are worth as much, or rather as little, as anyone else's. C.S. Lewis said it right:

"You must make your choice. Either this man was, and is, the son of God: or else a madman or something worse… Now it seems to me obvious that He was neither a lunatic nor a fiend: and consequently, however strange or terrifying or unlikely it may seem, I have to accept the view that He was and is God." From this follows that, if Jesus is indeed the Son of God, then all the things Jesus tells us must be true as well. No priest can start his sermon by saying, "The Lord Jesus once said… And I think He is right." Jesus *must* be right because He is Jesus.

Another implication of denying that Jesus is God is perhaps even more detrimental: if Jesus was only *like* God, then someone else who is more like God might arise somewhere someday. If that might happen, then Jesus was only an "interim" rather than a definitive revelation of God. If so, then the revealed truth so far might be less than that of later arrivals. If so, then all of Jesus's statements and commandments would have only temporary value. This would be contrary to what the apostles and the Church have been affirming over and over again—that Jesus was the definitive Word of God, that He was fully God and fully Man, and that His teaching, life, death, and resurrection were definitive, not interim, revelations from God.

The Incarnation speaks of a delicate balance between Jesus's divinity and his humanity—Jesus is the God-man, truly God and truly Man, fully divine and fully human. Jesus has two essential "poles" of being, so to speak. In the words of St. Paul (Eph. 2:5-7), "Christ Jesus, who, though he was in the form of God, did not count equality with God a thing to be grasped, but emptied himself, taking the form of a servant, being born in the likeness of men." The Catechism (464) adds to this that the Incarnation of the Son of God "does not mean that Jesus Christ is part God and part man, nor does it imply that he is the result of a confused mixture of the divine and the human. He became truly man while remaining truly God. Jesus Christ is true God and true man."

How do we balance these two sides? They are equally essential. On the one hand, had Jesus not been *human*, then the crucifixion was not real, but only an illusion. As Pope St. Leo the Great put it in 451, "Invisible in his own nature, he became visible in ours. And he whom nothing could contain was content to be contained." Therefore, His birth, crucifixion, and death must be real, not fake—they came with Jesus being human. The God-Man Jesus on earth prays as man, he obeys as man, and he suffers as man.

On the other hand, had Jesus not been *divine*, then He was only a prophet at best, and the whole economy of salvation would be up for grabs. No mere man can take away all the sins of the world, only a God-Man can. As the Letter to the Hebrews (10:4) puts it, "It is impossible that the blood of bulls and goats should take away sins." St. Proclus of Constantinople said in 429, "We do not proclaim a deified Man, but we confess an incarnate God." Jesus could only be our Savior by being the Son of God, an incarnate God, both divine and human. No one else could take away the sins of the world. John the Baptist could not have said it more clearly, "Behold, the Lamb of God, who takes away the sin of the world!" (John 1:29).

Therefore, there are also two sides to what happened on Calvary. On the one hand, to hold that the Son suffered only in His *divine* nature would mean that Jesus did not experience suffering the way human beings do. In other words, to place the significance of the Son's suffering within His divine nature is to relegate His human suffering to insignificance, and thus to demote all human suffering to insignificance.

On the other hand, to hold that the Son of God suffered only in His *human* nature would mean that He only suffered like every other human being suffers, which would make His suffering inadequate for the redemption of all humanity. The suffering of the Man Jesus would not be worth more than anyone else's suffering—only an incarnate God, a God-Man, can redeem all of us. Creation can only be renewed and redeemed by its Creator—that is, by the divinity of Jesus, an Incarnate God.

All this shows what reasoning can do for religion. It should not come as a surprise, though, that enemies of the concept of an Incarnate God used reasoning, too, to demonstrate what is wrong with that concept. A very influential group of these enemies can be found in Arianism. Arians defended their case by making some seemingly "logical" statements: if God is one, then Jesus cannot be God as well; if Jesus is the Son of God and also God Himself, then He cannot also be His own son (besides, what son is as old as his own father?); if Jesus is Son, then He was begotten; if He is begotten, then He had a beginning; if He had a beginning, then He is not infinite; if He is not infinite, then He is not God; if there was a time when the Son was not the Son, then He had to be created at some point. It is in logic and math that these lines of reasoning would be followed by QED [*Quod erat demonstrandum*]. It's as simple as that! Or is it not?

Where did the Arians go wrong? For one, they considered the terms "begotten" and "created" synonymous, which is a very questionable equation. C. S. Lewis explains the difference between "begotten" and "created" lucidly, as only he can: "When you beget, you beget something of the same kind as yourself. ... But when you make, you make something of a different kind than yourself. ... What God begets is God; just as what man begets is man. What God creates is not God; just as what man makes is not man."

Many other defenders of an Incarnate God had preceded Lewis some 17 centuries earlier. One of them was St. Athanasius, who saw in all clarity that the divinity of Christ is the cornerstone of our salvation. If Christ were only a creature, the Gospel would not truly be such good news after all. Jesus's suffering would end up being worth as much, or as little, as anyone else's suffering. As we said earlier, creation can only be renewed and redeemed by its Creator—that is, by the divinity of Jesus. No human beings could accomplish this on their own—only God can. That's why an incarnate God is an essential fact in Christianity.

From possibility to reality

Showing that some supernatural truth is not against reason means only that it is a possibility. But this doesn't automatically implicate that it is also a reality. The step from possibility to reality requires additional "evidence." The Catholic faith says supernatural truths are indeed an objective reality because they come directly from God. This is called Divine Revelation. It is a direct way of God communicating with us. The Bible testifies to this: "In many and various ways God spoke of old to our fathers by the prophets, but in these last days he has spoken to us by a Son" (Hebr. 1:1). That is how God can reveal supernatural truths to us. As we discussed earlier, if Divine Revelation were not possible, then God is not God.

Apparently, the seal of objective reality must come from a higher, Divine Authority, infinitely more reliable than any human authority can be. Of course, claims of supernatural truths must have passed the test of reason, otherwise they can't be a truth coming from on high. This means supernatural truths are in essence supernaturally revealed truths. That's the only way we can know for sure that God is a triune God, one God in three Persons. All Paul's letters and all four Gospels do clearly mention that Jesus was the Son of God, but it took longer, and the help of the Holy Spirit, to know the full truth of all of this: "These things

I have spoken to you, while I am still with you. But the Counselor, the Holy Spirit, whom the Father will send in my name, he will teach you all things, and bring to your remembrance all that I have said to you" (John 14:25).

Could we live without supernatural truths? Perhaps we could. Yet, they are life-savers on the way to Heaven. Think of this: the fact that all humans are mortal is a natural truth about their bodies, but the fact that they are also immortal is a supernatural truth that comes with their souls. No matter how good we are at validating them through reason, they need to be more than that, for we need ultimately divine, infallible, dogmatic certainty. Nothing, no reasoning, no proof can provide that certainty—only God can. Even what Jesus says comes from the voice of God. We need *the* truth, not just *a* truth or a *possible* truth. We need to be certain that the beliefs of our faith are true, for nothing merely human can be certainly true. That's why regular, natural truths come with confirmation at best, but never with certainty. What makes supernatural truths unique is that they are certain and infallible.

How was the supernatural truth of Jesus' resurrection confirmed? It was confirmed by the witness of those to whom the risen Lord had appeared. And we share in this witness by "hearsay." In a legal setting, "hearsay" evidence is not admitted if the source of that evidence is not available. But in the Bible, the original evidence came from the first witnesses and was handed on to later generations. That is not as uncommon as it sounds. Nearly all our historical beliefs, including our beliefs about where we were born and who our ancestors are, come from hearsay. Even the enterprise of science relies heavily on trustworthy "eyewitness" reports of others, largely in the case of special experiences and experiments recorded in articles and textbooks. Think of medical doctors who usually never had the diseases they treat.

Chapter 6: Made in God's Image

Their knowledge comes from "hearsay" during their training and from information received from the medical community. Something similar holds for what we know about religion.

In addition, the supernatural truth of Jesus' resurrection was also confirmed by God Himself. Picture this episode in which the apostles were put before the Jewish Council and one of its members, Gamaliel, a teacher of the law, held in honor by all the people, stood up and spoke these words (Acts 5:38-39), "I tell you, keep away from these men and let them alone; for if this plan or this undertaking is of men, it will fail; but if it is of God, you will not be able to overthrow them. You might even be found opposing God." Lo and behold, the followers of the apostles could not be overthrown for twenty centuries and are still around in high numbers. Apparently, even supernatural truths can be confirmed by natural truths in human history. What more confirmation could we wish for.

Let me put it this way: Just as scientists must submit their minds to the data of experiment, so must religious believers submit theirs to the data of Revelation. Divine Revelation is always progressive in nature—that is, over time, we are granted a fuller and fuller knowledge of God in general, including a fuller understanding of the meaning of prior Revelation. In other words, even religious knowledge, like secular knowledge, undergoes a process of gradual development and precision. Thus, it comes closer and closer to the full truth. For instance, the New Testament does not abolish the truth of the Old Testament but extends and deepens it. Many important religious concepts—such as the Incarnation and the Trinity—are not even mentioned in the Bible but were developed afterwards by the Church. This process of growth resembles the growth of a river—it gets wider and deeper, while remaining the same river. Another image compares this process with polishing silver: it does not change the silver but makes it clearer and brighter. The Catholic faith is a faith that makes you think, although we can never think it through completely.

A case in point is the concept of transubstantiation. To make the mystery of the Eucharist a bit more accessible and understandable, St. Thomas Aquinas used the concept of transubstantiation centuries ago. It hinges on the distinction between two sorts of change: accidental and substantial. Accidental change occurs when non-essential appearances change without a change in substance. Water, for instance, can take on the appearance of ice, while remaining the same substance. In the Eucharist, however, the substance changes from bread and wine into the substance of body and blood, without any change in appearance. This may be hard to believe, but we could point out that if a cow can change grass into milk, then God can certainly change wine into Jesus' Blood. St. Ambrose used a simple comparison: "If the word of the Lord Jesus is so powerful as to bring into existence things which were not, then a fortiori those things which already exist can be changed into something else." Obviously, we are dealing here with a supernatural truth which reason cannot prove but at least explain as best as possible.

Sometimes, natural truths and supernatural truths seem closely related. Take, for example, these two truths: the Crucifixion and the Resurrection. The Crucifixion of Jesus is a natural, earthly truth—which can be studied and corroborated by historians—whereas the Resurrection of Jesus is a supernatural, heavenly truth—which is authorized by God Himself and witnessed by those chosen by God. If the Crucifixion is true, then it is a fact, and denying it does not make it untrue. Another example of a natural truth would be the empty tomb that the women found on the third day after His crucifixion. It made sense to assume someone had removed the body until they were told, by Jesus and Angels, about the supernatural truth of His resurrection. Natural truths we can often claim "in the name of science and with the authority of science"; supernatural truths, on the other hand, we claim "in the name of God and with the authority of God."

Pope John Paul II makes a similar distinction when he said: "It may help, then, to turn briefly to the different modes of truth. Most of them depend upon immediate evidence or are confirmed by experimentation. This is the mode of truth proper to everyday life and to scientific research. At another level we find philosophical truth, attained by means of the speculative powers of the human intellect. Finally, there are religious truths which are to some degree grounded in philosophy, and which we find in the answers which the different religious traditions offer to the ultimate questions."

Obviously, when talking about supernatural truths, we are dealing with something usually called a "mystery." God being a Triune God is a mystery of faith. God being an incarnate God is another mystery of faith. A mystery is not something about which we can't know anything, but something about which we can't know everything. Just because it is a mystery does not mean we shouldn't spend time thinking about the Trinity, for instance. Dorothy Sayers (1893-1957) dryly noted that for many people, the doctrine of the Trinity is, "The Father incomprehensible, the Son incomprehensible, and the whole thing incomprehensible." Yet, the Trinity is something we can spend our entire lives thinking about it and never come to the end of it. In that sense, it is certainly a mystery, which in turn leads us to other mysteries such as the Blessed Virgin Mary, who is the *Theotokos* ("God-bearer." How can one believe in the Trinity—and, therefore, in the Incarnation—and not venerate the one through whom God became man?

The reason that there are mysteries is that God is infinite, which we know by reason, whereas our intellects are finite, which we know by experience. If miracles are possible—which they are, as we argued earlier—then mysteries must be possible as well. Although mysteries of faith may be beyond reason, they are not unreasonable; they can be explained and defended, although not proven, by arguments based on reason. As said earlier, God gave us brains and expects us to use them to understand even the mysteries of faith, to the extent such understanding is possible. Sometimes that requires heavy, precise terminology—often hard to digest. But that doesn't take away from how real they are.

The will is the voluntary part of the soul

Truth is an absolute concept, as we found out in the previous chapter. It is related to the intellectual part of the mind. But there is another absolute principle: goodness. It is based on the voluntary part of the mind, the human will. Blessed Cardinal John Newman was very emphatic in warning us not to make the mistake of separating intellect and will. We tend to think that intellect is the key thing—that if we *know* what is right, we will pursue it. But this fails to acknowledge that there is also weakness of will—that is, when we know what is right but fail to do it. The Bible makes no bones about it: "He who says 'I know Him' but disobeys His commandments is a liar" (1 John 2:4). All efforts of the intellect also require efforts of the will. That is why having a free-will does not guarantee that we do the right thing.

Morality in shambles

To do what is good and right is part of morality. Morality has come under attack from many sides these days—probably more

Chapter 6: Made in God's Image

so than ever before in history. It seems to be a slow-motion form of moral decline, yet it is a persistent process. I realize, of course, that morality has *always* been under attack—actually from the very moment Adam and Eve caved in to the first attack in history. But nowadays, there is more going on than just weakness of the will.

Many cultural, philosophical, and even scientific efforts are being made to undermine the very foundation of morality. What they all seem to have in common is the idea that our moral values are undergoing constant change, and therefore are subject to various cultural and historical fluctuations. If this were true, morality would just be a matter of emotions, personal preferences, cultural trends, and majority votes. That explains why we seem to be living in a world of disposable moral values—sometimes called the "transvaluation of values." As a consequence, morality has been subject to various misconceptions and false claims.

What are these misconceptions and false claims? Let's briefly tackle the most flawed ones and show how they deceive our thinking about morality.

Here is deception number one: Morality comes from past bad experiences. It does not. Why not? Well, killing is indeed morally wrong—but certainly not so because we discovered so after we had killed some people or had seen some killings. That would mean we would have to do something wrong before we could know what is wrong. A moral command comes before what it commands, not after. Morality may be corroborated by past experiences, but it is not created by such experiences—in fact, it aims to prevent them. There is mounting evidence that babies as young as six months old make moral judgments and can tell right from wrong. Their sense of fairness begins at a very young age. Researchers have found that, when they studied kids with a test that was unfairly rigged so that one child receives more rewards than others, they found children will ensure that a reward is fairly split, whereas animals usually fight for the largest piece.

Babies also know the difference between "good guys" and "bad guys"—despite little or no previous exposure to such situations. Based on this natural feeling of right and wrong, they can later be taught more specific rules about "bad guys", such as the "underwear rule": not be touched by others on parts of the body usually covered by their underwear, and not to touch others in those areas. Still, children sexually abused at a very young age know "intuitively" that they experienced something morally wrong. This tells us moral values and moral laws are not discovered through empirical observation but are somehow "inborn" from early childhood on.

Then there is deception number two: Morality comes from the animal world. It does not. Animals do not have morality and cannot have morality. The relationship between predator and prey, for instance, has nothing to do with morality; if predators really were guided by morality, their lives would be pretty harsh. Animals have social behavior, but not moral behavior regulated by a moral code.

Consequently, animals never do awful things out of meanness or cruelty, for the simple reason that they have no morality and thus no cruelty or meanness. They follow whatever "pops up" in their brains—and no one has the right to morally blame them. When animals seem to do awful things, it is only because we, as human beings, consider their actions "awful" according to our standards of morality. As said earlier, we will never arrange court sessions for grizzly bears that maul hikers, because we know that bears are not morally responsible for their actions. If animals truly had moral rights, their fellow animals, too, would need to respect those "rights."

Then there is deception number three: Morality comes from our genes. It does not. It would in fact be hard to claim that our genes tell us what is morally right or wrong. Here is why. First of all, those who believe that morality is rooted in their genes must face the possibility that this very belief then is also rooted in their genes—which makes it a belief that comes back like a "boomerang" to hit whoever launched it. Second, in the world of genes, there is material substance (DNA), but no truths and untruths that are immaterial—and hence, no intangible moral rights and moral wrongs either. DNA is physical "stuff" that can be long or short, light or heavy, but morals cannot be any of these—they have no mass, size, or color. Third, if morality were in the genes, why would we need articulated moral rules to reinforce what "by nature" we would or would not desire to do anyway? Under such circumstances, a moral code would be completely redundant. Instead, the opposite could be argued: Morality has the power to overrule what our genes dictate—passions, emotions, and drives. This seems to indicate that morality is at a level "above" the level of genes.

No wonder, then, that far too many people are willing to break a moral rule when they can get away with it. It is hard to believe that they are going against their genes. Everyone knows about moral laws, yet everyone breaks them repeatedly, as genes do not seem to prevent this. Unlike the laws of nature, moral laws can be ignored. We have here another flawed attempt at converting moral behavior into a non-moral phenomenon. The rules as to what is morally right and what is wrong do not and cannot come from genes. It is hard to see how non-moral causes such as evolution and DNA could ever produce a moral effect; they are of a completely different nature—as different as the rules of playing chess are different from the pieces on the chess board.

Then there is deception number four: Morality is something acquired—through upbringing, training, disciplining, or education. Well, it is not. No doubt, discipline is part of morality. People who are at the mercy of their lusts, drives, and passions may not do the good they ought to do, because they are not disciplined enough to resist their lusts. But that does not mean that morality is merely a matter of being educated, taught, and disciplined.

Think of this. The laws of nature, such as the law of gravity, may have to be taught to us in a physics class or biology class, but that doesn't make them only a matter of training and teaching. It is partly through schooling that we know about them, but the laws themselves are not a product of schooling. In a similar way, while parents may help us understand moral laws and prepare us to do what is morally right, the distinction between right and wrong is not a matter of upbringing.

Then there is deception number five, a very common trap: Morality is a matter of feelings. It is not. It may seem appealing to think that our gut feelings tell us what is right or wrong, but the word "feeling" carries a strong subjective overtone—some have it, some do not. This opens the argument up to attacking morality as not real, but only as something in a person's mind—a thought famously expressed as "many heads, many minds." George Bernard Shaw, for instance, spoke of "different tastes," as if there are many moralities. Seen this way, killing may be wrong for you but not for me. If morality were merely a matter of taste, no further discussion would be possible. The best we could say would be that some people have a better taste than others.

In contrast, "good" in morality is not a matter of what *feels* good. Feelings can never be the standard for judging morality, for then we would have to decide next who has the best "gut feelings." It is in fact the other way around: Morality is the standard for judging feelings. Feelings of revenge, for instance, need to be curbed by morality. Everyone can claim that intuition told him or her what ought to be done, but that in itself does not make such

Chapter 6: Made in God's Image

an action morally right or wrong; if that were the case, all defendants in court would be entitled to claim that they followed their "gut feelings." Again, it is in fact the other way around: a moral code determines which moral intuitions are right or wrong.

Then there is deception number six: Morality is a matter of conscience. It is not. Like intuition, conscience may indeed seem to be a good tool to guide our moral behavior. That is in fact a very popular view nowadays. One's conscience is often heralded as the ultimate source of moral good and evil. Ironically, even moral relativists, who deny that morality has any absolute authority, still hold on to at least one moral absolute: "Never disobey your own conscience." They should therefore ask themselves where the absolute authority of a human conscience comes from. How can a person's personal conscience possibly be an infallible guideline for morality? We cannot validly justify that the way we acted was morally right by claiming that our conscience tells us so. Were the Nazis "good" people because they followed their conscience? Both sides in a war conflict believe in conscience and claim that they are right—yet they contradict each other. Both cannot be right at the same time.

Moral relativists, on the other hand, consider themselves in charge of the moral terminology they use, and they manipulate it according to their needs. They replace, for instance, the old term "abortion" with the new term "selective reproduction." Or they determine on their own what the term "human" means by demarcating whoever qualifies for this predicate: perhaps only Arians, only white supremacists, only the biologically fit, only those who are not a burden to society. From then on, everything becomes relative to the criteria relativists invent on the spot, all by themselves—perhaps even supported by one's conscience. They plainly adjust their moral vocabulary to make it sound politically correct.

Then there is deception number seven: Morality is a matter of creating more happiness for more people. It is not. In this view, something is considered morally right depending on its effects—that is, if it leads to "the greater happiness of a greater number of people." This makes something morally right if it gives more happiness to more people around us. Seen this way, society exists above all to provide for the individual's comfortable self-preservation, but then in the greatest possible numbers. In other words, a moral code must ultimately be judged by measuring quantities and qualities in our direct surroundings. That is easier said and done. Lenin and Mao, for instance, were not awfully good at making arrangements for the happiness of hundreds of millions of people.

If it is quantity that matters, then it leaves the question unanswered as to what to make of those left behind in the minority. This comes close to survival of the fittest. On the other hand, if it is quality that matters, then it fails to tell us what happiness is. There are many ways to "define" happiness. Is it perhaps another word for pleasure? This is the solution *hedonism* gives us: feelings of pleasure are the only intrinsically good things in the world and feelings of pain the only intrinsically bad things. If this is true, then moral goodness is not truly good; it is good only to the degree it leads to pleasure. And moral badness is not truly bad; it is bad only to the degree that it leads to pain. So there is a pleasure-seeking morality versus a pain-avoiding morality. If so, then the pleasure of one person may cause the displeasure of someone else. We are back again with a morality of feelings according to which a person is a good person only if he or she is happy and *feels* good. However, feeling good does not make you a morally good person. If this is all morality is about, we would end up with an empty shell of feelings again.

Then there is deception number eight: Morality is based on

the so-called Golden Rule. It is not and cannot be. In its negative form, the Golden Rule says, "Do not do unto others as you would not have them do unto you." Its positive form is "Do unto others as you would have them do to you." True, this Golden Rule can be found in Islamic, Buddhist, and Confucian texts, among others; it is also mentioned in the Bible (Tobit 4:15; Matthew 7:12; Luke 6:31).

But is the Golden Rule a good moral code? I have my serious doubts, for its starting point is quite self-centered: what is morally good depends on what I want or not want for myself. It is aimed at one's comfortable self-preservation. It starts from and ends with "me, myself, and I." Besides, this makes "I" the maker of its own moral code. If I happen to have a weird preference for certain acts, do I have the moral obligation to do those also to others? Or do others have the moral duty to do those to me? In this view, my personal preferences have become the standard of morality. We end up with an empty shell again, this time a shell of preferences.

Then there is deception number nine: Morality is a matter of non-moral criteria. It is not. David Hume famously said that we cannot derive how things *ought* to be from the way things *are*. Some have tried to get around this problem by using the trick of *defining* moral terms in purely natural terms. But this leads to another fallacy, the so-called "naturalistic fallacy," which is the erroneous idea that what is natural can be defined as good in moral terms. Seeking pleasure for pleasure's sake, for example, may be natural but is not necessarily something that is morally good.

We can and should always ask the question as to whether things like "being pleasant" and "being desirable" are the same as "being good." We can only equate them by mere definition, but that brings us back to what we wanted to equate. A moral concept cannot be redefined in non-moral terms, for then it loses its specifically moral aspect. By "redefining" morality in non-moral terms, we inevitably lose its distinctive moral character.

Then there is deception number ten: Morality is based on demands put up by society. It is not. As a matter of fact, moral laws are different from the positive laws that society or its government has enforced. Driving under the influence is a moral issue whereas driving with an expired driver's license is not. Legal, civic, or positive laws are enacted and put in force by a specific political community. In ideal cases, the law of the land should be a reflection of the moral law. That is the reason why Martin Luther King Jr. called any unjust legal law "a code that is out of harmony with the moral law." Seen from a purely legal point of view, for example, it would not have been right, or even possible, to bring to trial and punish the Nazi perpetrators who had applied the laws that were created and implemented by a regime that had come to power through legal channels. They defended themselves as being just law-abiding citizens following the law of the land. But seen from a natural law perspective, their "lawful" actions were atrocities committed against humanity and morality. That's why we cannot easily equate *legal* laws to *moral* laws. Even if something is legal, it may still be immoral. Slavery, for instance, was legally right at one point, and now abortion is in many countries, but that doesn't make them morally right.

Obviously, the relationship between morality and legality is rather intricate. When *moral* consensus fades—as it did, for instance, in St. Thomas More's time, and as it does now in ours—we usually turn to law. But when morality is no longer widely shared, legal laws begin to falter as well, making society and culture teeter on the brink of chaos. In other words, legal laws cannot and should not be divorced from morality. Without morality, legal laws may easily get in trouble. The same might happen in a society without religion, as religion is a vital source of morality, of what is good and what is wrong. Consequently, legal laws, moral laws, and religion are strongly intertwined. When religion begins to fade in society, a cascade of effects sets in and starts a dangerous domino effect.

There are probably more misconceptions about the nature of morality. But at least the ones mentioned above do cover what morality does *not* stand for. Therefore, we need to find out what it is that morality does stand for. Let's try.

The amazing world of morality

The moral laws of morality come with some the following very peculiar characteristics: they are unconditional, universal, timeless, absolute, and objective. Let me explain what that means:

1. Moral laws are unconditional. Most rules we are familiar with are conditional upon a certain goal—they are means-to-other-ends: if you want Y, you must do X; if you do not want to attain that goal, the rule does not work. For instance, if you want to learn biking, you must do certain things; if you want to recover from a cold, you must do so-and-so, etcetera. Not so with moral rules and laws. They are unconditional: just do X, for you *ought* to do X—no matter what, whether you like it or not, whether you feel it or not, whether others enforce it or not. Therefore, when it comes to morality, we cannot just pick whatever we want.

Morality tells us what ought to be done; it obliges us to pursue unconditionally what is good and right—no more ifs; no more questions asked. The legendary US President Abraham Lincoln put it well when he challenged the Nebraska bill of 1820 that would let residents vote on whether slavery should be legal in their state: "God did not place good and evil before man, telling him to make his choice." In brief, there is no "pro-choice" in morality. Put differently, choice does not determine what is right or wrong, but it is morality that determines which choices are right and which are wrong.

What does it mean then for something to be called "good" or "wrong" in moral terms? I think we need to make an important distinction first. Something can be called "good" in relation to a given goal or objective. Medical rules and medical procedures, for instance, are "good" for the purpose of medical care. I would rather call them rules, norms, or standards—but not values in the strict sense. Some people, though, like to call them *instrumental* values. That is fine with me. But what remains true is that these values are always *conditional*, relative to what we need to do in order to attain something else. Cardiopulmonary resuscitation (CPR), for instance, is a "good" procedure to manually preserve intact brain function. It is "instrumentally" good to attain something else—the preservation of human life. If anyone ever wonders why a certain act is "good" in this instrumental sense, we can provide an explanation in terms of its objective: Does the act meet its objective, yes or no? If it does, it is considered "good." And every action that does *not* meet the objective is consequently "wrong." But I must emphasize this doesn't mean that those actions are also right or wrong in a *moral* sense. Abortion may sometimes be medically right, but that does not automatically make it also morally right.

From this follows that there's nothing "useful" about moral values. If anyone ever wonders why a certain act is "good" in a moral sense, we have no explanation to offer and cannot refer to other ends; all we can say is, "It's evidently right to do so." It is a matter of self-evidence! The moral value of human life is self-evident, whereas the technique of CPR is only right if it works to reach its objective. This means we have a "moral eye" that sees values in life, just like the "physical eye" sees colors in nature. Moral values are definitely real, but not so in a physical sense.

Chapter 6: Made in God's Image

Some among us are able to clearly discern certain values and evaluate them properly, whereas others are not. Anyone who does not see their evidence is "blind." Just as there are color-blind people, there may also be value-blind people.

2. Moral laws are universal. This means they apply to *all* human beings—regardless of age, race, ethnicity, nationality, culture, or political affiliation. Morality is not regulated by popularity, interest groups, or majority votes, but it is universal in scope—it demands the same of everyone everywhere. Moral laws are as universal as the law of gravity is universal. C. S. Lewis once said about moral values, "The human mind has no more power of inventing a new value than of imagining a new primary color."

Think again, for instance, of the Nuremberg trials that took place after World War II—or of any other international court, for that matter. Seen from a purely legal point of view, it would not have been right, or even possible, to bring to trial and punish the Nazi perpetrators who had applied the civil laws that were created and implemented by a regime that had come to power through legal channels—for they were just "law-abiding" citizens following the law of the land. However, seen from a universal moral code perspective, their "lawful" actions were atrocities committed against humanity. We could ask about Nazi death camps whether they were morally wrong, or just wrong in the eyes of nations other than Germany after World War II.

Some may argue that the facts seem to contradict the universal character of morality. There seem to be many varieties of morality among various cultures and beliefs. However, this perception may be very deceiving. As a matter of fact, there is not a great deal of difference between a Christian morality, Jewish morality, Hindu morality, Muslim morality, Buddhist morality—although there is a great difference in these religions. C. S. Lewis, for example, published a list of universal moral principles which he called "Illustrations of the Tao or Natural Law." Peter Kreeft compares this variety with the diversity of different languages: Beneath the different words of different languages, you find common concepts—this is what makes translation from one language to another possible. In the same way, he concludes, "we find similar morals beneath different mores."

Again, morality does not come with a specific race, ethnicity, nation, party, or church—it is a common property that belongs to *all* human beings. Only moral values and rules that are universal can transcend differences in culture, era, and personal interests. That's why the Catechism can state that a moral law is universally valid, as "it obliges each and everyone, always and everywhere" (2261).

3. Moral laws are timeless. Those who object to the idea of a timeless morality might claim that moral rules and values have repeatedly been subject to change during the course of human history. However, this objection is based on a mix-up between moral values and moral evaluations. Moral evaluations are our personal feelings or discernments regarding moral values and laws at a certain point in time. Many erroneously think that, in making moral evaluations, we create moral values in accordance with these evaluations. Hence, when evaluations change, the moral values and laws are said to change as well. However, moral evaluations are merely a reflection of the way we discern timeless moral values and react to them at a given time.

In other words, moral evaluations may change over time, but moral values do not—they are timeless and were always there, even when we did not yet discern them. The law of gravity, for instance, was already true before Isaac Newton discovered that law, but before him, we just did not know yet it was true. Something similar holds for moral laws and values. Slavery is a case in point. A few centuries ago, slavery was not evaluated widely as morally wrong, but nowadays it is by most people. The moral law did not change, but for a while many were "blind" for that law. Think of this comparison: although a visually impaired person cannot see the trees outside, the trees are still there, as the existence of the trees does not depend on whether a blind person perceives them or not. In a similar way, a morally blind person cannot see the moral laws and values "out there," yet they are there, for their existence does not depend on whether a person with moral blindness does perceive them.

In contrast, moral evaluations are merely our personal feelings or discernments regarding timeless moral values. However, the moral value itself ("being a value") should be distinguished from human attitudes toward values ("being valued"). "Having value" is not the same as "being valued." As said earlier, in making *evaluations*, we do not create *values* in accordance with these evaluations. That's why *political* correctness is very different from *moral* correctness Think of this comparison: We shouldn't confuse our current understanding of physical laws with the way those laws really are as we may find out some day. In a similar vein, do not confuse our current moral evaluations with the way the moral laws really are. Morality is not a function of the clock.

Let me illustrate this point a bit further. A few centuries ago, slavery was not evaluated as morally wrong, but nowadays it is by most people. Did our moral values change? No, they did not; but our evaluations certainly did. Only a few people in the past—St. Anselm was one of them, and then Pope Eugene IV (in his 1435 Bull *Sicut Dudum*) as well as Pope Paul III (in his 1537 Bull against slavery, entitled *Sublimis Deus*)—were able to discern the timeless value of personal freedom and human rights (versus slavery), whereas most of their contemporaries were blind to this value. The latter were value-blind, because they didn't "see" that one is obliged to be "color-blind" when it comes to racial issues. They could and should have known better! The 7th Commandment forbids acts that lead "to the enslavement of human beings, to their being bought, sold and exchanged like merchandise, in disregard for their personal dignity" (CCC 2414). No wonder, St. Paul directed a Christian master to treat his Christian slave "no longer as a slave but more than a slave, as a beloved brother, [...] both in the flesh and in the Lord" (Philem. 1:16).

Something similar holds for the moral value of monogamy. Many people in the past were blind to this value—and some still are. But the moral rule of monogamy is universal, even if not universally acknowledged and enforced. The way we "discover" moral laws is comparable to the way scientists discover scientific laws: typically. they both require the "genius" of especially gifted people. For religion and morality, such "gifted" people are Moses, the prophets, and Church authorities—and ultimately Jesus, the Son of God. As Jesus would say, "You have heard that it was said [...] But I say to you [...]"—which means, whether you "see" it or not, this is the way it ought to be in this world, for this is the way this world was created and designed. Moral laws, rules, and values are forever—not a function of the clock.

4. Moral laws are absolute. Because of its absolute character, morality cannot be based on anything that is relative and nonmoral by nature. Many, however, have tried to do just that. As we discussed earlier, some consider something morally right depending on its effects—that is, if it leads to "the greater happiness of a greater number of people." If this were true, we would not be morally obligated, but would only *feel* obligated. Contrary to this view, there is nothing "useful" about moral laws. Instead, they are absolute. Killing a human being is inherently wrong; stealing is inherently wrong; lying is inherently wrong—no matter who you are and where you are, regardless of your status in society, and regardless of any personal circumstances. Moral absolutes are like

unchanging rocks beneath the changing waves of feelings, preferences, and practices.

Such an absolutist view is not as bizarre as you might think. It is in fact a standard attitude in science: Our understanding of scientific laws did need, does need, and will need revision until we reach a better understanding of those laws the way they really are—just keep searching for the correct laws. Like moralists, scientists are basically absolutists. They are ultimately in search of absolute laws of nature, but they realize they may not be there yet. In morality, we should strive for something similar. Just as we may be oblivious to laws of nature that we didn't know yet, we may violate moral laws we are not aware of.

Let me explain this point with an example used by President Abraham Lincoln again. It seems to me that Abe put things better than I ever could when he was talking about slavery. In his own, rather technical words,

> *If A. can prove, however conclusively, that he may, of right, enslave B.—why may not B. snatch the same argument, and prove equally, that he may enslave A?—You say A. is white, and B. is black. It is color, then; the lighter, having the right to enslave the darker? Take care. By this rule, you are to be slave to the first man you meet, with a fairer skin than your own. You mean the whites are intellectually the superiors of the blacks; and, therefore have the right to enslave them? Take care again. By this rule, you are to be slave to the first man you meet, with an intellect superior to your own.*

President Lincoln's point is clear. All the answers you might come up with to defend your *moral* claim use criteria that are morally irrelevant, such as a darker skin color or a lower intelligence. Because those criteria are *relative*—someone with a lighter skin or higher intelligence would have the "moral right" to enslave you. And the same holds for the value of human life. This value cannot be based on biological standards, since those are per definition relative—and therefore, morally irrelevant. Yet, in the abortion debate, some judge the value of human life to be based on the use of biological criteria, such as the extent of cerebral activity. They use a "moral argument" based on relative criteria: the more cerebral activity there is, the more value a human life has, and therefore, the more protection it deserves. For others, viability is the criterion to determine the humanity of an unborn child. However, the biological criteria adduced here are relative—and therefore, morally irrelevant. We cannot use *relative* standards of intelligence, viability, maturity, health, fitness, and the like to measure or judge the *absolute* value of human life.

Instead, we need the moral, absolute standard of old that says whatever is born of human beings is human life and deserves absolute protection—irrespective of its extent of cerebral activity, its level of intelligence, or the number of its "defects." The Catechism puts it unmistakably: "*Human life is sacred* because from its beginning it involves the creative action of God" (2258). This viewpoint would imply that all human life deserves moral protection—from womb to tomb, from conception to natural death, from orphanages to mental institutions, and at all stages of its development. Just like no one can be halfway pregnant, no one can be halfway human or half a human being. Each human being bears the image of God—which is a gift, not an accomplishment achieved through maturation.

There is no space here for relative criteria. Yet, many people still need an ultrasound to see that abortion is wrong. Again, that is using *biological* criteria to make a *moral* decision—something like "the adult is more important than the unborn baby," or "independent human life outweighs dependent human life," or "a full-grown person is worth more than a growing fetus," or "a full-grown brain is worth more than a brain in development," and so on. In contrast, moral values are absolute ends-in-themselves—not disposable means-to-other-ends.

5. Moral laws are objective. As said earlier, "objective" means that something is real, regardless of whether or not we know it to be real. In other words, moral laws are not inventions of our minds, but they must be discovered the way they are in reality. They are "out there" and exist outside of us, in the sense of being independent of our thoughts and wishes. They are not merely a matter of "different tastes," as some think they are nowadays, thus changing moral laws into man-made laws. In this view, "I, me, and myself" has become the standard of good and right, the maker of one's own moral code. The new claim is that no one has the right to tell me what I ought to do or ought to avoid—I am fully autonomous. So, nothing and nobody should stop me from doing what I decide is "right" to do.

The idea that one's mind creates the laws of morality is as flawed as the idea that one's mind creates the laws of nature. Not only is there a physical order in nature but also a moral order. While the physical order is based on the laws of nature, the moral order is based on the laws of morality. What both kinds of laws have in common is the fact that they are based on objective reality. The main difference is that laws of nature *can't* be ignored, whereas laws of morality *shouldn't* be ignored. Yet, in both cases, ignoring them can have serious consequences.

My point is that the laws of morality are objective entities that exist in the real world, just as laws of nature are objective entities that exist in the real world. They are beyond human authority. No one had to invent them; they were already there for us to be discovered. They are not creations of the human mind, but entities which the human mind can fetch. As to moral laws, they tell us what we ought to do, no matter what. Rejecting them is like rejecting the law of gravity. That is why morality is a very demanding issue—it demands absolute authority. In the words of the Catechism (1751), "Objective norms of morality express the rational order of good and evil."

Let's sum up this discussion. All characteristics of the laws of morality on which the moral order of this world is based are similar to the characteristics of the laws of nature on which the physical order of this world is based. Both kinds of laws are universal (applicable to everyone everywhere), absolute (without exceptions), timeless (even if we do not know the underlying law yet), and objective (a given, independent of us and of any human authority). They are objective, universal, timeless, and absolute standards—no matter whether we are talking rationality, in terms of true and false, or morality, in terms of right and wrong. Just as "truths are true," even when we do not know yet they are true, "rights are right," even though we may not realize yet they are morally right. That's what our *intellect* tells us. Now it is up to our *will* to act upon this.

Where does morality come from?

The most common and popular idea nowadays is that morality is something coming from our genes, from the animal world, and from our evolutionary history. We discussed this idea earlier already and dismissed it as flawed. However, that leaves the question as to where morality does come from unanswered.

I can see why this discussion is confusing, especially so for people with a scientific background. Only science is supposed to give us "facts," or what we take the facts to be at a particular point in time. So, where do those moral values and rules suddenly come from? They do not seem to be facts, for there is no straight path from scientific facts to moral values. "Scientific maps," including maps of the human genome, tell us *how* to get some-

Chapter 6: Made in God's Image

where, but they do not tell us *where* to go—they do not contain moral directives. If science is all you believe in, then there is no discussion anymore in terms of "right and wrong." So, science seems to have blocked the road to morality altogether. It is scientism on its way again.

My fundamental rebuttal against this alleged scientific claim is as follows. If we are supposedly moral "by nature," why would we need an articulated *moral* rule to reinforce what by nature we would or would not desire to do anyway? If we were indeed moral "by nature"—that is, controlled by our genes and our evolutionary history—we would not need any articulated moral rules anyway, for our genes would take care of everything. Therefore, my conclusion is that moral laws tell us to do what our genes do *not* make us do "by nature."

Apparently, morality is about something that is outside the scope of biology, far beyond the reach of science. That's why science has nothing to say about morality. Albert Einstein was right to speak instead of "the moral foundations of science." He added, "You cannot turn around and speak of the scientific foundations of morality.... Every attempt to reduce ethics to scientific formulae must fail." In other words, one cannot explain moral behavior in terms of genetics or science in general. Instead, science itself must be judged by a moral code, for not everything that is scientifically possible is also morally permissible.

We argued earlier that the laws of nature cannot explain themselves nor their own existence, so they must come from a Divine Lawgiver who implemented them. Something similar can be said about the laws of morality, too: they cannot explain themselves nor their own existence. They come from a Divine Lawgiver who implemented them and made them part of this world. In both cases, the Divine Lawgiver is one and the same, the Creator of Heaven and earth. God gave the world not only laws of nature but also laws of morality, not only a natural order but also a moral order. Moral rules and values summon us to action, to what *ought* to be done, no matter what. This is a *moral ought*. Therefore, we ought to do what we ought to do—for Heaven's sake!

This means that human behavior is subordinate to a moral code. And this moral code cannot be fully understood without reference to God, for without God, everything would be permitted, even in science. Morality can interrogate science, but science cannot question morality—it is beyond its reach. Morality, however, cannot be properly understood without pointing to God. Our task isn't to *decide* what's right and what's wrong—God settled that at Creation. Our task is to *do* what's right and avoid what's wrong. As G.K. Chesterton put it, "I don't need a church to tell me I am wrong where I already know I'm wrong; I need a Church to tell me I am wrong where I think I'm right." And that's where the voluntary part of the mind, the human will, comes in.

Well, if we are not moral "by nature," then there must be something else that makes us moral beings, right? Let me say it one more time, morality is not rooted in our genes, it is not the product of natural selection, it is not the result of any legislation, it is not a scientific conclusion, and it is not based on anything useful or beneficial such as "the greater happiness of a greater number of people." All these substitutes are morally irrelevant, since morality includes a new dimension that only morality has access to—its moral dimension. And that is where we need "divine help." Why? Nature can only contain moral norms, if the Will of an Authority had put them there—which fact presupposes a Creator God whose Will has entered nature. Hence, morality must be from "Above." It is "the work of divine Wisdom" (CCC 1950). How could there be moral laws if there were no moral

Chapter 6: Made in God's Image

Lawgiver? Morality is written in our hearts and minds, guiding us to make the right choices in life. As the prophet Isaiah said, "Woe to those who call evil good and good evil" (Is. 5:20)—that's beyond their human authority.

The Russian writer Fyodor Dostoyevsky was entirely right when he showed us in his book *The Brothers Karamazov* that, without God, all things are permissible. Without God's eternal "Beyond," there wouldn't be eternal moral laws and we would be mere animals. Let me make clear that Dostoyevsky is not claiming that there would be no moral rules if God does not exist, for even in atheist societies there are some moral rules. What he does claim, through Ivan, is that nothing would be *always* and *everywhere* wrong for the simple reason that everything would be, at least at some point and under some circumstances, permitted. Without God, moral absolutism becomes moral relativism. In other words, if God is dead, Ivan himself must take ultimate responsibility for the moral order of the world. When God is absent, Ivan would become the moral commander-in-chief, all by himself.

A similar conclusion is phrased also by the late French philosopher Jean-Paul Sartre.: If atheism is true, he said, there can be no absolute or objective standard of right and wrong, for there is no eternal heaven that would make values objective and universal. Without God, there wouldn't be any objective moral standards. In his own words, if God does not exist, "there disappears with him all possibility of finding values in an intelligible heaven." In addition, Friedrich Nietzsche was another philosopher who clearly understood how devastating the decline of Christianity and its morality has been to society. If we are only the fortuitous effects of physical causes, we have no other moral measures but ourselves. That is why Nietzsche could say that humanism and other "moral" ideologies shelter themselves in caves and venerate shadows of the God they once believed in. In other words, they are only holding on to something they cannot provide themselves—mere shadows of the past.

Even the non-religious German philosopher Jürgen Habermas expressed as his conviction that the ideas of freedom and social co-existence are based on the Jewish notion of justice and the Christian ethics of love. This doesn't mean, of course, that people who do not believe in God cannot act morally. They surely can, for most people do condemn murder, whether they have religion or not. Nietzsche would probably say that they shelter themselves in caves and venerate shadows of the God they once believed in. Pope Benedict XVI went beyond this thought when he said to the world religious leaders gathered in Assisi on October 27, 2011: "The horrors of the concentration camps reveal with utter clarity the consequences of God's absence." And in his address to the German Parliament in 2011, he quoted St. Augustine, "Without justice—what else is the State but a great band of robbers?"

I would like to end this section with a question that is profoundly philosophical. Where do natural truths and supernatural truths reside in this world? Where do the laws of nature and the laws of morality reside in this world? They cannot just be in the minds of people. They cannot just be around us like objects that we can bump into. So, where then are they?

If abstract objects such as concepts, truths, and laws do not depend for their existence on the material world or on the human mind, then there is only one rational option left: they must exist in a "third realm" that is neither material nor mental. This idea may sound outlandish, but it is certainly not new; it is usually associated with the Greek philosopher Plato, who mentioned this third realm long ago in his theory of forms. However, Plato's position faces multiple, rather technical problems, which we will not discuss here. But there is a much more acceptable version of this third realm—arguably the only valid one—which goes basically back to St. Augustine and was later elaborated by philosophers such as Gottfried Leibniz and Gottlob Frege. In this version, abstract eternal entities or objects do indeed exist, but they can do so only in an infinite, eternal Divine Intellect. That takes us back to our original claims about morality.

Human rights

Morality comes with rights and duties. They are tightly connected: rights always come with duties. What we owe others, in moral terms, are our *duties*; what others owe us are our *rights*. Duties and rights have a natural reciprocal relationship—they go hand in hand and keep each other in tow. For example, the right to defend one's own life comes with the duty to protect someone else's life; the right to seek the truth goes with the duty to allow others to seek the truth; the duty to honor the *dignity* of human beings is what we owe others as a duty, and it is something others owe us as a right. In other words, without duties no rights, and without rights no duties. For example, no one has the duty to have children, so no one has the right to have children; no one has the duty to be married, so no one has the right to be married.

Obviously, "duties" and "rights" are very specific moral concepts. They are connected with another concept, human *dignity*. The idea that human rights come with human dignity is certainly not new. It is basically and fundamentally a Judeo-Christian concept, based on the religious fact that humans are made in the image and likeness of God. It did get a fresh look, though, after World War II when the first photographs of inhumane atrocities in the Nazi concentration camps surfaced. Thus, in 1948, the UN affirmed in the *Universal Declaration of Human Rights* that "all human beings are born free and equal in dignity and rights."

However, the UN assumed a generally shared understanding of "human rights," going back to its Judeo-Christian roots, but failed to define them. It must have assumed, though, that these rights are not man-made, but God-given—though the drafters famously left the term "right" vague in order to achieve passage. The Catholic philosopher Jacques Maritain, who was actively involved in drafting the U.N. declaration, said paradoxically, "We agree on these rights, on condition that no one asks us why." Obviously, the concept of human dignity had become what Adam Schulman called "a placeholder for whatever it is about human beings that entitles them to basic human rights and freedoms." It had become a placeholder for a man-made morality.

However, the fact remains that morality is God-given, not man-made. Without God, we wouldn't even have any moral *rights*. The US *Declaration of Independence* states very clearly that our human rights are *God*-given rights—otherwise we wouldn't have any: "We hold these truths to be self-evident, that all men are created equal, that they are endowed by their Creator with certain unalienable Rights, that among these are Life, Liberty and the pursuit of Happiness." These are divine birthrights. You cannot earn or forfeit your human dignity and human rights; human descent is enough to merit human dignity and human rights, both in living and in dying, because they are given by God to every human being. Without God, we would have no *right* to claim any rights.

The late President John F. Kennedy put it well in his Inaugural Address: "[T]he rights of man come not from the generosity of the state, but from the hand of God." In response to those who say that we should act in a way that is moral "even if God does not exist," Pope Benedict XVI argued that we should do the opposite, living a moral life "as if God existed." Without God, there could be no absolute or objective standards of right and wrong, we found out earlier. If human rights really came from men, and not God, men could take them away anytime—and they certainly have tried and will try again. Since we received our rights from *God*, let no one, and certainly not the government, decide how to exercise those rights. And let no one tell you that the *State* gave you those rights and can therefore decide how to exercise them.

Yet, what we see happening around us now is that the declaration of human rights was put at the mercy of special interest groups. These have hijacked the term "human rights" for their own agendas. They have come up with *new* "rights," practically invented on the spot. They used it as a placeholder for a man-made morality. New sexual and reproductive "rights," such as abortion, for example, were invented, and so were the new "rights" of scientists to experiment with human embryos, as well as another invention, the "last civil right" to die. But one of the problems is that these reproductive rights do not come with reproductive duties, and therefore cannot be rights.

Just think of how abortion was renamed many times. They are constantly coming up with new fuzzy euphemisms (choice, women's health care, reproductive justice, etc. etc.) to prevent the public from realizing that they're talking about killing and dismembering babies in the womb. How could abortion ever be called a "reproductive right," for after reproduction, abortion has already taken place. Once we start to call abortion and abortive contraceptives "*health* care" issues, we find ourselves in a terminological jumble, for none of this has anything to do with the health of the mother, let alone the health of the unborn baby to be aborted. On the contrary, morality is not about the choices that we have but about the choices that are morally right. Therefore, morality obliges us to go for pro-life and pro-abolition positions.

What we have lost here is the awareness that human rights are God-given. The only reason why we have human dignity and human rights is that God has endowed us with them. And that makes them *universal.* If moral rights were not universal, that would have devastating consequences. For one, human rights could not be universally applicable to all members of any culture or ethnic group. If there were no God, we could not defend any of those rights we think we have the right to defend. Without a firm foundation in God, "equality in dignity and rights" would be sitting on quicksand, subject to the mercy of law makers and majority votes. If there were no God, we would have at best (legal) entitlements, which the government provides, but no (moral) rights, for only God can provide those. Moral laws are not the monopoly of special interest groups, but they are God's monopoly.

The ultimate source of all these mix-ups is that rights are being confused with entitlements. A right is a moral concept based on a moral law, whereas an entitlement is a legal (but not necessarily moral) notion based on a legal law. There are no sexual and reproductive rights; these are, at most, entitlements. Rights are God-given—so we cannot invent them on our own—whereas entitlements are man-made, invented and handed out by the government. Once we fail to differentiate between them, we end up in the mud of confusion.

Do we have a moral compass?

Is there a moral compass that can guide us safely through the maze of moral issues? Yes, many think there is such a compass. What they are usually referring to is the moral compass of our *conscience.* Even if they don't acknowledge that morality is about unconditional, objective, universal, timeless, and absolute standards, these people still honor the one and only absolute standard they claim to be valid: "never disobey your own conscience." Even the Catechism seems to agree with this when it calls the human conscience "man's most secret core and his sanctuary. There he is alone with God whose voice echoes in his depths" (CCC 1776). It is in this sanctuary that human freedom makes moral decisions, right or wrong. That seems to be perfectly in line with the slogan, "never disobey your own conscience." Or are we missing something? What is wrong with the absolute authority of our human conscience?

Well, we should ask the believers in this authority a pivotal question: where does the absolute authority of a human conscience come from? Do my genes, or other natural factors, have the right to demand absolute obedience from me? Of course not! Does society have the right to demand my absolute obedience? Certainly not! Does any person, including myself, have the right to demand my absolute obedience? None of the above! The only authority that can obligate me is something—or rather Someone—infinitely superior to me; no one else has the right to demand my absolute obedience.

This may stir up a hornet's nest, for there is a lot of confusion and ambiguity behind the idea of "following your conscience." Our conscience has often been compared with technical devices we are all familiar with such as a compass, a global positioning system (GPS), a barometer, an alarm, a gas gauge in a car—the list goes on and on. What these analogies do get right is that our conscience is indeed a monitoring device—it monitors what is good or bad, right or wrong. What they mask, though, is the fact that the devices referred to are merely tools that may not work properly or may even fail entirely—and the same may hold for our conscience.

Is that the end of our conscience as a moral compass? It depends. A real compass, for instance, functions as a pointer to the magnetic north, because the magnetized needle aligns itself with the lines of the Earth's magnetic field—that is, with something outside itself. But it should not be used in proximity to ferrous metal objects or electromagnetic fields, as these can affect its accuracy. At sea, for example, a ship's compass must be corrected for errors, called deviation, caused by iron and steel in the ship's structure and equipment. The compass itself may have a defect besides. And the gas gauge in your car may no longer go down because it is broken, yet the tank may be almost empty. Your GPS system may not work when something obstructs the connection with the satellite high above your head.

In other words, a person's conscience may indeed function like a compass or GPS, but these "monitoring" tools must themselves be monitored and aligned to an outside source, and the same is true of our conscience. Just as a compass must be aligned with the Earth's magnetic field and protected from surrounding interference, and a GPS system needs to be "aligned" to the right feed from satellites high in the sky, so a human conscience needs constant alignment. What then is the right "feed" for our conscience? How do we properly align it, and to what? In short, how do we "calibrate" our conscience?

The Catholic Church would say that human beings are created with a moral compass pointing, not to the magnetic North, but to the "Above"—to a place where justice reigns and moral laws originate. Therefore, our conscience is not a private "compass" that determines its own North Pole; it has to be aligned to the one and only real "North Pole Above"—otherwise we can easily go off track. Our moral compass cannot be a private compass that determines its own direction.

Chapter 6: Made in God's Image

Obviously, there is more to morality than having a conscience and following it. When people say, "Never disobey your own conscience," they forget that one can do things "in good conscience," but also "with a bad conscience." Therefore, a conscience on its own can be good as well as bad. When people are unaware that they have a moral compass or that they have a moral compass that is broken, they end up following their genitals in sexual affairs, their curiosity in biomedical research, or their personal desires in matters of life and death, no further questions asked. However, personal desires cannot possibly be the source of morality because it should be the other way around: morality judges our desires, feelings, and choices.

Therefore, someone's conscience cannot have absolute authority in and of itself. A person's conscience does not speak on its own but listens to "God whose voice echoes in his depths" (CCC 1776). A human conscience does not create moral laws and values, but merely receives them. Therefore, a person's conscience is not the highest moral authority there is. Instead, it is subject to the supreme authority of God. As Vatican II puts it, "in the depths of his conscience, man detects a law which he does not impose upon himself, but which holds him to obedience." Therefore, when people follow their conscience, it is important they listen to God's voice, not their own.

But do they really listen to God's voice? Probably not, for all of us are often guided by a darkened mind and a corrupted will. Which raises a pivotal question: How is it possible that our conscience steers us the wrong way? Well, because our conscience is dependent upon human reason, it is subject to all the weaknesses to which human reason is prone, having been damaged by Sin since the Fall in Paradise. A darkened mind may lead to error, which means that we cannot treat our conscience as an infallible guide to moral truth. And a corrupted will may not steer us to do what we ought to do.

Consequently, our conscience is like an alarm that alerts us before we sin; when it goes off, we must not ignore it. When a red warning light in your car lights up, have the problem fixed—not by disconnecting the light but by fixing what causes it to light up. It is the same with your conscience: Do not silence it. However, when "the alarm" does *not* go off, that doesn't mean there is an "all clear" sign, but we may have intentionally lowered its "volume" or ignored its upkeep. That is how we can manipulate or even damage our conscience. A gas gauge in the car that does no longer go down is broken, yet the tank may be almost empty. Have it fixed! When it comes to your conscience, have it "calibrated" again.

I am sure this is not the kind of conscience moral relativists are referring to when they make it their absolute authority. The Catholic Church tells us very clearly that conscience can be understood only in relation to the individual's duty to obey the divine law—not to give people the freedom to live as they please. In other words, our conscience needs to be taught and nurtured—which is done by the teaching authority of the Church. Hence, it shouldn't surprise us that the "education of the conscience is a lifelong task" (CCC 1784). At the XXIV World Day for Peace, Pope John Paul II spoke of "the grave duty to form [one's] conscience."

How different is this from the view philosophers such as John Locke and Jean-Jacques Rousseau have deceived us with. They tried very hard to make us believe that humans are born good, that a child is just a blank slate, uncorrupted and free of any predispositions. But I would point out that, without morality, life would just bring out the cruel, selfish, and bullying parts of our inborn animal nature. Just look around to see how these philosophers are deceiving us. True, humans were *created* good, but that doesn't mean they were also *born* good. Because of the Fall and the Original Sin, our sense of morality has been corrupted. And that is how we ended up "in a fallen state" (CCC 404). Sin and evil have entered our lives. To paraphrase G.K. Chesterton, as far as sin is concerned, there are two kinds of people: not, as you might think, those who sin and those who do not sin, but those who know they are sinners and those who do not know they are sinners. Not only is there so much good in the worst of us, but also so much bad in the best of us. We will study this more in detail in the next chapter.

What I have been trying to emphasize in this chapter is that morality is on its way out at the very moment we try to detach it from religion and the eternal Heaven that makes moral values objective and universal. When we lose religion, we also lose the foundation of morality, and from there on, it just goes farther downhill, as our moral compass no longer works in a proper way. Satan keeps encouraging us to eat from the "tree of good and evil," by making our own moral laws. The Book of Genesis says about that tree in Paradise,: "God knows that when you eat of it your eyes will be opened, and you will be like God, knowing good and evil" (Gen. 3:5). We should know better!

7.

How Evil Is Suffering?

When you ask those who believe in God what the biggest difficulty is for their faith, they often come up with the word "suffering"—suffering through natural disasters, wars, diseases. They often don't see how they can possibly reconcile this with their faith in a God who is "all-powerful" and "all-good." Yes, that is certainly a challenge for a "faith that makes you think." It gives many of us plenty of reason to question whether and how our faith can withstand the challenges evil and suffering cause for our belief in God.

As early as the 3rd century BC, the Greek philosopher Epicurus worded the problem as follows: "Is God willing to prevent evil, but not able? Then he is not omnipotent. Is he able, but not willing? Then he is malevolent. Is he both able and willing? Then whence cometh evil? Is he neither able nor willing? Then why call him God?" It is hard to deny that this is quite a challenge for our faith in God. No wonder, the skeptic David Hume later sided with him. And probably many people nowadays still do.

Confronting this challenge, theism strongly professes its faith in an *all-powerful* God. How can that be, given the fact that there is evil all around us? Does that really mean God is not able to prevent evil? In other words, how can we still believe in a God who is omnipotent? Or is God indeed powerless? Not so in theism! Since Catholics honor "faith and reason," they must be reasonable in their faith as much so as they must be faithful in their reasoning. Let's try to find out how that can be done.

In addition, theism also strongly professes its faith in an *all-good* God. This is in fact a vital part of the God of theism—completely different from what pantheism proclaims when it declares that god must be evil as well as good at the same time, for both are seen as part of God. Not so in theism! Theism believes that God is all-good—there is nothing bad, or missing, in God. It keeps stressing that God created good things, but He did not create evil. God is not malevolent! Let's try to find out.

In spite of was theism claims, the fact remains that there is *moral* evil—what *we* do to each other—as well as *natural* evil—what *nature* does to us. Both kinds of evil are all around us. How can that be under an all-powerful and all-good God?

Moral evil

Where does moral evil come from, if it doesn't come from God? The answer is rather simple: it comes from human beings. It's their doing, not God's. This shifts the focus away from God but does not take God off the hook, for this evokes the next question: Why does God allow human beings to do evil acts against each other?

Moral evil comes in many, many forms: war, genocide, torture, holocausts, racism, drug trafficking, human trafficking, sex trafficking, pornography, prostitution, rape, abortion, adultery, theft, fraud, murder, injustice, slander, abandonment, rejection, and the list goes on and on. Moral evil encompasses all the evil we do to each other. But the question behind each one of them is this: shouldn't God's omnipotence, omniscience, and supreme goodness completely rule out the possibility of doing such evil? Why would God ever allow us to do moral evil to other human beings?

The answer is to be found in human freedom and the human free-will. Since God created us in His image and likeness, human freedom too comes from Him. God lets the actors on the world stage be free actors, who may not act the way the "Author of the play" would like them to act. Dictators may take human freedom away, but God made us in His image and thus He created us, not as marionettes, but as beings endowed with freedom and free-will. Such is the biblical message according to a quote of St. Irenaeus: "Man is rational and therefore like God; he is created with free-will and is master over his acts" (CCC 1730). And it is for that very reason—because not everything humans do on earth is in accordance with God's will—that we must pray daily, "Your will be done on earth as it is in heaven." When we cause moral evil, we damage God's creation. That is what happened in Auschwitz, in the Gulag Archipelago, in Southern Sudan, on Ground Zero—murder, genocide, and destruction.

In other words, human freedom is a great *good* that may also lead to much *evil*, for we can abuse our freedom at any time. Freedom is always a two-way street, leading us either *toward* God or *away* from God. Human freedom doesn't force us at all to make a choice between human freedom and divine omnipotence, but it does force us to choose good acts over bad acts. In that sense, God has indeed limited His own power. As said earlier, being all-powerful doesn't mean God is able to do what is logically contradictory—namely, giving freedom without the potentiality for evil. God gave us the grace to choose, which in turn allows us to make good as well as bad choices in life. We can therefore go astray and cause much moral evil on earth. In response to Epicurus' question—"Is God able, but not willing?"—we can now say, God does not *will* evil, but He does *allow* it.

If the freedom God gave us can be so detrimental, was it really necessary to give us that freedom? Yes. How could God give us freedom without accepting its consequences up to the point of us freely choosing the wrong outcome, away from God? If you love a person, you accept the possibility that he or she doesn't return the love. C. S. Lewis could not have expressed this better when he said: "We can, perhaps, conceive of a world in which God corrected the results of this abuse of free-will by His creatures at every moment [....] But such a world would be one in which wrong actions were impossible, and in which, therefore, freedom of the will would be void; nay, if the principle were carried out to its logical conclusion, evil thoughts would be impossible, for the cerebral matter which we use in thinking would refuse its task when we attempted to frame them."

If such a scenario were the case, wouldn't that be the end of human freedom? Absolutely! Instead, God made us free "participants" and "co-workers" in His ongoing creation of the world (CCC 307). "God has freely chosen to associate man with the work of his grace" (CCC 2008). We should feel very much honored. God took us seriously, with all the consequences that come with it. Evil is something that God does not will, but that He does allow in the name of human freedom. Lewis is absolutely right when he states that if our world were fully preordained by God, our brains would automatically refuse to enforce what our free minds would like to do. That would be a travesty of human freedom. Fortunately, God takes His creatures seriously, which also entails that they can make the wrong decisions. And that they did and keep doing, including you and me.

It may be hard to accept that God does respect our freedom. He does so much so that He even needed Mother Mary's "fiat" to have His Son be born from her womb as our Savior. It was her "Yes" that counteracted Eve's "No" and allowed her to become the Mother of God. It was her freedom that made the Incarnation possible. That was certainly a "good outcome."

But what about the bad effects that human freedom has caused? Where and when did the evil part of morality come in? The Catholic Church teaches us, in line with the Book of Genesis, that this kind of evil is a consequence of the Fall in Paradise, as we discussed already several times. After God gave the first humans rationality and morality, they fell for God's adversary, Satan. They wanted to be "like God" in the sense of "next to God," but not "under God"; they wanted to be creators, not creatures; they wanted to be their own commanders-in-chief. The Fall shows us that Adam and Eve didn't like God's Commands, because they didn't want to be commanded. And that's why we are often are often guided by a darkened mind and steered by a corrupted will.

It is then and there that moral evil entered the scene. And it was passed on to the next generations—which is called the *Original Sin*, as we explained earlier. In other words, *sin* can no longer be explained "as merely a developmental flaw, a psychological weakness, a mistake, or the necessary consequence of an inadequate social structure, etc. Only in the knowledge of God's plan for man can we grasp that sin is *an abuse of the freedom* that God gives to created persons so that they are capable of loving him and loving one another" (CCC 387; italics are mine). Epicurus did not know about the Original Sin when he attacked God's omnipotence and benevolence. David Hume, however, could have known better but chose to ignore it.

This shows again, in another way, that we do make choices in life. However, we are never alone in making free choices. We may think we are, but we are also being pulled by two opposite forces—the good force of God and the evil force of Satan. We are permanently "under the influence"—under the influence, that is, of good Spirits and of bad Spirits. We live under constant attention of both God (with His Angels) and Satan (with his fallen Angels). And don't be fooled, Satan never sleeps. Whereas good Spirits strengthen our virtues (such as faith, hope, and love), bad Spirits incite our vices (such as lust, doubt, despair, violence). Neither force controls us by making us act like puppets; they only entice us. But we ourselves decide which force we want to go with. Hume, for one, went for the wrong force when he attacked God being all-powerful and all-good.

Besides, be aware that free choices also have consequences—good choices have good consequences, bad choices have bad consequences. Because we are free human beings, we will be held accountable for our choices in life. Moral evil is a matter of bad choices; and bad choices not only affect our own lives but also those of others. That is where a final judgment comes in. If there is no *instant* repayment for good or bad actions and choices, there must be a *final* repayment (2 Mac. 6:26; 7; 44:46; Wisd. 2:16-20; 5:4-5; 5:14-16). If there is salvation, then there must also be damnation. We need and deserve to be judged, for God is also a *just* God, who rewards good actions with Heaven, and bad ones with Hell. As Pope Benedict XVI put it, "'unconditional forgiveness' would be that 'cheap grace' to which Dietrich Bonhoeffer rightly objected in the face of the appalling evil encountered in his day." We will get back to this later. Let's address first the more difficult issue of natural evil.

Natural evil

Like moral evil, natural evil too comes in many forms: earthquakes, tornadoes, hurricanes, flooding, drought, epidemics, infections, diseases, cancer, genetic defects, accidents, pains, chronic illnesses, disabilities, mental illnesses, death, and the list goes on and on. Unlike the case of moral evil, there is no perpetrator to blame other than God. That's what insurance companies do when they call calamities "acts of God." But are they really coming from God? If not, then where does natural evil come from? Some might respond that it does come directly from God, but in an *indirect* way, through the laws of nature which God gave to this world. Do they have a point?

Earlier, we explained the difference between Primary Cause and secondary causes. This explains, for instance, that God, the Primary Cause, keeps the Sun in existence, but the Sun melts ice independently of God. Perhaps the best well-known secondary cause is the force of gravity, which follows the physical law of gravitation. By allowing a secondary cause like this to operate, God made a universe in which He does not have to be the direct cause of every stone falling to the ground—for that would make God a secondary cause. We do not have to wonder about God's will every time a stone falls to the ground, even if it strikes us on the head. God has given us a secondary cause—the force of gravity—which is the direct cause of each stone's plummet to the earth.

Perhaps this gives us an opening to deal with natural evil in terms of good and bad effects. Natural *pain* is perhaps the easiest case—a warning sign that the body is in trouble. That in itself is a good outcome, but it also comes with bad effects as we all know (so we came up with painkillers). Gravity is another example of something good—it prevents me, everyone, and everything else from falling off the earth. However, if I defy or ignore gravity, then I could be in for a dangerous fall. Should I then blame gravity for the pain it causes, just like when a kid cries, "You bad floor!"? Blame gravity and yourself instead. Arithmetic is another case of something good, for it helps me to make calculations and predictions. But if I make a mistake in my calculations, should I blame arithmetic, or rather myself? The weather is one more example of something good—it provides us with sun, rain, and air for our food. But when it causes tornadoes, tsunamis, and flooding, we cannot blame the weather, but only ourselves who have not taken enough precautions.

Obviously, the forces of nature can cause results that are

lovely as well as cruel, and beautiful as well as ugly. Volcanos can create beautiful islands and mountains, but also devastating destruction. The power of growth makes flowers and babies develop into something beautiful, but it also makes tumors grow bigger and bigger. The weather may be the cause of a gentle breeze as well as a destructive tornado. Mutations gave us the diversity of life forms that we see around us, but they can also destroy what they had once produced. It is our task—given by our Creator as well—to get more and more control over these secondary causes and make them "work for the good." Obviously, nature is a combination of forces which can be both constructive and destructive. It is we ourselves who must learn how to control forces like these —not God, although we could certainly benefit from God's help.

Apparently, we live in a world where nature follows its own, God-given laws. But we are funny creatures. We love those laws if they go our way but detest them if they don't. We love the law of gravity for preventing us from falling off the earth, but we hate that law when it makes our homes collapse during an earthquake. Yet, that's the way nature was built. When we jump off a cliff, for instance, we can't expect God to intercept our fall. Thanks to the laws of nature, our bodies work beautifully and respond in very predictable ways. We can breathe, eat, etc. But the laws of nature regulate also that poisons, radiation, and mutagens can disrupt this beautiful mechanism. When we smoke cigarettes, we disrupt that mechanism. That's not God's doing—at least not in a direct way. Just like we must distinguish between the Primary Cause and secondary causes, so we must also distinguish between what God *wills* and what He *allows*. In response to Epicurus' question—"Is God willing to prevent evil, but not able?—our response is that God doesn't will earthquakes but allows them when they are a consequence, or "side-effect," of the laws of nature—in the same way as God doesn't will wars but allows them when humans use their freedom to start them.

But this may raise new questions: doesn't the idea of evil as a "bad side-effect" of something good trivialize the seriousness of natural evil? In a way it does. Natural evil is such a serious problem for religious believers that they have tried other explanations of natural evil. So, let us look then at another explanation. This one comes from St. Thomas Aquinas who stressed that the problem of good and evil must be seen in a wider context. His point is that if there were no natural evil, such a fact would diminish the good of the universe. To explain this seemingly enigmatic answer, St. Thomas uses the example of the lion that could not live without killing its prey. As he puts it, "if all evil were prevented, much good would be absent from the universe. A lion would cease to live if there were no slaying of animals." Whatever may be evil for the individual, the prey, is good for the larger picture, the universe. Consequently, if there were no natural evil, such a fact would diminish the good of the universe as a whole.

Environmentalists are very aware of this fact; even "dangerous" animals such as poisonous spiders and snakes play an essential role in their ecosystem—removing them would disrupt the system. There is always a delicate balance between what looks "bad" in detail and what is "good" in the larger picture. The Catechism follows this line of reasoning by saying, "God permits evil in order to draw forth some greater good" (CCC 412). I think the main point of this discussion is that God did not *create* evil—certainly not moral evil, but not even natural evil. Evil is not like the things that the Creator created. Neither did this make him a powerless God.

Yet, the enigma remains. We still have the problem that "misfortunes" are so *unpredictably* distributed: They strike the just as well as the unjust, believers as well as unbelievers, the good and the bad alike. There is no pattern! We all seem to have the same chances to be stricken by evil and suffering; no one is exempt; one's religion doesn't seem to make a difference. In addition, we have the problem that "misfortunes" are so *unequally* distributed: Some people have to stomach so much more than others; some receive one blow after another, whereas others are apportioned poorly. At times, you meet people who remain erect in the hurricane of misery; then again, you come across people who lament endlessly about trifles. Anyone eager to build a system explaining all of this will eventually be buried under a collapsing house of cards. Nothing fits, nothing makes sense.

But in addition to the above reflections on natural evil, I think there is a much more important, often overlooked, consideration. When speaking of natural evil, we find ourselves already in a mental, spiritual, even moral context. By stating "evil exists," we are asserting somehow that evil "should" not exist, which means we are using already ethical, moral standards. To use the terminology I mentioned earlier, the existence of suffering could be seen as a natural truth, but the existence of *evil* is a supernatural truth.

Let me put this more strongly: if there were no humans, there wouldn't be any evil—not even any natural evil. Since animals, on their part, do not have any moral considerations, they follow whatever pops up in their brains. Hence, the relationship between predator and prey, for instance, has nothing to do with morality or evil; if predators really had a conscience guided by morality, their lives would be pretty tough. The prey doesn't consider the predator "evil"—perhaps painful, but not evil. Let me say it again, there's no natural evil in the animal world, because the word *evil* implies already human evaluation with existing moral, ethical standards. As a consequence, natural events only become evil when we assess them as evil and dub them as evil. The "thorns and thistles" may have always been there, but since the Fall and because of the newly fallen consciousness of human beings, they were felt not only as painful but also as distressing, as *evil*. When animals give birth, they may experience pain but not evil. Humans, on the other hand, usually do! Hence, the cause of all evils is ultimately sin. Without sin, evils wouldn't rankle or embitter us. That's quite a different perspective on evil.

Only humans take diseases and catastrophes as something that shouldn't be, as something that even seems to be acting against them personally. Animals may "dislike" these things, but they do not question them in terms of "Why me?" Only humans know of God, so they tend to ask the question "Is something wrong between God and me?" or "Why, God, do bad things happen to good people?" Since animals do not know about God, nor about good and evil, they cannot ask why bad things happen to good animals. Only humans can ask that question—and they can find the answer to their questions at the beginning of the Book of Genesis: "of the tree of the knowledge of good and evil you shall not eat, for in the day that you eat of it you shall die" (Gen. 2:17).

C. S. Lewis said basically something similar in his book *Mere Christianity*, "My argument against God was that the universe seemed so cruel and unjust. But how had I got this idea of just and unjust? A man does not call a line crooked unless he has some idea of a straight line. What was I comparing this universe with when I called it unjust? [...] Of course I could have given up my idea of justice by saying it was nothing but a private idea of my own. But if I did that, then my argument against God collapsed too—for the argument depended on saying the world was really unjust, not simply that it did not happen to please my fancies." Lewis is stating here that calling the universe cruel (natural evil) and unjust (moral evil) must already assume that we have a moral and spiritual standard deriving from Heaven—and that is the place where God resides. Asserting "evil exists" would imply an ethical standard of how to define good and evil; and such a standard implies the existence of God. Without God, we couldn't even speak of evil. Thanks to God, we know what the world "should" be like. We know of "evil" because we have an idea of "good" and of what things should be like, if everything were indeed "good." There is the all-good God again.

Having heard all of this, perhaps we need to change our perspective on evil. If I ask myself why evil strikes *me*, I could ask myself as well why evil would *not* strike me. Realizing suffering is everywhere may help us de-center from our own suffering. Take the example of an infection. We tend to be surprised each time we get an infection, but we should rather be surprised that we usually do *not* get an infection. The real wonder comes from our beautifully designed immunity system—another wonderful piece of creation, but perhaps not perfect. The same is true of the tantalizing question as to why bad things happen to *good* people. We could as well ask why good things happen to *bad* people. Who is to say we are good people, anyway? Aren't we all bad due to the Original Sin? Asking things this way gives us a completely different perspective on evil and suffering: We are no longer "good" people who suffer "bad" things but "bad" people who enjoy so many "good" things. As Jesus once said, "No one is good but God alone."

Ultimately, religion is the only place where we could search for an answer to the problem of evil in all its forms. Science tells us that we don't know what the future holds, but faith tells us that it is God who holds the future. Faith tells us that God has the power to use evil for a better purpose, His purpose. In everything that happens, we can discern God's "hand"—not a hand that *causes* all the bad things that we read about in the newspapers, but a hand that *holds* all these things together by saving them for a better purpose and destination. Thank God, our faith has so much more to tell us about the mystery of good and evil.

The man Job

It won't come as a surprise that the problem of evil did not go unnoticed in the Bible! The Bible starts with the problem of evil in the Book of Genesis, and it ends with the problem of evil in the Book of Revelation. But more significantly, there is the Book of Job which focuses entirely and almost exclusively on the problem of suffering. Apart from the Gospels, the Book of Job is probably one of the best-known books in the Scriptures with respect to suffering and evil. But do not let this book fool you. It is one of those cases in which taking one sentence out of its context can easily and completely deceive you. Let's find out more.

Here is what the account of Job's suffering tells us. A good and happy family living in the land of Uz (Edom?) is stricken by one disaster after another, with no end in sight. A magnificent man, Job, loses everything he has and is left to sit on the ruins of his life. Forever, Job will be the unforgettable image of the just man unjustly afflicted. He is the central figure of a story that has intrigued generation after generation. We watch how all hell breaks loose in Job's life. What is reported to him by his servants sounds like a devastating litany of bad news for Job: robbers came, took your cattle and killed your servants; a thunderstorm came, the sheep and servants were consumed by lightening; enemies attacked us, raided your camels and killed your servants; a big storm arose and struck the house of your oldest son, all your children were killed.... All in all, it's a litany of bad tidings, several in a row. The end result is this: Job is completely ruined.

The devastation could not have been more complete. And

yet, Job's reaction is royal. He does not get bitter but better. He stands up, tears his robe, shaves his head, falls upon the ground in worship, saying: "Naked I came from my mother's womb, and naked I will depart." He even utters, "The Lord gave, and the Lord has taken away; may the name of the Lord be praised" (Job 1:21). In fact, Job has nothing left but his bare and naked faith, which makes him speak out: I don't understand it, I cannot make sense of it, I don't know what to do with it—and yet, I refuse to abandon God.

But the troubles are not over yet for Job. All that had happened so far was the loss of material things, not his health, neither physical nor spiritual. But now Job himself gets hit. The result is a sick and pitiful little creature, smitten from head to toe with painful sores which caused his skin to turn black and gave him a fever. Look at Job, completely covered with sores. People around him watch him with horror and disgust, as do his friends. There is nothing beautiful or noble about his misery. He is just plain dirt, unpleasant to look at, broken to the core. Not only has he lost everything he had, but now he is a wreck of a human being himself. This man is ruined for life, plunged into deep misery.

We see Job sitting on the ruins of his life. How more broken can one be! Now watch his wife approach. Isn't she true to life in the way she reacts: Where did all your faithfulness get you? Damn God and die! We understand her only too well. Wasn't Job's misery also hers? Weren't his children also hers? And what about this pitiful human being himself—her husband of all people! Yet, Job's response (Job 2:10) is magnificent again, "You speak as foolish women do. We accept good things from God; should we not accept bad things too?" Somehow Job is saying: I always accepted the good things received, so shouldn't I be willing to receive the bad things as well?

The book could have ended after these edifying words. However, the story goes on because it's time now for the real tribulations. They don't come from Job's enemies but from his friends—Job's "comforters"! Isn't it true that prosperity makes friends, and adversity tries them? Job's friends are the ones who have all the answers to the horrible riddles of his tragedy. However, their words turn out to be more painful than the sores on his body. Job still has depths to cross, deeper than his inexplicable and unreasonable misery.

Job's comforters resemble some people we often encounter ourselves: they are the ones who give a quasi-religious twist to human suffering. So does one of Job's comforters who basically tells Job that one gets what one deserves and that one deserves what one gets. A second one explains that suffering is God's punishment for what we ourselves did wrong. A third one stresses that God's wisdom through suffering is entirely beyond human understanding, because God's justice is not like ours. Then a fourth one strikes a different tone and explains suffering as a divine form of education, bringing people back to their senses. Sure, all nice trials, but do they satisfy Job?

After hearing all their semi-pious words and semi-religious explanations for his suffering, Job can no longer hold back (Job 19:2): "How long will you torment me, and break me in pieces with words?" He had expressed earlier (Job 3:3): "Perish the day on which I was born, the night when they said, 'The child is a boy!' May that day be darkness. [...] Why did I not die at birth, come forth from the womb and expire? Why did knees receive me, or breasts nurse me?" These are indeed harsh words, especially when coming out of the mouth of a devout believer such as Job. But let's not be too quick to judge Job. To begin with, notice that it is not God whom he curses, but the day of his birth and the fact that he is alive. He doesn't say: Oh God, there is no God! What he does say is this: I wish I had not been born! He doesn't question, Is God really there for me? Actually, he is asking, why am I here and why did God create me?

This tells us that Job hasn't removed God's address from his list; God remains the only address for him to come to with his why-questions. He does not reject that God is all-powerful and all-good. If there is any answer, any solution, or any explanation available, then they are to be found with God. In fact, arguing with God makes for a more religious attitude towards life than having a philosophy that doesn't acknowledge God at all. The person arguing with God is not someone who has lost faith, but someone who does the ultimate to hold on to God, even in times of disaster.

Nevertheless, for Job, there is still this tremendous question, the most distressing question there is: "Why is light given to those in misery, and life to the bitter of soul?" (Job 3:20). Job must have thought, why was I given life if it holds so much misery? I don't remember asking for it. What is the purpose of this misery? And why is this broken world in existence, why all of our history, why this long martyrdom of countless broken people? Why did all of this happen—a broken world with broken generations, broken families, broken hearts, broken souls?

In response, Job keeps repeating that a God who hits back is not the God he knows. And the entire Bible stands behind him: Evil and suffering do exist but perhaps shouldn't exist; they may be part of life but not of God's creation. Job's "comforters," who have all the answers to his piercing questions, turn out to be in fact his "adversaries," who provide cover-ups for all the suffering in the world—thereby basically changing God into an enemy. The apostle James makes a very strong case: "Let no one say when he is tempted, 'I am tempted by God'; for God cannot be tempted with evil and he himself tempts no one" (Jas. 1:13). It is the devil who tempts us, not God. (That's why the Book of Job starts with introducing the devil.)

Job, for his part, keeps repeating to his friends that he did not lose his faith in God. No, Job hasn't lost God at all when he exclaims those eternal words well known from Handel's Messiah: "I know that my Redeemer liveth" (Job 19:25)—which means "I know..." that God is God-*with*-us (Emmanuel), not God-*against*-us. For many people, Handel's Messiah has one of the most touching pieces of music ever composed. It is an Easter song. Not too many people realize, though, that this beaming profession of faith has been snatched from between the harsh lamentations and bitter questioning uttered by the afflicted Job, suffering under his pain and grief, and suffering from the semi-pious words his friends had voiced as explanations for his troubles.

The text speaks of a "redeemer," a familiar concept in the Old Testament. Even when you have gone aground, even when you must sell your land, even when you must sell yourself as a servant, never will you be lost forever. The Law of Moses commands your closest relatives to buy your land, or to ransom you as a person, someday. A redeemer, or vindicator, is someone who releases you from your desperate circumstances. If you happen to die without having children—that is to say, in Jewish terms, without having a future—the redeemer has the duty to marry your widow, thus ensuring you a next generation. It is through his belief in an ultimate Redeemer that Job remains firm in his stand, in spite of all his setbacks, both materially and spiritually, He tells his friends that the God he knows would never do what they are telling him. Evil and suffering are too serious and too devastating to blame God for them. Therefore, Job keeps asking for God's personal answer instead.

Well, did Job really get an answer from God? Yes, Job did receive an answer from God—perhaps not at first sight. Near the end of the book, God Himself seems to bombard Job's questions with a cascade of counter-questions: Where were you, Job, when I did this? Where were you when I did that? It is turning Job's repeated question of "Where were you, God, when I was stricken by misery?" into a counter-question of "Where were you, Job, when I created this world?" In fact, it is not an answer but a long-winded question, consisting of a collection of sentences, all of them devastating questions, until the very end.

However, do not read God's torrent of questions the wrong way. It is not anticipating an answer like "you were nowhere, and you are nothing." God's answer is not meant in a demeaning way. We would seriously be mistaken to stick to our first impression, to consider this to be a sarcastic way of putting Job in his place, by giving him a description of the majesty and grandeur of the Creator and His creation in comparison to the smallness of Job and his suffering. Something else is at stake here. A few sentences may put us on the right foot: "Who shut up the sea behind doors, when it burst forth from the womb?" (Job 38:8). "Have you ever given orders to the morning, or shown the dawn its place?" (Job 38:12). "Have you an arm like that of God?" (Job 40:9). In other words, God is asking Job the following question: Don't you remember how I shut up the sea, a menace to life, how I created light in the darkness to light up your path, and how I use my arm to protect people like you? Have you forgotten all of that, Job? Have you forgotten, Job, that God's creation was good, from day one on?

To come straight to the point: God is expressing his intense concern over His creation, especially over His people. It's for them and for their sake that everything exists. God made the Earth their home. In fact, it's a colossal home furnished with tender loving care. In other words, it is I, a caring God, who created all of this—a home furnished with TLC. God is in fact asking Job: You, human being, have you ever looked at it this way?

Have you ever read My heart this way? Such is the very question God is asking Job, out of mere concern. In short, there is no sarcasm here at all.

So, God's answer to Job was not really an answer the way we understand it. Besides, if Job was told that God's creation was done with TLC, there is still the question left where evil stems from in what God has created. The Book of Job comes up only with the beginning of an answer to that question. It mentions the role of Satan at the beginning and at the end of the book. In other words, evil is not something God created, but God's enemy does. It's just a dawning insight, perhaps not even a clear answer yet. But it puts Job's often quoted, "pious" sounding statement of "The Lord gave, and the Lord has taken away" (Job 1:21) in a different light. Did the Lord really take away what He had given? After hearing God's answer, Job would come to regret his choice of words, "I spoke of things I did not understand" (Job 42:3).

Let me put it differently: Did Job really expect an answer? To have all riddles solved and all questions answered, is that indeed what Job was waiting for? Job does not need the kind of God who gives us all the answers. What he needs is a God who is in fact answering him, just that. He needs to know where he stands with God; he needs to know whether God is with him, or against him. And it's that very need that God met. Job understands. He understands what he hears: Job, I am on your side; you should know that! At last, Job gets it; he gets the answer in its fullness: "I had heard of thee by the hearing of the ear, but now my eye sees thee" (Job 42:5).

In summary, the Book of Job may seem like a long winded debate between Job and his so-called friends, but it is basically one long protracted charge against the misconception that calamities and afflictions are meant to *punish* us, to *test* us, to *discipline* us, to *correct* us, to *purify* us, or to *teach* us a lesson. All we can say is that God may *use* those afflictions for His purpose, but He did not *produce* them for that reason. At least we have got one vital answer: God did not create or cause evil and suffering. God doesn't strike us with afflictions, but whenever evil strikes, God may use it for a better purpose. The bottom-line is this: God is God-*with*-us (*Emmanuel*), not God-*against*-us.

And the entire Bible stands behind Job: Evil and suffering *do* exist but *shouldn't* exist; they may be part of *life* but not of *creation*. You might be surprised that the rest of the Bible is also very critical of the "cheap" explanations Job was confronted with by his "friends." Here are a few:

- The simple slogan of "Evil suffered is evil deserved" is challenged, for instance, by the prophet Jeremiah: "Why does the way of the wicked prosper?" (Jer. 12:1).
- The idea that people must pay for the sins of their ancestors is also contested: "Our fathers sinned and are no more; and we bear their iniquities" (Lam. 5:7). Even prophets protested against such simple views by assuring their audience that the son is not punished for his father's iniquities (Ezekiel 18; Jeremiah 31:29; John 9:3).
- The book Ecclesiastes questions the idea that the misery of good people will soon turn for the good: "there is a righteous man who perishes in his righteousness, and there is a wicked man who prolongs his life in his evil-doing" (Eccl. 7:15). Think of it this way: Some people do return to God because of a tragedy, but that doesn't mean God would ever *send* them tragedies to *force* their conversion.
- St. James makes a very strong case in his letter: "Let no one say when he is tempted, 'I am tempted by God'; for God cannot be tempted with evil and he himself tempts

no one" (Jas. 1:13). It is the devil who tempts.

In the meantime, the Bible moans and groans under the pain of suffering. The best I can do at this point is repeating what the Catechism says: "God is infinitely good and all his works are good. Yet no one can escape the experience of suffering or the evils in nature which seem to be linked to the limitations proper to creatures; and above all to the question of moral evil" (CCC 385).

Job testifies to this. He got God's answer to his questions, although it may not look like an answer in the technical sense—it is not even God's final answer. That final answer came much later. God's ultimate answer would come in the form of a Person, coming directly from Heaven: The God-Man Jesus. In Jesus we find the ultimate answer and cure for our broken hearts and our broken world. God's "answer" does not come from words but from a Person, the Son of God, the God-man Jesus. It is an answer that comes in fact from the Man of Golgotha: God is love—and love wants to share to the very end, with all its consequences. God's love wants to personally share everything with us, even our sufferings.

The God-man Jesus

The Incarnation is the mystery of the God-Man Jesus. It's the greatest story ever told: the one, true God taking on human flesh. That means the God-man is the son of a human mother, and a human woman is the mother of the God-man. The light of the world entered the darkness of a woman's womb. Isn't that hard to believe? The God-Man Jesus came to be among sinners and came to die so that we, the sinners, might live.

Like Job and Abraham and countless others, Jesus learned what it means to live in a broken world. He was betrayed by Judas. He was abandoned by His other followers. He was taken captive by a mob. He was deserted by His disciples. He was falsely accused and rejected by the Jewish leaders. He was mocked and abused by Roman guards. He was spat upon and beaten up. He was falsely accused by those in authority. He was rejected by the crowd. He was scourged. And finally, He was crucified between two thieves—the cruelest method of execution we know of in human history.

This explains why Christianity is the only religion where suffering is at center stage. No wonder then the Cross of Jesus is a touchstone for Christians, but at the same time a stumbling block for non-believers. St. Paul was right when he called Christ crucified "a stumbling block to Jews and foolishness to Gentiles" (1 Cor. 1:23). Pope John Paul II put this in his own words: "Many of our contemporaries would like to silence the Cross. But nothing is more eloquent than the Cross when silenced!" How right he was! The God-Man Jesus went to the full depth of sin and suffering on Golgotha by identifying Himself with our suffering so as to eradicate the effects of sin. This is the mystery of the Incarnation, and thus of the Crucifixion—the fact that the God-Man Jesus comes to us, weeps with us, and suffers with us. That's God's answer to Job's questions as well our own questions about evil and suffering.

God's "solution" to the problem of evil that Job has asked for, is His Son Jesus Christ—not an intellectual but an existential "solution." The Father's love sent His Son to die for us in order to defeat the power of evil in human nature—which is the heart of the Christian story. To humanists, socialists, and Buddhists, suffering is as painful as it is to Jews and Christians, but the former are not haunted with this piercing question, "Why does God abandon *me*?" Believing in a God of *love* and in a *good* creation causes the pain of suffering to penetrate to a deeper level—to the level of "Is something wrong between God and me?" In response, the Gospel of John tells us, "God sent the Son into the world, not to condemn the world, but that the world might be saved through him" (3:17).

Peter Kreeft rephrases this as follows: "How do we get God off the hook for allowing evil? God is not *off* the hook; God *is* the hook. That's the point of a crucifix. That's why the doctrine of the Divinity of Christ is crucial: If that is not God there on the cross but only a good man, then God is not on the hook, on the cross, in our suffering. And if God is not on the hook, then God is not off the hook. How could he sit there in heaven and ignore our tears?"

Let me quote Peter Kreeft once agaib: "He didn't give us a placebo or a pill or good advice. He gave us himself. He came. He entered space and time and suffering. He came, like a lover. Love seeks above all intimacy, presence, togetherness. He came. [...] He did the most important thing and he gave the most important gift: himself. Out of our cry, 'My God, my God, why hast Thou forsaken me?' he came, all the way, right into that cry." Pope Benedict XVI summarized this during his *Urbi et Orbi* blessing on Christmas Day 2011 with one single sentence: "Jesus Christ is the proof that God has heard our cry." It is a cry coming out of a broken world and answered by the God-man Himself.

A broken world—broken by moral and natural evil—can only be healed by the one who created this world, God. In one of his interviews, Pope Benedict XVI made the same point. After mentioning all the evils we have witnessed now and in the past, he continues, "This mass of evil cannot simply be declared nonexistent, not even by God. It must be cleansed, reworked and overcome.... God simply cannot leave 'as is' the mass of evil that comes from the freedom that He Himself has granted. Only He, coming to share in the world's suffering, can redeem the world."

No wonder then that there is "power" in the Cross. In Dan Schutte's Easter Triduum Hymn, every stanza ends with the words, "Let us ever glory in the Cross of Christ." You might wonder how there could ever be glory in the Cross. How could the Cross ever triumph over human brokenness? That's something hard to believe, until we realize that we do have reason to speak of the "Glory of the Cross," because it was not the cross of a man called Jesus, but the Cross of the God-Man Jesus. At the Cross, the God-Man Jesus took on the brokenness of the entire world, of all generations, of all families, of all hearts, and of all souls.

Cardinal Timothy Dolan of New York City once mentioned how he visited a man in great pain, dying of cancer, and no longer able to talk. He stood by his bedside, spoke to him and prayed with him and his wife. When he noticed the man was getting agitated, he asked his wife if he had said something wrong. She shook her head and told him, "By where you stand, you're blocking my husband's view of the crucifix on the wall." That crucifix had been his constant support during his long battle. He was able to fight his battle as long as he could keep his eyes fixed on the Cross of Jesus, which the crucifix on the wall represented.

In other words, when the God-man Jesus came to earth, he did not come to abolish but to sanctify suffering with His presence. Jesus did not save us *from* the cross, but instead he saved us *by* the Cross. Anyone who offers love without sacrifice, anyone who offers Christ without the Cross and the crucifixion, is just trying to sell snake oil. Even in suffering—or particularly in suffering—we can find the Glory of God, for Jesus is the human face of God—and a human face comes with tears. Our tears are His tears, for God is not a God of evil but a God of love.

Chapter 7: How Evil is Suffering?

Through the Incarnation, God entered space and time, which also includes suffering.

In other words, Golgotha has become a "meeting place" for all those who suffer. From now on, in the words of the Catechism, "Suffering, a consequence of original sin, acquires a new meaning; it becomes a participation in the saving work of Jesus." (1521). In Him, we "offer up" our sufferings, for we are participants and co-workers in God's creation. Where else would we go if not to Jesus? More than intellectual understanding do we need personal acceptance. God speaks to us from the Cross. St. John Vianney, often referred to as the "Curé d'Ars" (i.e., Parish Priest of Ars), told us about a man whom he saw every day in his church, without rosary or book, his lips not moving, his gaze fixed on the crucifix. One day the priest asked him, "What are you doing?" The man replied, "I look at Him, and He looks at me." He was right: that's where our answer comes from.

Therefore, there are two sides to what happened on Calvary. On the one hand, to hold that the Son suffered only in His *divine* nature would mean that Jesus did not experience suffering the way human beings do. In other words, to place the significance of the Son's suffering within his divine nature is to relegate his human suffering to insignificance, and thus to demote all human suffering to insignificance. On the other hand, to hold that the Son suffered only in His *human* nature would mean that he only suffered like every other human being suffers, which would make his suffering inadequate for the redemption of all of humanity. The suffering of the Man Jesus would not be worth more than anyone else's suffering—only an incarnate God, a God-Man, can redeem all of us.

Jesus' suffering also gives us a completely different perspective on suffering. Suffering is a two-way street: When you look with the eyes of Satan, it is pure evil that takes us away from

God, but seen through the eyes of God, it may turn into salvation and redemption that brings us closer to Him. Thus, suffering has this mysterious potential of redeeming us, transforming us, transfiguring us. You might think the less we suffer, the closer to God we will be—but it might actually be the opposite. Let me quote St. Rosa of Lima: "Apart from the cross, there is no other ladder by which we may get to Heaven." And isn't Heaven the final destination we should all be striving for on our journey from life to after-life? Life-saving answers to our life-size questions come only from God. When God is absent, nothing is good!

More than other Judeo-Christian traditions, it is Catholicism that emphasizes suffering as a source of redemption. Just think of the Catholic crucifix with its naked corpse, in contrast to the Protestant cross with its vacant wood or the Orthodox icon with its gold. This Catholic conception is not born from stoicism, which is the mere tolerance of suffering, neither is it born from a form of masochism which derives pleasure from pain and suffering. Instead, it invites us to transform suffering into a source of redemption. Trust and surrender—that is a Catholic motto. The coming of Jesus was like D-Day, the day of invasion into enemy territory. But ultimately, there will be V-Day, the day of victory. But this will take redemptive suffering. Even in suffering—or particularly in suffering—we can find the Glory of God, for Jesus is the human face of God—and a human face comes with tears.

A matter of life and death

Because we are free human beings, we will be held accountable for our choices in life. Moral evil is a matter of bad choices; and bad choices not only affect our own lives but also those of others. That is where a final judgment comes in, as we said earlier. If there is no instant repayment for good or bad actions and choices—and there usually isn't—then there must be a final repayment (2 Mac. 6:26; 7; 44:46; Wisd. of Sol. 2:16-20; 5:4-5; 5:14-16). If there is salvation, there must also be damnation. We need and deserve to be judged, for God is also a just God: Good actions are rewarded with Heaven, bad ones with Hell.

With Hell? An eternal Hell, really? Yes, an eternal Hell can be the ultimate consequence of the freedom we were given. As Peter Kreeft says, "We freely choose hell for ourselves; God does not cast anyone into hell against his will. No sane person wants hell to exist. No sane person wants evil to exist. But hell is just evil eternalized. If there is evil and if there is eternity, there can be hell." God in Heaven welcomes all people—but so does Satan in Hell. C. S. Lewis called Hell "the greatest monument to human freedom." The Catechism confirms this very emphatically: "Mortal sin is a radical possibility of human freedom […] it causes […] the eternal death of hell, for our freedom has the power to make choices for ever, with no turning back." In other words, Hell is not so much a place somewhere but first of all a state of "definitive self-exclusion from communion with God" (CCC 1033). As a matter of fact, people who commit grave injustices condemn themselves. As St. Augustine put it, God "did not will to save us without us."

Indeed, Jesus speaks about Hell more than anyone else in the Gospel—which is the Book of the Good News. He told His disciples that weeds will be in the field of the world until the end of time, but then the King of Justice will throw those weeds "into the fiery furnace" (Mat. 13:50), so grave injustices will not go unaddressed. The Catechism puts it this way: "The Last Judgment will reveal that God's justice triumphs over all the injustices committed by his creatures" (1040). A final judgment is the answer to many questions we might have had in life. What about all those people who have experienced so little joy in their lives?

What about all those victims of genocide, gas chambers, torture chambers, wars? What about all those people who cannot be called back to life again to receive a bit more warmth and love? What about those intentionally left behind by their spouses or their parents? So many people had hoped for something good but received so much evil and suffering instead. What are we to do with all these people?

Put differently, there are too many debit accounts that still need to be settled. I am not talking about those little accounts that you might like to settle with your neighbors, but about those enormous accounts that caused sorrow, tears, afflictions, and disasters to millions of people. If there were no final judgment, those accounts would remain unsettled. In a world without God, there is no hope those issues will ever be addressed. Yet, the earth is crying out for justice! Thank God, we have a loving God who is also a just God. That is why we need judgment. There is a particular judgment at the end of each one's life, and there is a final or last judgment at the end of time (CCC 1021). The last judgment takes place when Christ returns in His glory to "pronounce the final word on all history" (CCC 1040). In His presence, "the truth of each man's relationship with God will be laid bare" (CCC 1039). During this final judgement, Jesus will judge us according to our deeds (Mt. 25:31-34).

You may agree with me that God's justice does call for judgment. But does the verdict have to be with such an extreme contrast? Must it really be either Heaven or Hell? Yes, because no one can enter Heaven if not completely clean. That's what the Book of Revelation tells us about Heaven: "nothing unclean shall enter it" (21:27). That means nothing unclean can enter the presence of God face-to-face. So where does this leave us? Well, since are all sinners (Rom. 3:9, 5:12), would this mean everyone is barred from entering Heaven? Yes, unless....

Unless there is a purgatory. Purgatory is a place or condition of temporal punishment for those who depart this life in God's grace. The Catechism says about purgatory: "All who die in God's grace and friendship, but still imperfectly purified, [...] undergo purification, so as to achieve the holiness necessary to enter the joy of heaven" (1030). Purgatory is a place or state where human imperfection is corrected in the "fire of purification." Joseph Ratzinger, the later Pope Benedict XVI, wrote: "Purgatory is not, as Tertullian thought, some kind of supra-worldly concentration camp where man is forced to undergo punishment in a more or less arbitrary fashion. Rather it is the inwardly necessary process of transformation in which a person becomes capable of Christ, capable of God, and thus capable of unity with the whole communion of saints."

I think this is best explained by an example the legendary Mother Angelica of EWTN uses: If a prostitute had a profound conversion and decides to enter Mother Angelica's convent, a one-day transition would definitely be too short a period for such a person to make the transition—a massive shock actually—in spite of all her good intentions. Indeed, for most of us, the transition from a life on earth to a life in Heaven would be so dramatic that we would need some extra purification time. No wonder, the Catholic Church has always stressed the importance of a purgatory where we can see in all clarity who we were and where we came from before we can enter the eternal glory of God. The late Fr. Benedict Groeschel has expressed this well, "Purgatory is not a temporary hell, but a preliminary heaven." Holiness is certainly not an over-night thing.

Some might counter that purgatory is merely a Catholic invention. It certainly is Catholic, but in no way an invention. Yet, some Protestants call purgatory a Catholic money maker, probably going back to the time the Protestant reformer Martin Luther was (rightly) attacking the Church for her "selling" of indulgences. At the beginning of the Reformation, there was still some hesitation, especially on Luther's part, as to whether this doctrine of a purgatory should be retained. However, as the breach widened, the denial of purgatory by the Reformers became universal. Modern Protestants, while they avoid the name purgatory, now do often speak of "the middle state." Orthodox Christians speak in terms of a "theosis," a journey of transformation.

Many Protestants keep stressing that the word "purgatory" cannot be found anywhere in the Bible. However, that objection in itself is not valid because many other words—such a "Bible," "Trinity," and "Incarnation"—cannot be found in the Bible either. Does that mean there is no foundation for them in the Scriptures? No, of course not. As to purgatory, we do find indications of purgatory in both the Old and New Testament. The clearest text in the Old Testament is 2 Maccabees 12:46: "It is therefore a holy and wholesome thought to pray for the dead, that they may be loosed from sins." One of the strongest lines in the New Testament can be found in Matthew 5:25-26, when Jesus ends one of His parables with the following statement: "you [will] be put in prison; truly, I say to you, you will never get out till you have paid the last penny." Well, we know that in Heaven no last penny needs to be paid, and from Hell there is no liberation at all; hence this reference must apply to a third place—purgatory, that is. Many are not good enough to be fit for Heaven immediately; many are not evil enough to fully deserve Hell. Purgatory is the place of their last hope. Probably it is better to speak in these cases of a "state" of being rather than a "place." Heaven, Hell, and purgatory do not occupy some remote geographic corner of the physical universe. As Hell is a state of eternal damnation, Heaven is a state of eternal salvation, and purgatory is a state of preparation and transformation.

We find also indications of purgatory very early in Christianity. Graffiti in the catacombs of the first three centuries mentions prayers for the dead. Some of the earliest Christian writings also refer to the Christian practice of praying for the dead. Saint Perpetua, who was martyred in 202, was encouraged in a vision to pray for her brother, who had died in his eighth year. Among Church writers Tertullian († 230) also mentioned prayers for the dead: "The widow who does not pray for her dead husband has as good as divorced him." Then there is St. Augustine's mother who asked her son to remember her soul in his Masses. St. Ambrose said about the deceased, "We have loved them during life; let us not abandon them until we have conducted them by our prayers into the house of the Lord." Such prayers would make no sense if these early Christians thought the souls of the dead were already in Hell or in Heaven, for they could no longer benefit from prayers. Besides, the Bible speaks of "the limbo of the Fathers," where the just who had died before the redemption by Jesus were waiting for Heaven to be opened to them. Doesn't that come close to a purgatory? In other words, the concept of purgatory may have been further clarified and defined over the years, but it is certainly not new to the Bible and the Church.

It is quite obvious that both Hell and Purgatory are connected with the moral evil in this world. We discussed already that the origin of moral evil must be traced back to Satan. Never forget that the question "How real is evil?" runs parallel with the question "How real is Satan?" The more we deny his existence, the better he can hide by being outside the limelight. The Catholic Church doesn't want us to forget that Satan is a real force to reckon with. If there is no Satan, then there is no evil; if there is no Satan, then the Cross is a hoax; if there is no Satan, then the whole economy of salvation is up for grabs. No wonder Christianity sees the history of humanity as a perpetual, cosmic warfare between God and Lucifer, between good and evil, between the Light of God and the darkness of evil, between God calling us to be like His image and Satan enticing us to be our own image. Not only does this cosmic warfare occur on the large scale of history, but it also rages on the small scale of one's inner self where decisions are being made for or against God. Those tiny, personal decisions shape history as well.

We had encountered this evil force already in paradise, deceiving Adam and Eve. The serpent (or snake, or dragon in Rev. 12:9; 20:2) has typically been identified with God's antagonist and adversary—the satanic one (Satan), the diabolic one (the devil, the demon, the divider). The Book of Wisdom says, "through the devil's envy death entered the world" (2:24). The serpent is the smooth voice of the big lie, "a seductive voice, opposed to God, [...] a fallen angel" (CCC 391). It is the voice of God's enemy, saying that you can only be yourself by leading your own life, by being number one rather than number two, by making God look like our biggest rival, by stealing the fruit from the Owner's tree of life and death. Satan is the "father of all lies." This makes moral evil part of a much larger picture. It is God's aim for each one of us to attain Heaven after death, whereas Satan's aim is to ensure that as many people as possible miss that eternal goal and end up in Hell.

When praying "Deliver us from evil," we are not asking God to take something, a thing, away, for evil is not a "thing." Unfortunately, our current translation of this sentence is not explicit enough. When Matthew (6:13) cites how Jesus prayed the Our Father, he uses the word evil (*poneros*) in a way that can be neuter or masculine, but according to New Testament parallels, should be taken as masculine: the Evil One—which makes even more sense in connection with the previous line that says "And lead us not into temptation" where Matthew is not speaking of God tempting us but of the final ordeal of this world (*peirasmos*). This last word is also used when Jesus tells his followers on His last night on earth, "Pray that you may be spared the test" (Mk. 14:37, Mt. 26:41, Lk. 22:4, all use the word *peirasmos*). Jesus is speaking here of the temptation led by Satan that comes with the final ordeal. That's why the Passion of our Lord Jesus Christ is such a crucial event in human history.

Apparently, sin is a key issue in human history. History began with sin and sin will still feature at the end of history during a final judgment. So, we need to find out what is considered sin. Probably the best guidelines come from the Ten Commandments. What do they tell us? That is our last issue in this book.

8.

God's Prescription for Happiness

The main pillars of Judeo-Christian morality are the Ten Commandments. God, according to St. Augustine, "wrote on the tables of law what men did not read in their hearts." These Ten Commandments are vital for each individual and for our society at large, although the Supreme Court has ruled that it is illegal to display them in public schools. Yet, they are chiseled into the facade of the Supreme Court building, at the very place where this decree was made! Well, not only did those vital Ten Commandments lose their prominent position on the walls of our court houses (your tax dollars at work), but even—what is much worse—"on the walls" of our conscience. What is at stake here? The answer is short and snappy: the happiness of eternal salvation!

Happiness? Our society is obsessed with the search for happiness; some have declared it the only guideline for morality. And yet, there seems to be so little of it. The other day, I found a brochure for nutrients in our mailbox featuring in big letters: instant happiness delivered at your door. We all know better, I hope. Happiness is not for sale in tablets! God has a much better prescription for happiness: two of God's tablets a day—that is, the two tables holding the Ten Commandments. They are not ten suggestions, not even ten options, but Ten Commandments, Ordinances, or Statutes. They are not nutritional supplements but "nutritional essentials." Well, those vital Ten Commandments have lost their prominent position in the lives of most people nowadays. That is why our happiness is in trouble, more so than ever.

In other words, they are more than "Ten Words of Wisdom"; they are "Ten Laws of Life"—one for each finger. We certainly have got our hands full with them. Let's find out in this chapter how we can get our health and happiness back with the right "nutrients."

Why "ten words"?

The table below shows three different traditions of numbering the Ten Commandments or Decalogue: 1. Talmudic (T); 2. Orthodox and Calvinists (O); 3. St. Augustine, Catholics, and Lutherans (C). There are two versions of the Decalogue in the Bible: Exodus 20 and Deuteronomy 5. All traditions use the version given in the Book of Exodus.

The Catechism describes the Decalogue—literally the "ten words"—as "the gift of God himself and his holy will. In making his will known, God reveals himself to his people." (2059). God's Revelation tells us who God *is* for us and what God *wants* from us. These two are thoroughly intertwined with each other: What He *wants* of us is related to the Person He *is*, a God of Love who fell in love with us. Not only is God all-powerful, all-knowing, and all-good, but also all-loving—with a love that surpasses all the kinds of love we know.

The Ten Commandments are, in themselves, the covenant between God and His people. They used to be kept and carried around in the Ark of the Covenant. They are the terms and conditions and guidelines of a covenant (CCC 2058)—or more specifically, of a "spousal" relationship. The terms and conditions and guidelines are as follows: "I will be your God; you shall be my people"— and here is how we will treat each other. Thus, it is within the context of a *Covenant* that the Ten Commandments take on their full meaning.

Chapter 8: God's Prescription for Happiness

T	O	C	Exodus 20
1	1	1	2 I am the LORD your God, who brought you out of the land of Egypt, out of the house of slavery;
			3 you shall have no other gods before me.
2	2		4 You shall not make for yourself a carved image, whether in the form of anything that is in heaven above, or that is on the earth beneath, or that is in the water under the earth. 5 You shall not bow down to them or worship them [...]
3	3	2	7 You shall not make wrongful use of the name of the LORD your God, for the LORD will not acquit anyone who misuses his name.
4	4	3	8 Remember the Sabbath day and keep it holy. 9 Six days you shall labor and do all your work. 10 But the seventh day is a Sabbath to the LORD your God; you shall not do any work [...]
5	5	4	12 Honor your father and your mother, so that your days may be long in the land that the LORD your God is giving you.
6	6	5	13 You shall not murder.
7	7	6	14 You shall not commit adultery.
8	8	7	15 You shall not steal.
9	9	8	16 You shall not bear false witness against your neighbor.
10	10	9	17 You shall not covet your neighbor's wife...
		10	...you shall not covet your neighbor's house... ...or male or female slave, or ox, or donkey, or anything that belongs to your neighbor.

The table above shows three different traditions of numbering the Ten Commandments or Decalogue: 1. Talmudic (T); 2. Orthodox and Calvinists (O); 3. St. Augustine, Catholics, and Lutherans (C). There are two versions of the Decalogue in the Bible: Exodus 20 and Deuteronomy 5. All traditions use the version given in the Book of Exodus.

You may wonder why there are *two* tablets instead of one? Well, Jews usually place five Commandments on each tablet or table, as if they represent the five fingers on each hand, whereas Catholics follow St. Augustine who has three Commandments on the first tablet and seven on the second one (CCC 2066). Either split is based on the idea that the first tablet has "love God" commands, and the second one "love neighbor" commands. That is a nice thought, as long as we do not lose sight of the fact that all ten commandments are simultaneously ten ways of loving God and ten ways of loving our neighbor. They go hand in hand: "The two tables shed light on one another; they form an organic unity [...] One cannot honor another person without blessing God his Creator. One cannot adore God without loving all men, his creatures" (CCC 2069).

St. Paul also stresses the unity of the two tables (Romans 13:8–10): "Owe no one anything, except to love one another; for he who loves his neighbor has fulfilled the law. The commandments, 'You shall not commit adultery, You shall not kill, You shall not steal, You shall not covet,' and any other commandment, are summed up in this sentence, 'You shall love your neighbor as yourself.' Love does no wrong to a neighbor; therefore love is the fulfilling of the law." Love is apparently the key word of God's Covenant with us. After all, He is an all-good and all-loving God. Indeed, loving your neighbor is ultimately based on loving God; it begins with loving God before we can love our neighbor. (And the "neighbor" is not just the person living next door!) Notice how, just like the Ten Commandments, the *Our Father* also begins by establishing the primacy of *God* in its first half, which then leads naturally to finding the right way of being *human*. As Pope Benedict XVI put it, "The first thing we must do is step outside ourselves and open ourselves to God. Nothing can turn out right if our relation to God is not rightly ordered." The

Chapter 8: God's Prescription for Happiness

rest flows from there.

My point is that "Love God" and "Love your neighbor" go in fact hand in hand. Why? The fact that my God is the Creator of all people is also good for my neighbor, since we are all neighbors of each other—that is, brothers and sisters from the same Father. As a consequence, the Commandment that I must not kill my neighbor is also good for God, because He is the giver of my neighbor's life as well, which makes every single human life precious in God's eyes. Put differently, we cannot honor other people without blessing their Creator, and we cannot honor God without loving all His people (CCC 2069).

If that is the case, shouldn't we then think of the Decalogue as being on *one* tablet? Interestingly enough, Rabbi Gamaliel, who was the Jewish Law teacher of Saul before he became Paul, does mention that "the Sages say ten on one tablet and ten on the other." That may very well have been the case, because the Ten Commandments establish a covenant between God and His people. So, it is possible that both tablets were complete replicas of each other—one for each party in the Covenant. This can be compared to diplomatic treaties of Ancient Egypt, in which a copy was made for each party. In a love relationship, like in a covenant, each party should have a copy of what the duties and rights are; it is like "give and take," in good and bad days.

Therefore, we could say that it is our *duty*, as an act of love, to make God the only one (Commandment #1); but it is equally true to say that God has a *right* to sit on that divine throne in our lives. Next, it is also equally true to say that God alone has the *right* to give and take human life and that people have a *duty* to respect that right. The Decalogue brings to light the duties and rights inherent in a covenant. There are always two sides to the story, as long as we realize it is a covenant of *love*. So, it doesn't really matter whether we were given one tablet or two tablets.

By the way, speaking of rights and duties, the Ten Commandments seem to be more about duties than rights in the eyes of most people. True, eight of them begin with "You shall *not*..." No wonder that many people think the Catholic Church is the church of "No." Cardinal Seán O'Malley likes to tell this story about one of his community members who wrote a book on moral theology and was teased by one of the friars with the question "350 pages just to say no?" The message is clear: We think the Church is saying no to numerous moral issues—no abortion, no euthanasia, no divorce, no blasphemy, no perjury... But in fact, the Church is really about saying "Yes": saying yes to God, yes to love, yes to life, and yes to other people.

Therefore, we should take the Decalogue as a *dialogue* between God ("I") and Man ("You"). As a matter of fact, all Commandments are stated in the first person—"*I* am the Lord..."—and addressed by God to another person—"*You* shall..." Unlike most other European languages, English does not distinguish between "you" singular and plural, but the original texts of the Ten Commandments use only the singular version: each one of you. In other words, God makes His will known to each person individually, so that each person can respond to His love. Therefore, it is only through each individual person that God speaks to the whole people (CCC 2063). So, in essence, the Decalogue brings our *religious* and *social* lives into unity, as the Catechism puts it. The Decalogue stands for the "ten words" that connect God to humans and humans to God. They are "Ten Words of Wisdom"—a manual of how to treat one another as one people under God. This was well put by Pope Benedict XVI when he said, "that we give God his just due and, in so doing, discover the criterion for what is justly due among men."

This raises the question as to where these Ten Commandments came from. The best and shortest answer is that they came directly from God. But as to *how* they got to us, the Bible is more ambivalent. According to Deuteronomy, it was God who personally wrote them on the two tablets of stone, with His own finger and in a special handwriting (Dt. 5:22; 10:2-4). The Book of Exodus, however, has a different, more down-to-earth version: It was Moses himself who wrote down on the two tablets of stone everything God had told him on the mountain (Ex. 24:4; 34:27). Jeremiah goes even one step further when he says that God will write His law upon the hearts of people, rather than on tablets of stone. Apparently, the message is not *how* God gave them to us, but *that* God gave them to us. No matter how they got to us, they do come from God.

Because they come from God Himself, any violation of the Ten Commandments is called a *sin*. The Church calls them even *mortal* sins; they are like a "spiritual death penalty"; yet they are not a penalty coming from *God*, but a "lethal" consequence of *sin* itself. You may want to think about these "ten laws" or "ten words" as if they were traffic signs. The sign "*Wrong Way. Do Not Enter*" can obviously be ignored, but if you do ignore it, you will most likely experience a "mortal penalty." What kills the violator is not this traffic law or the maker of this law, of course. The law was made by lawmakers to prevent actions that are by nature potentially deadly; that is the reason why the act was made illegal. The Church takes sinful acts as "mortal" because they "kill" our relationship with God. It is not God withdrawing from us, but the sinner pulling away from God.

In addition, we should say that some sins are not "mortal" but "venial"; they "wound" but do not "kill." They rather resemble traffic rules such as "*10 minutes parking limit*." Violating this kind of regulations is illegal but does not kill. Examples of this would be things like petty theft, lies of convenience, mild laziness, etc. St. Thomas Aquinas considers a mortal sin to be "*against* the law," whereas a venial sin is considered to be "*out of step* with the law." In short, the Ten Commandments keep us on the right path, from which so many people tend to deviate given their darkened mind and corrupted will.

What does each "word" command?

I think it is best now to just look at the individual Commandments and discuss what each one entails, so that we know what we ought to do. Please follow me on this path of discovery.

#1: I am the Lord your God: you shall not have strange gods before me

What this Commandment says is basically the following: Do not honor or revere creatures in place of their Creator. Away with any human being, any object, any deity before God! Do not bow to anything and do not shudder before anything. Do not believe that anything in the world has the power to heal you or ruin you. Why not? God answers that question very directly: "For I am the Lord your God." This reminds me of what God said to St. Catherine of Siena, "I am God, but you are not."

There is a clear reason why the First Commandment is first. Get that one wrong and what follows is a moral trainwreck of such immensity that no human engineer can rectify it, for from then on, life would be without any authoritative standards—only based on personal preferences and choices. Without absolute moral standards, we necessarily turn to anything that suits ourselves. C.S. Lewis once stated that "From the moment a creature becomes aware of God as God and of itself as self, the terrible alternative of choosing God or self for the center is opened to it." Once people remove God from their lives, the residue is self-celebration, egomania, "me, myself, and I." Such people live in an echo-chamber, where they keep hearing only themselves. Instead, we should choose God as the center of our lives—that's God's right and our duty.

We talked about this earlier in connection to the first creation account in Genesis. In the light of God's countenance, all entities that call themselves "god," or deem themselves to be a god, fade away and shrivel up. Their masks are torn off. Just look at what some call the mysterious power of Mother Nature—it turns out to be a tiny piece of God's creation for the mere use of human beings. Watch the lights of Sun and Moon and Stars—they are merely lamps created to give people light and to show them what time it is. Or take King and Government—they are nothing-but human institutions curbed by human limitations; their assignment is temporary and their power transitory. Don't ever bow for them!

But there are so many other idols and deities that we venerate more than God. Think of "the god of pleasure"—pleasure in its many forms, from sex to alcohol, from sports to gambling. Its worshippers are "lovers of pleasure rather than lovers of God" (2 Tim. 3:4). Think of "the god of materialism." The worshippers of material possessions "cannot serve God and mammon" (Mt. 6:24), because "the love of money is the root of all evils" (1 Tim. 6:10). Or take "the god of appetite" who lures us into over-eating and binge-drinking. Or take "the god of self-worship" venerated by people who idolize themselves and their Ego, because of their talents, education, title, or career. They venerate "I, me, and myself," and choose to live in splendid isolation, as far as isolated from God.

The Catechism expands on this theme: "Idolatry not only refers to false pagan worship... Man commits idolatry whenever he honors and reveres a creature in place of God, whether this be gods or demons (for example satanism), power, pleasure, race, ancestors, the state, money, etc." (2113). The Catechism also mentions various forms of divination: the use of horoscopes, astrology, palm reading, clairvoyance, mediums, and so on. (2116). If you thought these were gods, you must not be in your right mind! A coin may hold the emperor's image, but you and I carry God's image. Thank God, the Bible has cleared the sky of all those fake and misleading deities who like to put us in bondage. They only enslave and degrade us, for they are extremely addictive.

The things that imprison us can easily deceive us. St. John of the Cross put it this way: "A bird can be held by a chain or by a thread, still it cannot fly." Even those tiny threads can hold us earthbound; they may hold us as firmly as if they were made of steel. No matter what, we end up being shackled. With our very own eyes, we notice how people prostrate themselves before these gods and how these gods bind our world hand and foot to their relentless and gruesome tyranny.

So let the real God stand up please! No doubt, Baal is dead, Jupiter is dead, the Pharaohs and the Caesars are dead. But what about Israel's God, the God of Jesus? Many people no longer ask this question nowadays. They have lost even God through the various forms of atheism that we discussed at the beginning of this book. Are we really on our way to live without God? Having no God means the sea has been drunk dry, the fourth dimension has been taken out of our lives, the bottom has fallen out, and our sixth sense is gone. Everything is just the way it is, as they say—only a matter of historical facts and laws of nature. These people can no longer look beyond the natural to see the supernatural, beyond the physical to see the metaphysical, beyond the visible to see the invisible, beyond the present to see the eternal. As G.K. Chesterton put it, "when we cease to worship God, we do not worship nothing, we worship anything."

No matter how essential the First Commandment is, certain churches have a different version of it. What St. Augustine and Catholics combine into one Commandment—"You shall not have strange gods before me"—is split by other traditions into two separate commandments—"You shall have no other gods" and "You shall not make an idol." The reason for combining them into one commandment is that idols easily become "strange gods" that tend to take over God's place in our minds. The Bible is in a constant battle with "idols." An idol in itself can do nothing; left alone, it will deteriorate, rust, rot, or chip. Scripture calls idols literally "nothings" when it says, "For all the gods of the peoples are idols" (Ps. 96:5). So where does their power come from then? Although the idol itself is nothing, every idol has a demon associated with it. Demons are the spiritual agents acting in all idolatry. We can find these demons all over the Bible: "They sacrificed their sons and their daughters to the demons" (Ps. 106:37) and "They sacrificed to demons which were no gods" (Deut. 32:17).

And then there is the worst idol of them all, atheism. We talked about that already at the beginning of this book. Atheists like to occupy God's throne that they had declared vacant. All idols, including the idol of atheism, keep doing what they used to do in the past. They are still trying to put clouds between the living God and us, to alienate us from God, from one another, and from ourselves. Perhaps we should reconsider and take these gods seriously again; and yet we should take them for what they really are: nothings! No wonder then that the Catholic Church combines "other gods" and "idols" into one single Commandment, for they all try to take God's place, but they are actually "nothings"! Once we realize that we belong to God, everything else loses the allure of divinity.

#2: You shall not use the name of the Lord your God in vain

Every once in a while, you may read the following words on a highway billboard: "Speak out about God, but do not abuse His holy name." It makes many of us think of the 2nd Commandment, because abusing His name is often interpreted as "swearing." I do admit swearing is a very annoying habit. If the names of God and Jesus mean anything, one wouldn't use them in and out of season. However, I must add that this common interpretation seems to miss the key point of the 2nd Commandment—if only because our manner of swearing hadn't been invented yet when Moses was around.

There is much more serious stuff at stake in the 2nd Commandment. It is about the Divine Name that God made known to us. The first Name that is used for God in Scripture is *Elohim*, "gods," not really a name but a plural word for majesty and divinity. That name is used in the very first sentence of the Bible: "In the beginning God [*Elohim*] created the heavens and the earth." This is the God of gods, the One who began it all, and no other god. What is in a term, you might ask. Sometimes a lot! No wonder then, in Ex. 3:13-22, Moses asks God what His "name" is. Moses is not asking "what should I call you;" rather, he is asking "who are you; what are you like; what have you done?" That's when God gave Moses a more specific name: the four-letter Name represented by the Hebrew letters YHWH (Yahweh). Although nothing in the Bible prohibits a person from pronouncing this Name of God, it is often substituted by the Name *Adonai*.

What a name that is: I am; I am the I-am; I am who I am; I am present as I am. Well, from now on, God has been introduced to us! God has divulged His deepest secret to us! God has given us the right to use His name, so He is no longer a stranger to us. He has become a very "personal" God, who wants to associate with us. We all know how important a personal name is; even when someone misspells your name, you feel personally offended. So imagine, we may call Him by His Holy Name, as if He were our partner and friend. We are allowed to claim that God is with us—Emmanuel! We know His Name, and He knows the name of each one of us, for He has written the name of each one of us in the palm of His hands (Is. 49:16).

That is why we shouldn't use God's name for shallow and deceitful purposes. Don't pull God down by His name. Don't cause harm to God's concern—that is, God's dedication to people and their well-being—by abusing His Holy Name. Words like slander and fraud come to mind. Those are the real issues that the 2nd Commandment is about. As Pope Benedict XVI worded it, "Do I take care that God's companionship with us will draw us up into his purity and sanctity, instead of dragging him down into the filth?"

Sure enough, human history is one long-winded, miserable story of all the things we have done and not done—supposedly in God's name and with God's support, turning *our* concerns into *God*'s concerns. At one time, someone was even sentenced to death, to death on a cross—and again, it was done in God's Name. Too many people thought horrors like these were the right thing to do, in God's Name. They forgot that when Joshua drew his sword and asked God's angel, "Are you for us, or for our adversaries?" the angel answered, "Neither!" (Joshua 5:13). And yet, we cannot but use His Name, calling upon His Name—but without abusing His Name. We do have to keep praying to Him—"Hallowed be Thy Name"—so that our relationship doesn't get damaged, or even broken, by mere negligence. We have a Covenant, remember?

The Bible says several things about calling upon God's Name when we pray to Him. First, it tells us that by using His Name, we are permitted to be familiar with God, for He is always eager to listen. God is only a prayer away. On the other hand, how rotten can such a relationship be if I look out only after myself and my personal interests, if I talk without listening? What is the use of prayer if we plan to live our own lives anyway? In other words, what is the use of prayer if it doesn't change us? Prayer is meant to change *us*, not *God*. Prayer is not sending a to-do-list to God. He is not a cosmic vending machine. Imagine that you would pray for patience and demand it right now on the spot.

Second, since God confides his Holy Name to those who believe in Him, the gift of a name belongs to the order of trust and intimacy. So, in our own talk and prayers, we should never use His Name except to bless, praise, and glorify Him. Therefore, never abuse God's Name, whether it is in blasphemy—when uttering against God words of hatred, reproach, and defiance (CCC 2148)—or in false oath calling on God—by being witness to a lie (CCC 2149)—or in perjury—when making a promise under oath with no intention of keeping it (CCC 2476).

The third thing about God's Name is that others should believe in God as well. The Holy Name should become known among people, for His Name is not something you keep to yourself. His stories with us should be passed on—which is a precarious undertaking. It is in His Name that people go to the sick, to lepers, to the poor, and even to the ones in prison. But times are changing; nowadays, it may be even more of a concern whether God's Name will still be used at all and whether present-day people will ever have a chance to hear from others how beautiful it is to still have faith in God, to be part of His Church. "Hallowed be Thy Name" is a cry of the human race that comes from a deep hunger for God. It is a cry that should never be silenced. How different it is in our highly secularized society, in which we see a new 2nd Commandment arising: "You shall not use the Name of

God, *unless* you do so in vain." Somehow, we have lost the reverence for God's Name. His Name has become a forbidden word in many circles, politically incorrect. But even if there were no one left crying out His Name, "the very stones would cry out" (Lk. 19:40).

When God gave us His Name, He took the risk that we may also abuse His Name, may neglect or even reject His Name. As a matter of fact, many people nowadays live in a vacuum that was once filled by faith in God. This has left a "God-shaped hole" inside of them that only God can fill—nothing else can. In his *Pensées*, Blaise Pascal describes what man does with this hole: "What else does this craving, and this helplessness, proclaim but that there was once in man a true happiness, of which all that now remains is the empty print and trace? This he tries in vain to fill with everything around him, seeking in things that are not there the help he cannot find in those that are, though none can help, since this infinite abyss can be filled only with an infinite and immutable object; in other words, by God himself." And thus, we are back again at the 1st Commandment: "You shall not have strange gods before Me, for *I am the Lord your God.*" Hallowed be that Name!

#3 Remember to keep holy the Lord's Day

For Jews, that holy day is the Sabbath—the seventh day of the week, a day of rest, following the six days of creation. For Christians, the Sabbath would be replaced by the eighth day—the day the Lord Jesus Christ was resurrected. On the eighth day begins the new creation (CCC 349, 2174). That is the day when humanity was re-created in Jesus Christ. This is now called the "Lord's Day" by Christians. It is the *first* day of the week when Christians come together for the breaking of the bread. In the words of St. Luke (Acts 20:7), "On the first day of the week, when we were gathered together to break bread, Paul talked with them."

We find reference to the "Lord's Day" already in the *Didache* written at the end of the 1st century: "But every Lord's Day gather yourselves together, and break bread, and give thanksgiving after having confessed your transgressions, that your sacrifice may be pure." Another early reference comes from the St. Ignatius of Antioch in his AD 108 letter to the church of Magnesia: "those who were brought up in the ancient order of things have come to the possession of a new hope, no longer observing the Sabbath, but living in the observance of the Lord's Day, on which also our life has sprung up again by Him and by His death."

Keep one day a week "holy," says the 3rd Commandment. This one particular "day off" that the 3rd Commandment speaks about—this one holy-day per week—is really a great "invention." It is a gift from the God of the Bible, which has been given, through Israel, to all people who didn't have a holiday at the end or the beginning of the week. The Sabbath was the completion of the old creation, but for Christians, a new day has dawned: the day of Christ's Resurrection.

In most cultures at the time, it used to be that people labored seven days of the week—each day was exactly the same. There was no stopping, for as the saying goes, "such was life." Life was laboring until death came. It was "slavery" for everyone. That is how most people lived their lives for centuries, not knowing any better. Living is laboring, right? For what else could it be? Until a voice said something to this effect: "One day is Mine—and I want to give this day to you too. It is meant to be a pleasant day. It is a reminder of our Covenant, old or new. On that day, you do not need to work; and what is more, on that day, I do not allow you to work, because I want you to rest, to find yourself, and to

Chapter 8: God's Prescription for Happiness

discover what I gave you. Plus, I want you to share this day with others, your personnel, your cattle." Isn't that a miracle!

Do we still consider Sunday a gift, let alone a miracle? It is quite strange that nowhere in the Bible are we ordered to work hard. Instead, the Bible says we should be able to *stop* working; it asks us what we have experienced from God's creation by the time we die. Did we notice God? Did we have a taste of life? We just keep running, but God tells us to stop and think, for we have a faith that makes you think. Let's give our God, ourselves, and our fellow people a moment's thought and prayer. The Catechism calls it "a day of protest against the servitude of work and the worship of money" (2172). To put it in a nutshell, being the richest person in the cemetery shouldn't be our main concern.

Well, what then *should* we do on Sunday? We should rest with the Lord and thank Him for the six days of creation that He gave us. The best way to do so is by celebrating the Holy Eucharist (CCC 2177), as a testimony of belonging to and of being faithful to Christ and His Church (CCC 2182). In so doing, we proclaim that all there is belongs to God through Jesus. Humans do not live to work, but they work to enjoy the gift of life—or in Jesus' words, "The sabbath was made for man, not man for the sabbath" (Mk 2:27). Put differently, do not mingle this one holiday of the week with other weekdays.

A day of rest doesn't mean we should lie in bed, sit on the couch, or walk the golf course all day. This day off was given to all of us together, as each one of us needs such a day just as badly. That is why Sunday is also a day of service to others—to those who do not have much to live for, those who are drowning in their work and in their worries, those who are unemployed because of social or personal circumstances, those for whom Sunday is the most difficult day of the week because they have no one or have only painful memories. That is why the 3rd Commandment wants *everyone* to have a Sunday, not only you and me (CCC 2186).

This must also be the reason why Jesus heals the sick on this very day of rest. Now we may better understand those Gospel stories in which Jesus, on the Sabbath of all days, does several things that are forbidden, or at least seem unnecessary. Luke 13:10-17, for instance, tells us that Jesus healed a woman severely stricken with rheumatism. He "happens" to heal her on the Sabbath. Could Jesus not have waited one more day? Why this act of provocation? Was it meant to get a rise out of the religious hair-splitters? Was it meant to show people how open-minded and broad-minded He was? Was it meant to demonstrate how *in*significant the Sabbath is? No, none of the above! Jesus did what He did for none of these reasons. Rather, He did it out of respect for the Sabbath and for the God of the Sabbath. Here was a woman for whom it was never Sabbath; all her days were painful; all her days were drab. Jesus gave the Sabbath back to her when He healed and liberated her. At last, she could enjoy the day that everyone deserves. Finally, there was a Sun-day in her life! That is the crowning glory of God's creation.

#4: Honor your father and your mother

This Commandment looks very straightforward—something like this: You shall not give up those parents of yours, who spent their whole life toiling for you. Although they may no longer be able to do anything and may even have become useless and needless, you shall not treat them like dirt; you shall not throw them on the dumpster of life; you shall take care of them as they have taken care of you, in a God-like manner. You shall honor and value them as any human being deserves to be honored and valued, to the very end.

Chapter 8: God's Prescription for Happiness

Not so in these days, of course, you might counter. Haven't we wrapped our folks in comfortable cotton? They have their pension plans, their social security benefits, and so on. They have their elderly homes and nursing homes. What more could they wish for? Yet, we should ask ourselves as to whether an honorable place is still left in our midst for them. Do they still feel that they are a part of everything, that they are worthwhile and have some say in what is going on? Of course, there must be much more to the 4th Commandment. In fact, much more! Some, following St. Augustine, place this Commandment on the 2nd tablet, the "love neighbor" section, whereas other traditions think it belongs on the 1st tablet in the "love God" section. There is some profound truth to either position. Let's discuss the "love God" interpretation first.

Parents are our lifeline to God. They were, or should be, the first ones to tell us about God and about all we know about Him. The Catechism stresses this very clearly: "we should honor our parents to whom we owe life and who have handed on to us the knowledge of God" (2197). What our parents hand on to us is the rich tradition of the Catholic Church. Tradition means literally: something we "pass or hand on." Unfortunately, our culture doesn't appreciate what has been handed on because it is often considered "second-hand." Indeed, the material things that we pass on usually deteriorate with age. But the tradition that the 4th Commandment refers to doesn't deteriorate; it is more like gold that doesn't tarnish; it is definitely "first-hand"—coming directly from God. However, it came to us through our parents. Consequently, honoring our parents means giving them the weight they have received from God; not the weight they have given themselves!

But the 4th Commandment is also part of the "love neighbor" section, especially when it comes to the parents. Although this commandment is addressed specifically to children in their relationship to their father and mother, it covers in fact a much wider range of "neighbors:" We should respect all those whom God, for our good, has vested with His authority (CCC 2197). "This commandment includes and presupposes the duties of parents, instructors, teachers, leaders, magistrates, those who govern, all who exercise authority over others or over a community of persons" (CCC 2199).

In short, what is essentially at stake in the 4th Commandment is the continuation of God's cause, of God's concern for humanity, but through the channel of other people. Parents and others with authority are like people on a mission—in fact, an important mission. Their concern is to ensure that God's history with His people continues. That is the mission the Bible talks about. Hence, we can call them God's representatives. In time, children will be representatives for the new generation. Therefore, you cannot just leave current and previous generations out; they deserve reverence, because they are part of a continuing chain. Do not think the world began with you! However, the opposite side of the coin is that those before you should also be *worthy* of reverence! We owe respect to those who earn respect.

This all sounds nice, but what if our parents didn't earn respect and failed in their mission? Indeed, some parents failed because they never passed on much of God's story. But fortunately, God's reliance on parents is a relative one. And then there are parents who think they failed because their children didn't accept the "tradition" they handed on to them. There may be many reasons. Sometimes, evil forces from outside the family took over. Sometimes, parents just failed to be there for their kids. At times, the black shadows of their views darkened the lives of their children. At other times, they stood in someone else's way. Let's face it, didn't they pass on the Original Sin to us as well? And yet, they tried to make sure the Good News had a sequel. You may not be able to *respect* your parents, but you are asked to *honor* them by loving them, even though they may have failed.

Let's put this in a wider context. Thanks to parents, there are families in our society. The family is the cornerstone of society. The Catechism of the Catholic Church calls the family "the original cell of social life [...] an initiation into life in society" (2207). As the philosopher Peter Kreeft noted societies have survived with very bad political systems and very bad economies, but not without strong families. Families are to society what cells are to a body. The family is the first place where children learn life's most important lessons. The family is the first place where children find protection and learn the role of being a male or female. None of these "lessons" are inborn; they must be taught and nurtured! Pope Benedict XVI stressed the importance of the family because, as he put it, the family holds "the authentic setting in which to hand on the blueprint of human existence. This is something we learn by living it with others and suffering it with others."

True, character formation may certainly be done in school too, but it begins in the family where you learn from your parents. They try to make sure that they place respectful and responsible children on earth. We cannot expect schools to correct what went wrong in the family for 24/7. Yet, schools do play an important role. The idea that schools should not only prepare students for careers but also help shape character is an idea that extends back to the ancient Greeks. Do not confuse this with indoctrination. If one believes that children have more than a biological dimension, then omitting any other dimensions from education is itself indoctrination of another kind. It is our duty to give our children the education that we consider best, including religious education. We shouldn't get fooled by the slogan that children of all ages ought to make such choices on their own. After all, parents did not let them choose whether they wanted to be born; parents even decided on their names and on so many other things.

As a matter of fact, the family is of vital importance in the development of human beings. Babies can tell mother from father as early as six weeks, or even three weeks after birth. Almost invariably, they make this same distinction, becoming calm in the presence of the mother, while being aroused and stimulated by the approach of the father. The interactions between infant and father, as between infant and mother, work in either direction and follow a pattern that transcends social class and cultural expectations. Children whose fathers help care for them have been shown to be less likely to become violent; they have higher IQs, better impulse control, and better social adaptations—in short, better psychological health. And as for the fathers themselves, studies with inner-city men who stay with the family have shown that fathers also learn from this experience and are less prone to commit crimes or join gangs.

Just as children learn to imitate language and gestures, they also mimic the moral practices they see at home. The Catechism of the Catholic Church (2207) calls the family "the community in which, from childhood, one can learn moral values, begin to honor God, and make good use of freedom." The popular saying, garbage in, garbage out, applies even here—and might also apply to what happens in dysfunctional families. Children do need and deserve a functional family. Good role models are essential, making every day a "school day" when it comes to moral development. Children who have never learned to be ashamed of certain behaviors are in real trouble, perhaps even for the rest of their lives. That's why the 4th Commandment is pivotal to each one of us and to society at large.

#5: You shall not kill

In the Bible, murdering or killing is more than knocking someone's brains out. Murder can actually happen much sooner—at the moment one doesn't acknowledge that someone else is equally worthwhile. When Cain shouted, "Am I my brother's keeper?" (Gen. 4:9), the Bible responds very clearly: "Yes, you are! What else would you be?" Essentially, that is the point at issue in the 5th Commandment. Because we all have one Father in Heaven, we *all* are His children on earth and are equally worthwhile. That is the very basis of the principle of human dignity, as we discussed earlier. Once we step out of the closed circle of "I" and surrender ourselves to communion with the other children of God, we truly become "children of God."

Jesus of Nazareth was the incarnation of this "rule of life." Life was always flowing from Him. To the hungry, He was bread; to the sick, health; to the enslaved, liberation; to the convicted, forgiveness; to the downtrodden, justice. Pope Francis once declared, "God never tires of forgiving us. It's we who tire of asking for forgiveness." God's No to manslaughter is not some kind of law designed to protect the abstract entity of "life." Saying No to manslaughter is God's way of saying Yes to tangible people. "Hatred of the neighbor is a sin when one deliberately wishes him evil" (CCC 2303). Instead, "To love is to will the good of another" (CCC 1766)—which is certainly more than not killing another person.

Taking the words "You shall not murder" seriously has much wider consequences. It means we have no good word to say about someone's inconsiderate attitude toward any form of human life—no matter whether the issue is abortion, euthanasia, reckless driving, or the arms race. Nevertheless, this world of ours has become murderous—it is becoming more and more people-unfriendly, less and less loving. Radio, TV, and newspapers keep bombarding us with violations of the 5th Commandment. We are exposed to such news for 24/7. The lives of individual human beings seem to have lost their value. All these horrible news reports and TV images have almost made us tone-deaf and eye-blinded for the reality behind murders and killings. They make it sound and look like these things are just part of human nature. Having been made in the image of God, you and I possess "the dignity of a person, who is not just something, but someone" (CCC 357).

I admit hospitals do fight an admirable battle for a patient's life; just think of the transplantations performed, the expensive devices applied, the number of doctors tending to the same bed! On the other hand, there are millions killed by abortion, euthanasia, traffic accidents, road-rage, famine, poverty, and war. Is life still worth living? Would there be any sanctuary left if even the womb of a pregnant mother is no longer a safe hiding place for an unborn child? Life was given to us by God; we cannot just take it away or refuse it on our own terms. Neither can the message of peace be spread by the sword.

Does this mean killing is never legitimate or right in moral terms? Although there are no exceptions to the prohibition of murder, sometimes murder can have a double effect: the preservation of one's own life and the killing of the aggressor—one intended, the other not (CCC 2263). Therefore, *self-defense* is legitimate "since one is bound to take more care of one's own life than of another's" according to St. Thomas Aquinas. This even holds for governments, as they have "the right of lawful self-defense, once all peace efforts have failed" (CCC 2308).

Aren't there other cases, though, in which killing is not a violation of the 5th Commandment? More and more people nowadays think there are. We see this most clearly in the abortion debate. How can abortion not be a violation of the 5th Commandment? Well, as we discussed already, we are masters of "massaging" our language with misleading and seductive terminology so that abortion is no longer killing a human being. Abortion is portrayed as simply a matter of conflicting interests, while subordinating the interest of the unborn to the born. But then, in a cunning twist, the woman's interest is turned into a woman's right. From then on, the woman has the "moral right of freedom" to do with her own body whatever is in her own interest.

But that raises another question: what about the baby's interest? To make sure pregnancy becomes a matter of a woman's interests *only*, the next step is to change the meaning of what it is that she is pregnant with. It is no longer a human being but mere "tissue," a "growth," a "tumor," a "clump of cells" foreign to the woman's body. Obviously, "clumps of cells" cannot express any desires or defend any interests—they are voiceless. From then on, there is no longer a conflict of interests—all that is left are the woman's interests. Abortion supporters simply define the unborn out of existence. Once the unborn child has become a "nothing," abortion has become something like the removal of an appendix. Some have even chosen to label abortion as a "cure" for the "disease" of pregnancy, thus turning abortion into a "health" issue. The new mantra is now, "It is my body, so I can decide whatever I want."

Indeed, we are masters of "massaging" our language with misleading and seductive terminology. We have done so also with euthanasia by changing it into "doctor-assisted suicide." Even the term "eu-thanasia" is part of a misleading vocabulary, for there is nothing "good" (*eu-*) about this kind of death. Suddenly, assisted suicide is no longer considered a form of killing, but merely an "aid in dying," while the term "doctor-assisted" is supposed to stand for "with merciful medical compassion." How deceptive words can be! Words like "mercy," "dignity," and "compassion" cannot alter the fact that "mercy-killing" is a form of killing. What they euphemistically call doctor-*assisted* suicide nowadays is in fact doctor-*prescribed* death.

It is certainly not "aid in dying," for we can never really help people by killing them. Those who do provide "aid in dying" at the end-stage of life are hospice workers, hospital chaplains, nurses, counselors, psychologists, and concerned relatives—but not those doctors who provide lethal drugs to their patients, who are usually not even their own patients. Providing lethal drugs is a disgrace to their profession and to the final stage of life's journey. We all have the moral duty to improve the quality of life, even at the end of life. Passionate doctors should end the patient's suffering, not the patient's life. When they decide otherwise, they make all people involved accomplices in a suicide—pharmacists, nurses, family members, friends, and even society itself.

In short, any kind of abortion or suicide is a violation of the 5th Commandment. The Catechism (2280-2281) says, "Everyone is responsible for his life before God who has given it to him. It is God who remains the sovereign Master of life. [...] We are stewards, not owners, of the life God has entrusted to us. It is not ours to dispose of. Suicide contradicts the natural inclination of the human being to preserve and perpetuate his life. It is gravely contrary to the just love of self." Therefore, the bottom-line remains this: You shall not kill or murder.

#6: You shall not commit adultery

In the 6th Commandment, marriage is the issue—not only marriage, but in fact the entire gamut of sexual morality. Marriage isn't easy. No matter how much we love our spouses, we will have our differences. They may be as minor as where to squeeze the toothpaste or as serious as having different religious beliefs. Marriage isn't easy and has never been easy, but times have changed. Since made easier by civil law, the number of divorces has been on the rise. It used to be rather common for parents to have four or more children; nowadays it is rather common for children to have four or more parents.

That makes me appreciate even more what this older, witty, and long-married man used to say to people he introduced his wife to: "Did you ever meet my first wife?" She was, and ever would be, his first and last wife—it was his way of joking. His unspoken message was, there is nothing more nourishing than love. No wonder the Gospel is a love story, in which everything revolves around love, the love of God and the love of Jesus for everyone He met. Nothing else shows the beauty of a human being so clearly and gives meaning to life so deeply as love does. God who created us out of love also calls us to love—the fundamental and innate vocation of every human being (CCC 1604). At last, it was also out of love that He sent His Son to the world. "For God so loved the world that he gave his only and unique Son" (John 3:16).

However, love is a two way street. On the one hand, it means "someone is there for you." On the other hand, it also means "you are there for someone else." The very essence of love demands that we give it away, for love cannot exist in the same space as possessiveness and selfishness. As said earlier, families are grounded in the rights and duties of a marriage: Only if you marry me and stand by me, can you count on me to bear and help raise your children. This requires a commitment on both sides. No involvement without commitment. It is in the loving bond between two parents that their children can blossom.

Love is the keyword here. However, we probably all know that nothing is more precarious than love. Indeed, this very same love—or should we say lust—makes people leave their families and neglect their duties. Love can create the deepest problems and practically incurable wounds when it is refused, trampled upon, or just not returned. Love is like a beautiful river that turns into a menacing torrent once it exceeds its bounds. Yet, this very love urges people to make one of the most important decisions in life: the decision to marry, to take another's side for good, to share every part of life from then on with someone else. In fact, love is the only valid reason to do so. Otherwise, having the other person always around will gradually become more and more of a nuisance.

The Church makes it very clear that the husband and wife themselves are the ministers of the sacrament of marriage to each other. The ceremony itself does not bring about a sacrament, but the full and free consent of a man and a woman does—the priest is only the official witness. However, if the gift of self is not given, no sacrament takes place. That is the reason why a marriage can be annulled. An annulment does not destroy the indissoluble bond of marriage, but it acknowledges that no marriage may have taken place if, at the time of the vows, there was something either present or absent that made the consent invalid.

What a valuable gift this sacramental bond can be! What a valuable gift it is to have someone beside you, in good and bad days! Didn't Genesis 2:18 say about Adam, "I will make him a helper fit for him"? A more accurate translation would be: "I will make him a helper as his counterpart and opposite." How can a helper be an opposite at the same time? Well, a helper is not a servant; Jesus called even the Holy Spirit a Helper. Instead, the helper given to Adam is going to be his "other half" or "significant other," but with opposite attributes—not just a replica—a person who gives you an answer and makes you answer. Love is not meant to be kept to oneself but must be given away.

How do we make such a marriage work? Obviously, the Bible doesn't offer us recipes as to how to make a marriage successful. The Bible has only one story to tell, not in one or some of its sections, but in all of them, from Genesis 1 to Revelation 21. It is the story about the covenant between God and God's people. A covenant is like a marriage, according to the Bible. As a matter of fact, a marriage is a reflection of the Great Covenant between God and us. It is a covenant between two people who have accepted the call to give to each other the gift that God gives to all human beings—happiness, nurture, and support. Put succinctly, "God himself is the author of marriage" (CCC 1603).

If that is indeed the case, then the word *love* is no longer sufficient in itself; another word is needed, namely the word *fidelity*. These two words, love and fidelity, mark the covenant. However, fidelity means more than what we usually think it does; it expresses constancy in keeping one's given word (CCC 2365). Most people believe in the idea of a "soul mate," someone who is always there for them, ready to meet their every need. But many forget there is another side: They should also be there for their soul mate as well—not "as long as we both shall *love*" but "as long as we both shall *live*." Fidelity is a gift, not a choice. God allows infidelity but wills fidelity.

All of this is closely connected to *chastity*. The Catechism explains that "Chastity means the successful integration of sexuality within the person and thus the inner unity of man in his bodily and spiritual being" (2337). It tolerates neither a double life nor duplicity in speech. It matures through self-mastery, which is a form of training in human freedom by ridding oneself of all slavery to unruly passions (CCC 2339). Make no mistake, chastity applies to each and every human being, whether it is a spouse, a widow, or a virgin. It doesn't mean abstinence of sexual intercourse, but it includes it. It means *purity*: pure sex, right sex, not twisted sex. Since our corrupted will often tempts us to kinky sex, chastity requires self-control, self-mastery. It leads to a breach of covenant.

However, there are many things that can cause a breach of this covenant. First of all, there are many ways one can commit an offense against chastity. The Catechism mentions several: lust, masturbation, fornication, pornography, prostitution, and rape (2351-2356). In addition, there are other seemingly minor things, although they can have life-lasting effects: attachment to our jobs or our hobbies is one of them, as are our ingrained opinions, our unwillingness to listen to that other person, our persistent selfishness, our apathy and lethargy when our marriage needs work. The list could go on and on—exploiting one another, letting one another wither, tearing one another's heart out, tying up one another, overlooking one another. These are the silent kinds of infidelity, which may last throughout a marriage. They make for a marriage that is everything but a covenant. That is where the 6th Commandment calls us to order.

But I also need to mention that we tend to put so much emphasis on being married that those who are single might get the impression they are not quite normal, that they are only half a person. Do singles have any place left to go to, or any person left to call on, without the risk of being merely endured or trampled upon? I believe we should just say out loud that marriage is not the only way to function as a human being. It is better to refuse a marriage than to enter a bad one. Besides, there are so many other ways to be "productive." The Church has a high esteem for all those celibatarians in priesthood and religious life, and all those singles, widows, and widowers in regular life. These people have so many immaterial goods to offer to humanity, and to the Church in particular. Just think of those who forgo marriage in order to care for their parents or brothers or sisters, to give themselves more completely to a profession, or to serve other honorable ends. In their own way, they "can contribute greatly to the good of the human family" (CCC 2231).

#7: You shall not steal

I admit that hearing about armored trucks and ingenious tricks to break into bank safes makes for fascinating stories. However, stealing may be quite annoying, especially when we ourselves are the targets. Yet it is usually not all that dramatic, for it is only about money, made of paper or metal. Even the Bible doesn't make much of a fuss about such kind of stealing. Somehow offenses involving someone else's property are not taken too seriously in the Bible. There is no question of cutting off hands as punishment, the way it is still done in some societies. According to the Bible, all one is expected to do, in cases like these, is to pay compensation, albeit manifold (Ex. 22:1-4). Although we do have property rights (CCC 2401), it is apparently not true that our properties are utterly inviolable. Jesus blesses Zacchaeus for making his pledge of saying, "if I have defrauded any one of anything, I restore it fourfold" (Lk. 19:8).

Let us be clear, though, that there is also nothing wrong with having property or even being wealthy either. St. Francis de Sales used to stress there is a big difference between having poison and being poisoned. Pharmacists, for instance, deal with lots of poison without being poisoned themselves—as long as the poison is in their stores, not their bodies. The same with wealth: If you have wealth, make sure it is in your wallet and home, not in your heart. Whatever we do possess shouldn't possess us. Jesus had no preference for either rich or poor people, but He did have a preference for the "poor in spirit" who know they are in need of redemption.

The Catholic Church explicitly acknowledges the right of owning private property. In his encyclical *Rerum Novarum* [On New Things]—an epitome of the Church's social doctrine—Pope Leo XIII emphatically declares, "every man has by nature the right to possess private property as his own." Needless to say also that a person may lawfully abandon this property right; but the Church denies that humans can be forced to do so. The pontiff makes very clear that it's the role of the State to promote social justice through the protection of individual rights, while the Church must speak out on social issues in order to teach correct social principles. He defends the basic rights of the individual and the family and their priority with regard to the State.

But there is another dimension to the 7th Commandment. The Catechism places it in a much wider and more proper context: "The right to private property, acquired by work or received from others by inheritance or gift, does not do away with the original gift of the earth to the whole of mankind" (2403). Apparently, there is more at stake here than protecting our properties from violation by others, for it is also possible to steal from the whole of mankind. Think of this well-known story about that well-known person called Adam, the "gardener" in the Garden of Eden. That story is still being enacted today: This earth belongs to God; therefore, everything belongs to us together; what we have has been given to us as stewards; we should use it the way God has intended us to use it. The person who claims to be the boss, who keeps everything for himself or herself, is actually taking things away from God's purpose, keeping them away from God. Such a person is breaking away from God, refusing to be under God. Such a person is said to be a thief. In *Fiddler on the Roof*, this thought was used for a great joke: If the rich who do not want to die could hire the poor to do so for them, the poor could make a nice living. Well put!

Chapter 8: God's Prescription for Happiness

Now, we should be able to rephrase the 7th Commandment as follows: "You shall not steal" means "You shall not keep everything for yourself, but give each person what is badly needed, so that all people can make a living on God's earth." It shouldn't surprise us that the Catholic Church has always been very involved with charity in its double sense: "love to our neighbor" and "aid to our neighbor." Whereas thieves seem to think "what's yours is mine," Christians tend to reverse things, "What's mine is also yours."

It is important to note that, when Jesus prays for bread in the Our Father, He does not do so in the singular—give *me* my daily bread today—but in the plural: "Give *us* this day our daily bread." We pray for *our* bread—and that means we also pray for bread for others. From this comes the social teaching of the Church on "superfluous goods," those things of which there is more than is needed for our personal welfare. The 7th Commandment does require respect for the right to private property (CCC 2401), and yet a person is not entirely free with regard to personal possessions. At a certain stage of ownership, we may even lose the right to property of what is unquestionably ours.

In addition, there are probably other hidden forms of stealing in our modern society. One of them is *corruption* in its various forms: pinching at schools, manipulating declarations, defrauding the tax system, faking damage claims, abusing welfare, shoplifting, withholding lost items, lifting company goods, and swindling others. Actions like these seem to have become utterly normal nowadays. Isn't everyone involved in these "mild" kinds of stealing? Aren't these just "light" offenses of the 7th Commandment? Not so in the eyes of St. Augustine. He warns us, "If you take them for light when you weigh them, tremble when you count them." Suddenly, we find ourselves on a very slippery slope. When it comes to making money and making a profit, it is not always easy to remain a person of integrity, living in a world controlled by greed.

At times, though, one wonders whether one looks like an idiot when trying to be honest. There's no doubt, the dollar knows no bounds. Money has become the end to justify any means. But nothing corrupts more than money; it is an idol without equal. The Worship of Money, the Mammon, is the only "religion" that doesn't have to cope with apostasy. Not only is money called the root of all evil, but credit cards are next, as some consider them the devil's vehicle to the End Times. More than ever do we need the 7th Commandment, for being the richest person in the cemetery shouldn't be our main concern!

Therefore, it shouldn't surprise us that the 7th Commandment refers not only to material properties but also the people behind them. It requires respect for persons *and* their goods. Therefore, it also forbids acts that lead "to the enslavement of human beings, to their being bought, sold and exchanged like merchandise, in disregard for their personal dignity" (CCC 2414). Do not think slavery is something from the past. A modern-day form of slavery is human trafficking—the illegal and immoral trade of human beings for the purposes of reproductive slavery, commercial sexual exploitation, or forced labor. It shows us again how timeless the 7th Commandment is.

#8: You shall not bear false witness against your neighbor

The 8th Commandment touches on issues that are much more exciting than always telling the truth. It says: "You shall not give false testimony against your neighbor." A more literal translation would be: "Regarding your neighbor, you shall not act as a false witness."

The central question is this: Do we realize that someone's

honor, well-being, and happiness may depend on what we say, or fail to say? Do we realize that our words have the power to make or break one another? It does not matter so much *how* we hurt others with our words—behind someone's back or right in their face. Neither does it matter *where* we hurt others with our words—in court, in the family room, at work, in the newspaper, on radio, or on TV. That it does happen is enough to be a violation of the 8th Commandment.

The damage inflicted by malicious words can be as painful and as long-lasting as any physical injury. The victims usually cannot even combat a nasty lie; the louder victims protest, the more people are likely to believe the falsehood. The only thing that may help them is to remember that actions speak louder than words, especially false words. In his letter, St. James puts it very harshly (3:5-6): The tongue is a small part of the body, yet the most dangerous. We seem to be able to discipline every part of our bodies, but what about our tongue? We use the tongue to praise the Lord, and we use the same tongue to curse the people created in God's image. Apparently, the tongue is like a two-edged sword.

Isn't it amazing what such a tiny organ like the tongue can do! As tiny as it is, the tongue is proportionately the strongest muscle of the body. Isn't it disgusting to see how this tiny but strong organ can be used, in secret and in public, for gossiping, twisting the truth, for nonsense talk and empty talk, for hollow phrases and false rumors, for vicious gossip and black lies, for shallow opinions about others, for fake commercials and false propaganda? It is a cascade of words, hollow words, dangerous words. We hear lies all day—on radio and TV, on the internet, you name it. I always worry about our new generation, for when they grow up listening to lie after lie in commercials and broadcasting, twenty-four-seven, they must think this world revolves around lies and half-truths. Having been bombarded with lies, they do not know anymore what truth is like. Sadly enough, truth has become a relative and pliable commodity.

One single lie, or even a half-truth, can ruin someone else's life forever. Think of a politician who is being *falsely* accused of sexually harassing a staff member, or a priest who is being *falsely* accused of touching a minor. Sometimes it is done out of revenge or hate, sometimes for political reasons, sometimes out of self-interest. Even when the story is untrue, the harm has been done and the blemish will never leave the victims. St. Aquinas put it well: "Men could not live with one another if there were not mutual confidence that they were being truthful to one another. [...] one man owes it to another to manifest the truth." No wonder, Jesus teaches us the unconditional love of truth: "Let what you say be simply 'Yes' or 'No'; anything more than this comes from evil" (Mt. 5:37). Mean what you say and say what you mean.

Does this suggest that we are *always* obliged to tell the truth? Some people take great pride in always "talking straight from the hip," or "calling a spade a spade," or "saying things to someone's face"—even to someone on a death bed. They want the truth, the full truth, and nothing but the truth in plain terms—the bare truth, the cold truth, that is. Is that really the message of the 8th Commandment? Not quite. Has anyone given us the right to always say the cold truth to someone else's face? Who is being served by our words—that is the fundamental question at stake. In other words, the right to hear the truth and the duty to tell the truth are not unconditional. The precept of love in the Gospel requires us in concrete situations to judge whether it is appropriate to reveal the truth to someone who asks for it (CCC 2488). The Catechism uses here the term "discreet language," because "No one is bound to reveal the truth to someone who does not have the right to know it (CCC 2489).

The Greek word for truth is *aletheia*, which means disclosure and exposure. The Hebrew word for truth, however, is *emeth*, which means fidelity, reliability, and respect. What a world of difference between these two words and where they come from! The 8th Commandment is not about *aletheia* but about *emeth*. There are times when "the truth"—whatever that may be—should not be disclosed, because fidelity or respect is at stake. The real truth can resound only in love, otherwise it makes a false sound. "Speak your mind" is not a biblical motto; "Love one another" is what the Bible wants us to do instead. There are times, though, when a lie can be well-intentioned. A famous example is the case when the Gestapo is at your door, asking you whether you are hiding Jews. Or take the case of the people who exposed the actions of Planned Parenthood by falsely portraying themselves as being in need of help.

Can lies really be well-intentioned? The Bible seems to think so. Abraham, for instance, lies when he tells people that Sarah is his sister (Gen. 20:1). Jacob lies when he tells his father that he is Esau (Gen. 27:19). The Egyptian midwives, when asked by Pharaoh to kill the Hebrew boys on the delivery table, lie when they tell Pharaoh that Hebrew mothers are more vigorous than Egyptian women and will give birth before the midwives arrive (Ex. 1:15-19). Moses lies when he tells Pharaoh that he intends merely to celebrate a festival to honor the Lord of Israel in the desert (Ex. 5:1). Rahab must lie while keeping the Israelite spies hidden (Josh. 6:17). Samuel lies when he announces that he is going to Bethlehem to make a sacrifice, instead of anointing David king (1 Sam. 16). Jonathan lies when he tells his father that David is absent because of a family celebration (1 Sam. 20:6; 20:28). St. Paul lies, or at least tells a half-truth, when he tells the Sanhedrin that he is standing trial because of his hope in the resurrection of the dead (Acts 23:6). All these "lies" seem to be well-intentioned lies.

Shouldn't we be proud of those priests in the Vatican, I might add, who gave false passports to Jews during W.W. II?

Nevertheless, I still wonder whether it is right to lie in these cases by intentionally leading someone else into error, by thinking that good may come out of something intrinsically bad. The fact that lies are reported in the Bible doesn't mean they are sanctioned by the Bible. The Bible contains in fact a lengthy record of sinful acts, but that doesn't mean they received approval. You may not have the duty to tell the *truth*, but that doesn't give you the right to tell a *lie*. Once we allow bad things "for the greater good," every lie can be legitimized as a "truth." But the day may come when that lie catches up on us. Mark Twain put this in very practical terms, "Tell the truth. Then you do not have to remember what you said." In other words, do not lie but make sure, for instance, that your hiding place for Jews is well hidden. You shouldn't lie, but you may have to withhold the truth from people who have no right to hear the truth. Withholding the truth is very different from distorting the truth.

This may seem a radical interpretation, but it is fully in line with Jesus' instruction that we quoted earlier: "Let what you say be simply 'Yes' or 'No'" (Mt. 5:37). Both St. Augustine and St. Thomas Aquinas further elaborated on this radical interpretation. The Catechism says it very harshly, lying is "speaking a falsehood with the intention of deceiving" (2482) and it is "the most direct offense against the truth" (2483). If we do lie, we in fact take the side of Satan, who is the "father of all lies." Is lying a *crime*? Sometimes it is, but that is a legal issue. Is lying a *sin*? Always, but that is a moral issue. No wonder, the Catechism considers lying destructive to society by undermining trust among people and tearing apart the fabric of social relationships (2486). There is no way around it, although there may still be room left for so-called half-truths, because someone may not have the right to hear the whole truth or may not be helped by the full truth.

#9: You shall not covet your neighbor's wife

St. Augustine split the last Commandment of Exodus 20 into two separate Commandments (#9 and #10), as it is done in Deuteronomy 5. First of all, he didn't want to place the neighbor's *spouse* on the same line as the neighbor's *goods*—a spouse is not a property! Second, St. Augustine knew from his own experience how destructive sexuality can be, so he made sure there is a 9th Commandment, separated from the 10th. Plus, there is the 6th Commandment against adultery. Those two combined create a heavy load of sex and sexuality on morality. Perhaps, this gave the Catholic Church the blemish of being mostly—or even only, according to some—focused on *sexual* sins. As a teenager, I knew of a priest whose sermons dealt mainly with the 6th and the 9th Commandments; he seemed "obsessed" by these two, so we called him "six by nine."

The 9th Commandment is in essence about the twosome "marriage and sexuality." Nowadays, the society we live in seems to be more than ever fascinated with sexuality, or more accurately sex—that is, sexuality without marriage. It is the main ingredient of most books, magazines, TV shows, movies, and the internet—the opposite of what the 9th Commandment tells us. Don't take this commandment the wrong way, though. It is not about the neighbor next door but about everyone outside your marriage. It is a commandment for all times, but since Sigmund Freud, we know more than ever how strong our sexual feelings can be; Freud didn't really discover them but probably strengthened them. Ever since, the need for this commandment has become only stronger.

But there is another reason why the 9th Commandment has

become more needed than ever. Rather recently, we saw a dramatic twist in the debate about marriage and sexuality. The so-called "sexual revolution," unleashed in the 1960s, aimed to "liberate" human sexuality from the straitjacket of "traditional" morality, specifically the perceived "restrictive" morality of marriage in Christianity. The groundwork had been laid in the 1940s by Alfred Kinsey, who did what he called "scientific research" on human sexuality, published in his so-called "Kinsey Reports." But lo and behold, the supposedly "disinterested, impartial observers" of his team were encouraged by Kinsey to sexually experiment with each other, himself, his wife, and invited guests. Not surprisingly, some have speculated that Kinsey was just driven by his own sexual lusts; some critics have even called him a pervert.

Although Kinsey died in 1956, we are still living with the consequences of his actions. Since then, many have come to see sexuality as completely liberated from the bonds of marriage, monogamy, love, and fidelity. This is even reflected in the way news reports from the BBC, for instance, shifted their terminology from "committing adultery" to "being unfaithful," and soon thereafter to "having an affair." That's what the sexual liberation has done for us. As a result, we have become a culture ruled by Viagra, condoms, pornography, sexual abuse, and rape. They call this nicely the "sexual revolution," but it is time for a counterrevolution based on the 9th Commandment. We need to confirm once again that sex belongs to the domain of marriage, monogamy, and fidelity; that sex is for life, not just for fun; that the taming of the sex drive and harnessing it to the family are a necessary condition for social stability and long-term human happiness.

Instead, this so-called "revolution" has only led to growing numbers of children who are sexually abused and women who are beaten, abandoned, or raped by men who do not want to hear about self-control and who consider every subject they meet as a mere object for their own use or abuse. Mary Ellen Stanford of Christendom College asks the pivotal question: "Can today's adults—so very fixed on trying to find fulfilment through sex—accept the truth that they can survive without sex, but that children cannot thrive without the fullness of Christian marriage?" As soon as intercourse doesn't need the context of marriage anymore, and marriage is no longer directed toward the rearing of the next generation, marriage gets in trouble, ready for a speedy decline.

Indeed, more than ever, we need to counteract the effects of this "sexual revolution." We need to escape from behind enemy lines of the sexual revolution. At the moment "love" is detached from marriage, it becomes a menace and turns into "lust." This same love—or rather lust—makes people leave their families and neglect their moral duties. The fact is that love can create practically incurable wounds when it is refused, trampled upon, or not returned. As said earlier, love is like a beautiful river that turns into a menacing torrent once it exceeds its bounds. Yet, this very love urges people to make one of the most important decisions in life: the decision to marry your spouse, to take another's side for good, to share every part of life from now on with one's significant other. In fact, love is the only valid reason to do so. Otherwise, having the other person around for life will gradually become more and more of a nuisance. That's where the 9th Commandment stands as a warning sign at the door of every marriage.

The heart is the seat where our feelings and acts originate: "For out of the heart come evil thoughts, murder, adultery, fornication, theft, false witness, slander." (Mt. 15:19). We need to become masters of our feelings and emotions again. The Catechism calls this "The Battle for Purity" (2520). Purity of heart brings freedom from widespread eroticism and avoids entertainment inclined to voyeurism and illusion (2525). Very often the reason for a divorce is not located inside the marriage but inside the person—the lust of the flesh, the lust of the eyes, which leads to coveting a neighbor's spouse and thus disrupting and harming at least *two* marriages and *two* families. When sought for itself, lust is disordered desire for sexual pleasure, isolated from its natural purposes inside the marriage.

This takes us to another form of sexual pleasure that is sought for itself: pornography. Nowadays, due to the presence of computers and the internet, we get bombarded with pornography—the explicit portrayal of sexuality for the purposes of sexual arousal and erotic satisfaction. A multi-billion dollar pornography industry pours garbage into our homes every day through the Web and other media. Not only is it highly addictive, but it also detaches the body from the soul and thus poisons the human heart, imagination, and soul. It is like selling your soul to the Devil. It distorts the image of sexuality and demeans the person—man, woman, or child alike—by making them pure objects of lust and pleasure. It changes sex into a deity that wants to be idolized—which is in defiance of the 1st Commandment besides. The Catechism describes it as "removing real or simulated sexual acts from the intimacy of the partners, in order to display them deliberately to third parties" (2354).

Archbishop Charles Chaput of Philadelphia worded it this way: "Pornography is never 'innocent entertainment,' no matter how private it might seem. It turns human beings into objects. It coarsens our appetites. It darkens our ability to see real human beauty. It creates impossible expectations about sexual intimacy. It kills enduring romance and friendship between the sexes. And ultimately it is a lie and a cheat. Pornography is a cheap, quick, empty copy of the real thing — the real joy of sexual intimacy shared by a man and woman who have joined their lives in a loving marriage. [...] Pornography is poison. It should be controlled like any other toxic waste." That is when the 9th Commandment resonates loudly for those who are tone-deaf: Covet no one.

#10: You shall not covet your neighbor's goods

Like the 9th Commandment, the 10th Commandment also seems to deal with things residing *inside* of us. Again, it says you shall not *covet*. Well, coveting has something to do with your heart, doesn't it? We can keep our hands off things and we can swallow our words, but a covetous heart is much harder to control. Envy, for example, just comes upon you, whether you like it or not. It makes you desire to have what some other person has, or possibly more. Envy can poison you inside, by spoiling your enjoyment of what you do have at home, including a loving spouse. Who isn't familiar with such feelings? Can we really curb or stop them, as we can stop ourselves from killing, stealing, or lying?

Yet, the 10th Commandment refers more to our doings than to our feelings; at least it refers to what we *do* with our feelings. Loving is something we do with our hands, so to speak. It is not an emotion word but an action word. The same thing applies to coveting; coveting is something we do with our hands. Of course, what we do relates to what we feel, and what we do with our hands reveals what we feel in our hearts. Do not take this the wrong way. Nowhere has the Bible ever banned desire for things we do not yet have—a good house, a nice job, good friends, things that make life pleasant, and money to spend on fun things. Desire is an important drive in life; we work to achieve our desires. God wants to be part of the nice things in life as well as the more serious and profound aspects of life.

Coveting, on the other hand, means that you have set your heart on what belongs to someone else. Never shall you put your hands on it. Those who covet what someone else owns become ugly as sin, both on the inside and the outside. As a result, complete households can get ruined. Intrigues can become part of the life-threatening race to keep up with others or to get ahead of them, by fighting one's way up and letting no one stand in one's way. It becomes a rat race, a demonic drive. Of course, this causes accidents and may even cost lives!

Again, drives like these come from *within*. Jesus said it very clearly, "there is nothing outside a man which by going into him can defile him; but the things which come out of a man are what defile him" (Mk. 7:15). Once we are set free from the tiring need to look with jealousy at the things other people possess, we can begin a new life. Others do perhaps possess a little more, or even much more, than we do—but so what! Their possessions may do them good. "Rejoice in your brother's progress" says St. John Chrysostom. My own calling and my own chances are enough to handle. It would be a "sin" to miss out on all I do have.

What the 10th Commandment does forbid instead is greed, envy, and materialism; it doesn't want us to be possessed by possessions. How true it is that he who loves money never has money enough (CCC 2536). Envy can lead to the worst crimes. St. Augustine considered envy "*the* diabolical sin," for "through the devil's envy death entered the world" (Wis. 2:24). In history, it took on a more general form: envy of the rich who have more than others. Apparently, the 10th Commandment does not condemn the rich. Did we hear that right? As we discussed earlier, there is nothing wrong with owning private property—unless it is stolen. And there is nothing wrong with owning private capital—unless it enslaves us. That's why Pope Francis most recently stressed the moral dimension of private property and capital when he said, "Once capital becomes an idol and guides people's decisions, once greed for money presides over the entire socioec-

Chapter 8: God's Prescription for Happiness

onomic system, it ruins society, it condemns and enslaves men and women."

These thoughts are certainly not new. As early as 1891, Pope Leo XIII issued his encyclical *Rerum Novarum* [On New Things] in opposition to communism and unrestricted capitalism. This necessarily implied he also had to touch on the notion of private property: "To remedy these wrongs the socialists, working on the poor man's envy of the rich, are striving to do away with private *property*." This, he declared, is "emphatically unjust." It is a form of coveting our neighbors' goods. So, don't let the state do this for you—in the name of social justice—by taking "goods" from the rich and giving them to the poor. Social justice is a good goal to strive for, but it has little or nothing to do with "redistribution of wealth by a government"; it has nothing to do with "taking from the rich and giving to the poor."

The Catechism of the Catholic Church (1941) puts all of this together as follows. "Socio-economic problems can be resolved only with the help of all the forms of solidarity: solidarity of the poor among themselves, between rich and poor, of workers among themselves, between employers and employees in a business, solidarity among nations and peoples. International solidarity is a requirement of the moral order; world peace depends in part upon this."

In short, the 10th Commandment teaches us to be grateful for what we own, our private property, but it also tells us to respect someone else's property. Therefore, we should be happy, not envious, that someone else has different circumstances and may in fact have a few more or even many more possessions. Let's live our own lives, as unique individuals, and let them live their own lives. After all, it is not a question of the things we *own* but of the persons we *are*. As St. Augustine says, "The more one loves, the less one covets."

Coming to the end...

Not quite yet. I want to stress once more that the Ten Words are life-saving beacons in our lives and in our societies. They contain the moral values that should guide and shape our moral evaluations. But often they don't. Time and again, the Ten Commandments go against what the surrounding culture prescribes. The prohibition of polygamy is as countercultural in Africa as the prohibition of divorce is in America. As G.K. Chesterton put it, "I don't need a church to tell me I am wrong where I already know I'm wrong; I need a Church to tell me I am wrong where I think I'm right." Sometimes we think we know so much that isn't so.

Why do we need Ten Commandments? God gave us the commandments for us to obey—the best nutrients for our moral health. And yet, we don't need rules, only love. That same St. Augustine we quoted already several times had this famous motto, "Love God and [then] do what you will." If I love someone, then I shall quite certainly never steal anything from them or say bad things about them. In other words, if you truly love God and His will, then doing what *you* will, will amount to doing what *God* wills. But the grand question is: do we have that love already? Perhaps the Ten Commandments will help us to come closer to that love, closer to God's Heart. God's prescription for happiness is definitely "two tablets a day."

Indeed, "two tablets a day" are what the human soul needs for its voluntary part, as a gift from God. The Ten Commandments are God's law, the core and center of our moral code, guiding us through life between the Scylla and Charybdis of good and evil. They steer our actions and correct us when we veer off. They are the objective, universal, timeless, and absolute standards on which good moral behavior is founded.

So, what happens when we sin against God's Law? All those who violate any of the Ten Commandments disrupt their relationship with God. People who do so are playing with fire—the fire of Hell, that is. Is that final and forever? For Catholics, there is no "forever" in this life, as long as there is a Sacrament of Confession. We all need fire insurance for the afterlife. When G.K. Chesterton was asked "Why did you join the Church of Rome?" he answered that question in his autobiography with the words, "To get rid of my sins." Then he explained, "For there is no other religious system that does really profess to get rid of people's sins." How right he was; the Catholic Church is unquestionably a "hospital for sinners."

It seems to me that the best way to bring this book to a close is using a quote from Tom Peterson (*MyGodsBlog.com*) about Catholics and the Catholic Church:

> *Our family is made up of every race. We are young and old, men and women, sinners and saints. Our family has spanned the centuries and the globe. With God's grace, we started hospitals to care for the sick. We establish orphanages and help the poor. We are the largest charitable organization on the planet, bringing relief and comfort to those in need. We educate more children than any other scholarly or religious institution. We developed the scientific method and laws of evidence. We founded the college system. We defend the dignity of all human life and uphold marriage and family. Cities were named after our revered saints, who navigated a sacred path before us. Guided by the Holy Spirit, we compiled the Bible. We are transformed by sacred Scripture and sacred Tradition, which have consistently guided us for two thousand years. We are the Catholic Church, with over one billion in our family sharing in the sacraments and fullness of Christian faith.*

Index

A

abortion 22, 81, 187, 190, 192, 198, 207, 216, 254, 271-74
absolute 28, 29, 55, 57-9, 67-8, 71, 83, 137, 141-43, 149-51, 156, 161 169, 182, 187, 191, 196-200, 203, 206, 208-09, 211-12, 218, 256, 295
abstraction . 98, 152, 154, 165
agnosticism 1, 3-7
alleles 30, 32, 88
Ambrose 113, 180
Angelica, Mother 243
Anselm 173, 195
anthropomorphism 47
Aquinas 6, 28, 29, 33, 47-8, 57-9, 65, 74, 82, 100, 108, 113, 117, 130, 133, 137, 148, 154, 158, 161, 163, 168-69, 173, 180, 223, 255, 272, 284, 286
Arianism............................176
Aristarchus..........................114
Aristotle 114, 122, 128, 148, 158
assumptions 8, 123-24, 127
Athanasius..........................176
atheism 1-4, 6-7, 11-2, 14-25, 57, 203, 258-59
Atkins, Peter......................141
Augustine .... v, 1, 64, 113, 130-31, 133-34, 155, 162, 169-70, 205, 241, 245, 249-50, 252, 259, 267, 281, 286-87, 292, 294

B

Bacon, Roger 123-24, 126, 130
Barr, Stephen......................145
Barron, Robert 127
Basil the Great...................113
Bellarmine, Robert............116
Benedict XVI .... v, 2-3, 6, 64-5, 67, 71, 79, 130, 149, 204, 206, 220, 237, 243, 252, 254, 261, 269
Big Bang...... 132, 142, 144-45
blasphemy 81, 254, 262
Bochenski, Joseph 53
Bohr, Niels..........................106
Bonaventure 67
Bonhoeffer, Dietrich. 75, 220
Book of Nature 129-30,

132-34, 146
Book of Scripture 78, 129-30, 132-33, 146
brain.......... 40-3, 45-7, 94-104, 182, 184, 192, 198, 218, 224
Brenner, Sidney................... 86

C

Catherine of Siena 256
cells 31, 37-9, 86, 90, 99, 139, 155, 269, 273
chance 23, 30-3, 69-70, 144, 224, 262, 292
Chaput, Charles 290
chastity 277-78
Chesterton, G.K. 4, 50, 102-103, 151, 202, 213, 258, 294-95
Commandments 81-2, 174, 182, 249-56, 259, 287, 294-95
communism.....18, 52, 54, 293
Compton, Arthur.............. 103
concepts 8, 46, 64, 98, 144, 152-59, 171, 179, 194, 204
confirmation................... 20, 72, 172, 178-79
conflict theory........... 111, 119
conscience............ 187, 208-12, 224, 249
contingent .. 58-9, 69, 71, 109, 126, 135, 139, 160
Copernicus, Nicolaus 114, 118-19, 127-28
correlation 99
corruption 281
covenant 250, 253, 277-78
Covenant 77, 250-53, 261, 264, 277
creation 5, 19, 21, 80, 83, 120, 135-45, 147, 161, 169, 172, 177, 217-18, 226, 230, 232-34, 237, 239, 257, 263-66
Creation 59, 69, 128, 132, 135, 137, 145, 161, 176, 202
Creation account 132, 135, 137, 147, 257
creation out of nothing143-45
Crick, Francis . 10, 39-40, 101

D

Darwin, Charles 47, 97, 101, 164
Davies, Paul.................. 140-41
Dawkins, Richard . 16, 30, 32, 73, 76, 101
Decalogue 250, 253-54
deism...................................... 65

determinism............ 85-6, 89, 91-3, 103-107
Didache............................264
dignity.............25, 33, 80, 138, 196, 205-6, 208, 271-72, 274, 282, 295
DNA............. 10, 25, 33-9, 54, 80, 85-91, 167, 185
Dolan, Timothy.................238
Dostoyevsky, Fyodor........17, 161, 203
Drummond, Henry............75
Duhem, Pierre............. 124-25
Dulles, Avery.................22, 65
duties 49, 53, 205, 207, 253-54, 268, 275-76, 289

E

Eccles, John................. 96, 234
Einstein, Albert. 54, 101, 139, 141, 158-60, 201
Eiseley, Loren 129
empiricism 1, 9
entitlements 208
Epicurus.................... 219, 222
epigenetics 91
euthanasia .. 81, 254, 271, 273
evaluations 194-95
evil 15-21, 80-2, 187, 191, 200, 203, 213, 215-27, 230-46, 257, 268, 271, 282, 284, 289-90, 292, 295
  moral.......216-17, 219-20, 223, 225, 235, 240, 245
  natural.......... 216, 220-21, 223-25, 237
exorcism 20

F

facts........ 7, 10-1, 37, 50, 87-8, 112, 125, 144, 150, 152, 159, 162, 164-65, 169, 193, 200, 258
faith and reason....v, 131, 215
falsification.................... 10, 72
family..........227, 268-70, 274, 279-80, 283, 285, 288, 295-96
fidelity...............277, 285, 288
First Cause *See* Primary Cause
Five Ways........................ 58-9
Fodor, Jerry 96
Frankl, Viktor......................96
freedom 2, 43-4, 54, 79-82, 85, 87, 89, 93, 108, 120, 150, 169, 195, 204, 209, 212, 216-19, 223, 238, 241, 270, 273, 277, 290

free-will ...39, 43, 80-1, 85-89, 91, 93, 95-6, 102-05, 107-10, 216-18
Frege, Gottlob 205
Freud, Sigmund 11, 287

G

Galileo 112-19, 124, 127, 129, 159
Gamaliel..................... 179, 253
gender-identity 87
genes..........25, 30-5, 37-8, 55, 68-9, 80, 85-92, 103, 148, 166, 184-5, 200-02, 209
genetics...30-2, 80, 85, 91, 93, 166-67, 201
Gilbert, Walter 86
Gödel, Kurt 45, 60
Golden Rule 189
Gould, Stephen J. 32
Grant, Edward 123
Groeschel, Benedict 243
Grosseteste, Robert..........126

H

Habermas, Jürgen 204
Haldane, J.B.S. 101
Haldane, John 165
Hawking, Stephen 140-2, 144
hedonism 188
Heisenberg, Werner 106

heliocentrism 114-16, 132
Hell 20, 220, 241-46, 295
Hinduism 63
Hume, David............. 78, 189, 215, 219-20
Huxley, Thomas.................3, 5
hypothesis 4, 57, 72-4, 92, 116, 126

I

idolatry...............137, 257, 259
idols........... 137, 170, 257, 259
Ignatius of Antioch 264
immanence.................66-7, 83
Incarnation..........77, 155, 162, 171-4, 179, 235, 239, 244, 271
intellect ..vii-viii, 74, 100, 107, 109, 124, 131, 147-49, 152-53, 156-58, 162-4, 181-2, 197, 200, 205
Irenaeus 217

J

Jaki, Stanley.................. 120-21
Jesus 77, 133, 162, 168, 172-80, 196, 226, 235-42, 245-47, 258, 260, 263, 265-66, 271, 275-6, 279, 281, 284, 286, 292

Index 301

Job 133, 227-36
John of the Cross 258
John Paul II 7, 131, 181, 212, 236
judgment. 107, 148, 183, 220, 240-42, 247

K

Kant, Immanuel 157
Kennedy, John F. 206
Kepler, Johannes 113, 115-16, 128-29, 140
King, Martin Luther 190
Kreeft, Peter 5, 151, 194, 237, 241, 269
Kuhn, Thomas 122

L

language . 7, 41, 47-9, 69, 134, 194, 254, 270, 273, 284
Laplace 4, 72-3, 106
laws of nature 43, 66, 76-9, 140-3, 185-86, 197, 199-201, 204, 220, 222, 258
Leibniz, Gottfried. 45, 75, 97, 138, 141, 205
Leo the Great 175
Leo XIII 19, 131, 134, 280-293

Lewis, C.S. 22, 27, 78, 102, 173, 176, 193, 217-18, 225, 241, 256
Libet, Benjamin 93-5
Lincoln, Abraham 191, 197
Locke, John 212
Lord's Day 263-64
Luther, Martin 243

M

Maritain, Jacques 206
marriage. 274-79, 287-91, 295
Mary, the Blessed Virgin ... 77, 181, 218,
materialism 26-8, 42-3, 257, 292
matter 26, 28, 43, 61-2, 65, 98, 141, 143
mechanicism 43-6
Medawar, Peter 37
Mendel, Gregor 129, 140, 164, 166-67
metamorphosis 35
Middle Ages 112, 114, 123-28
mind .. vii, 5, 8-9, 11-2, 20, 26, 39-46, 49-50, 63-4, 67, 91, 95-104, 107, 116, 120, 122-23, 129, 131-32, 139, 149-52, 154, 156-159, 161, 163-65, 167-68,

179, 182, 186, 193, 199, 202-04, 211, 218-19, 256, 258-59
Minsky, Marvin 43
miracles 76-9, 182
monotheism 137, 155, 170
morality 3, 48-9, 54-5, 103, 148, 182-208, 211-13, 218-19, 224, 249, 274, 287-88
murder 204, 216-17, 251, 271-72, 274, 289
mystery 64, 162-63, 172, 180-81, 227, 235-36

N

naturalistic fallacy 189
nature-nurture 91
neuroscience 93, 96-7, 102
New Atheism 16
Newman, John Henry 33, 132, 182
Newton, Isaac 75, 98, 121, 129, 140, 194
Nietzsche, Friedrich ... 203-04
nothing-buttery 27, 48

O

objective 55, 123, 150-51, 157-58, 161-62, 165, 177, 191-92, 199-200, 203, 206, 208, 213, 295
omnipotence. 80, 168, 216-17
omniscience 109, 216
Oppenheimer, J. Robert .. 120 122
Original Sin 138, 148, 162, 213, 219, 236, 239, 269

P

Padre Pio 33
paganism 1, 2, 69
pantheism 66, 82-3, 215
paradise 138, 147-49, 211, 213, 218, 246
parents ... 82, 86, 88, 111, 186, 242, 266-70, 275, 279
Pascal, Blaise .... vii, 74, 127, 129, 148, 161, 263
Penfield, Wilder 95-6, 103,
perjury 254, 262
physical constants 143
Planck, Max 101, 129
Plato 204
polytheism 68, 170
Popper, Karl 104
pornography 216, 278, 288, 290-91
Primary Cause 29-30, 57-9, 61-2, 69-70, 73, 108, 110, 139, 141, 160, 221-22

Proclus of Constantinople 175
property............38, 106, 194, 279-81, 287, 292-93
purgatory................155, 243-5
Pythagoras.........................113

Q

quantum tunneling.....144-45

R

randomness..............32, 69-70
rationality..3, 36, 49, 54, 131, 148-49, 152, 154, 163, 200, 219
redeemer............................231
reductionism........27-8, 30, 34, 43-4, 46, 48, 54, 101, 104, 107
relativism...3, 149-52, 156-57, 203
Revelation..........15, 133, 155, 167, 169, 174, 177, 179, 227, 242, 250, 277
rights..........18, 47, 49, 51, 53, 184-85, 195, 200, 205-08, 253-54, 275, 279-80
Rousseau, Jean-Jacques....212

S

Sabbath................251, 263-66
Sacks, Jonathan...................17
Sagan, Carl......26-7, 142, 144
Sartre, Jean-Paul.......22-3, 55, 79-80, 161, 203
Satan.........1, 19-21, 213, 219, 233, 239, 241, 245-47, 258, 286
Sayers, Dorothy.................181
Schulman, Adam...............206
scientism........1, 12-5, 61, 101, 104, 107, 123, 130
secularism.....................2, 149
sexual revolution.........288-89
sexuality 91, 277, 287-88, 290
Shaw, George Bernard.......30
skepticism........................73-4
slavery...190-91, 194-95, 197, 251, 264, 282
Smolin, Lee........................142
social justice.......................293
Solzhenitsyn, Aleksandr.....17
soul.......19-22, 26, 43, 66, 82, 129, 147-49, 178, 182, 230, 238, 245, 277, 290, 295
Stark, Rodney....................121
suffering..........52, 175-7, 215, 224, 226-27, 229-32, 234-40, 242, 269
supernatural 62, 78, 168, 172, 177-81, 204

T

Tertullian.... 54, 171, 243, 245
theism. 16-8, 25, 57, 61, 65-7, 74, 82-3, 215-16
Thomas Aquinas. *See* Aquinas
thoughts 41-2, 45, 49, 97-102, 147-48, 150, 157-58, 162, 164-65, 199, 218, 289, 293
transcendence............ 63-4, 66
transubstantiation 180,
Trinity....... 64, 155-56, 170-71, 179, 181, 244
truth ..... viii, 4-6, 12-3, 17, 20, 27, 40, 44, 54, 60, 63-4, 74, 102, 112, 116, 131-32, 149-51, 156-64, 166-67, 169, 172, 174, 177-82, 205, 212, 224, 242, 267, 282-87, 289

U

unconditional .. 191, 208, 200, 284
universal 4, 14, 55, 98, 121-22, 142, 151, 153, 161, 191, 193-94, 196, 200, 205, 208, 213, 244, 295

V

values 55, 106, 142, 161, 183-84, 192-96, 200, 202-03, 211, 213, 270, 294
Vianney, John..................... 239
Vilenkin, Alexander........... 144

W

wave function..................... 107
Whitehead, Alfred North 107, 121
will
    free-will .. 39, 43, 80-1, 85-9, 91, 93, 95-7, 99, 101-05, 107-10, 182, 216-18,
    God's ... 66, 108, 217, 221
Wilson, E.O. 34, 122
Wittgenstein, Ludwig 7-8, 40,
Wright, Jonathan................ 127
Wyszynski, Stefan 17

About the Author

Dr. Gerard M. Verschuuren is a human biologist, specialized in human genetics. He also earned a doctorate in the philosophy of science. He studied and worked at universities in Europe and the United States.

Currently, while semi-retired, he writes about issues at the interface of

- science and religion,
- science and creation,
- faith and reason.

All his books can be found at:

www.where-do-we-come-from.com

www.ingramcontent.com/pod-product-compliance
Lightning Source LLC
Chambersburg PA
CBHW070527090426
42735CB00013B/2892